The Horizontal Oak

A Life in Nature

Polly Pullar

BIRLINN

First published in 2022 by
Birlinn Ltd
West Newington House
10 Newington Road
Edinburgh
EH9 1QS

www.birlinn.co.uk

British Library Cataloguing in Publication Data
A catalogue record for this book is available from the British Library.

Typeset by Initial Typesetting Services, Edinburgh

Printed and bound by Clays Ltd, Elcograf S.p.A.

For Freddy
With all my love

Contents

Introduction

There's a single oak high on the flank of Ben Hiant, overlooking the Sound of Mull. I have known this resilient tree since my early childhood. It's in a place I love very much. Massaged by the warmth of the Gulf Stream, battered by the wrath of the Atlantic and silhouetted by a thousand sunsets over the islands of Mull, Coll and Tiree, it is horizontal, its trunk fissured and colonised by tiny ferns. An oak sustains more life forms than any other native tree. Generally, we think of oaks as mighty: trees for building houses, boats or bastions; trees of grandiose parklands, their massive weighty boughs stretching to the heavens. The oaks of Scotland's rainforest on the western seaboard are different: diminutive, wind-sculpted. Many do not stay the course while others, like mine, grow strong and beautiful as they find succour between a rock and a hard place. Raven, hooded crow, buzzard and tawny owl frequently visit this tree. Sometimes it will be the little stonechat with his dapper black bonnet. And, from time to time, it is me, for its trunk, having withstood so much abuse, offers me support too; the horizontal oak, high on a hillside west of the sun.

*

Ordinary families like mine hide secrets, issues and struggles that cause pain. When my mother died, I knew that it was time to come to terms with the strains of my relationship with my parents. For far too many years this consumed me, spiralling out of control and leading to tragedy. I usually write about nature and have found writing about personal issues troubling, yet this journey has been burning deep in my heart for a long time.

In nature – in wild places, and through some extraordinary close relationships with animals and birds, both wild and domestic – I have found the peace that nurtures my soul. In particular, I have returned again and again to Ardnamurchan, a remote, mercurial peninsula flung west towards the setting sun, where nature embraces me in its many moods. And to that oak tree; it's as fine a place as I know for reflection. And calm.

Few are lucky enough to avoid life's emotional battles, but it is how we survive them that matters. Do we cling on and become more weathered and lined, like my horizontal oak, or do we instead blow over with the first hard gust of wind? Perhaps this nagging at our roots strengthens us, and maybe even leads us to a better understanding of the problems we all face.

My life and work are woven around nature. The natural world forms a vital part of this memoir and provides a continual counterbalance of hope. Hope and a sense of humour are essential emotional ingredients for life. Laughter helps us find ways to continue when things are testing. Here, then, is a little part of that story.

I

A Childhood Eden

'Polly, you are so lucky to have owls in your ovaries.' I was peering through the kitchen window watching tawny owlets in the aviary in the garden with a friend's eight-year-old daughter. Children do not realise the power and wisdom of their priceless statements. It was appropriate because wildlife has always been part of my very being, though perhaps not my ovaries. She was right; I consider myself fortunate to work closely with injured and orphaned wild animals and birds. As well as making me laugh, her statement brought forward a vivid memory from the annals of my mind, from Cheshire, around 1966: that morning when I discovered my first tawny owl.

The garden was an amphitheatre of birdsong. It drifted through my open bedroom window. Jackdaws were ferrying twigs to the collapsing chimney in the old stables next to the house. One of them had long wisps of sheep's wool in its bill – it looked like a Chinese wise man with a drooping white moustache. I listened to their effusive chatter, so many different calls, some almost human. The fireplace in the wood-panelled tack room bulged with sticks and twigs spewing forth onto the cracked stone floor. Sometimes I collected them for Mum to use as kindling. They were surplus to the jackdaws' requirements for they only used the ones at the top to create their shambling nurseries. In a continuous stream, more and more sticks were flown in, and the chimney echoed to the sound of their chortling, chakking communications with their voracious youngsters.

A dead jackdaw lay rotting in a verdant grave of emerging nettles close by. It had died a week earlier, but I didn't know why.

I'd found it when it was still warm, its smoky hood and glossed indigo-black plumage fresh, its eyes topaz blue. There was not even a speck of blood to reveal a fight with one of its kind; perhaps it had had a disease. I'd wished I could have saved it. I raced outside for another quick look before school. That day the bird's eyes were sunken, the blue faded to storm-cloud grey, and its feet clenched in a death grip, claws earthy under sharp nails. I turned it over with my foot, watching iridescent beetles and creamy maggots working on its decaying flesh. The smell was overpowering, but the bird was moving in an intriguing way. Beside the gruesome scene, there was a splash of brilliance: celandines and dandelions were opening their bright faces. The bird had flowers on its grave.

I heard a soft churring sound, almost inaudible, merely a whisper. It was close. I had never heard it before. I looked up and saw an owl perched in the open hayloft doorway above me, its burnished bronze plumage dappled with light rays that briefly illuminated festoons of lacy cobwebs around the corners of the opening. It was the most beautiful bird I had ever seen. It drew itself up tall as if to make itself invisible, narrowing its huge dark eyes to mere slits, and then it swayed its body over to lean up against the sandstone. I stood motionless, captivated.

Mum shouted, 'Pol, time to go.'

I pretended not to hear.

Then after a few minutes, she shouted again, 'Pol, will you *please* hurry up?'

I stood still, frozen to the spot, watching. It was so similar to Old Brown, the tawny owl that snatched Squirrel Nutkin's tail in the Beatrix Potter story Dad's younger brother, Uncle Archie, had read to me. Mum yelled again and gave one of her trademark whistles. This time she sounded cross. I ran round to meet her, stumbled over a heap of slates and cut my knee on a sharp edge. There was no time to fuss, but the blood oozed stickily into my sock and made me wince. Mum was revving the car engine; I grabbed my satchel from the path where I had dropped it and leapt in the back as we hastily departed for school.

I hated school, and Mum understood because she had hated it too. On the way, I told her about my discovery. 'I can't wait to show you when I get home. It's such a big owl and it's just sitting and staring. Do you think it lives there? Will it be there when I get home? Please, can we go back now and have a look? I have a bit of a tummy-ache, perhaps I should stay at home today.'

The day dragged longer than usual. I was lost in reverie. Such a beautiful, perfect owl! Every O or o on the blackboard reminded me of those big, darkly round eyes.

'Polly, will you please pay attention, what are you doing, you have not been listening to anything I have been saying, have you?' snapped the teacher, rapping the blackboard with her knuckles and tutting loudly.

I didn't like her; she was always irritable. The owl consumed me, and I wished it were time to go home. I wanted to venture up into the loft to see if I could get even closer, but the wooden stairs were collapsing and the slates were tumbling off the imploding roof. I wasn't supposed to go up there.

As soon as I was home, I gulped tea in a hurry and ran across the yard to the cottage close by, where my friend Alan was waiting. He didn't go to a boring all-girls school like me, and he arrived home earlier. Most days we raced out to play together.

'There's this gi-normous owl, we have to go and see it,' I told him.

Alan's eyes opened wide. He still had his grey uniform shorts on, had matching cuts on his knees, and a permanently dirty nose.

'Don't be late for your tea again!' shouted his old grandma from her knitting perch by the fire. Alan shoved his wellies on the wrong feet and left the house coatless, without shutting the door.

'Dad says she's a silly old bat,' said Alan, who ignored all instructions that didn't suit him.

We crawled around the corner of the stables on our hands and knees so as not to frighten the bird away. Miraculously it was still there – this was its chosen daytime roost.

From then on, every day after school we looked for it and sometimes saw it flitting silently through the trees. I became so absorbed by our woodland explorations that I never noticed how stung and scratched I was until I stepped into the bath at night, and then my stings and cuts made me yelp. We learnt that the blackbirds and other songsters gave the game away, scolding and revealing the whereabouts of owls or other birds of prey roosting deep in the surrounding woodland. We carefully followed their irate protestations and were usually rewarded. Then we discovered a heap of owl pellets beneath the hayloft window and began a forensic investigation of their contents. Alan borrowed a magnifying glass from his grandma, and Mum gave me an old pair of tweezers. Within the woolly grey casing, we revealed perfect little vole and mice skulls bleached white, tiny feathers and minute skeletons, as well as beetle cases. We also tracked deer, rabbits and hares, following their prints through muddy pathways where tripwires of brambles waited to snag bare legs. I grew increasingly feral as my desire for wildness blossomed.

My parents never minded that I was outside all day and only appeared for meals. I often missed those too. Mum, remembering her own free-spirited and outdoor childhood, could clearly relate to mine, whilst Dad worked long hours in his office in Liverpool, only returning when I was ready for bed. Dad loved nature too.

When the window was empty, the owl gone, we tiptoed up to the hayloft, barely putting our weight on steps like seesaws. Upstairs, it was stifling with the smell of rats; there were layers of dry grain husks and mould-covered droppings, fusty empty hessian sacks latticed with cobwebs and massive spiders emerging threateningly from every corner.

'There are probably vampire bats up here. It's the perfect spot for them,' Alan informed me as he led the way. He seemed brave and knowledgeable.

The gaps in the floorboards were wide as crevasses, and shafts of light revealed even more cobwebs, with struggling bluebottles fizzing out their last before succumbing to the spiders' efficient strangling shrouds. And then there were even bigger spiders. Startled pigeons clattered from the rafters as we leapt back and teetered on the edge of a gaping floor crack.

Bones lay in a heap by an upturned metal bucket plastered with white droppings. 'Do you think they belong to a dead person?' I asked Alan.

He laughed dismissively and replied, 'I bet they do.'

That attic made me feel uneasy and itchy, all the dust and rancid hay left in piles. It caught the back of my throat and scared me.

'My grandma says a tramp sometimes sleeps up here. She says he is an escaped *convick*,' Alan announced.

'What's a convick?' I asked.

But he didn't know either and shrugged. Even though I was frightened, the prospect of getting a little closer to my owl made it worth the terror. Little did I know then that owls, in particular the tawny, were birds that would continue to feature intermittently throughout my life, birds that I would come to know, love and understand quite well.

The only time we were not outside was when we watched the television series *Animal Magic* and *Daktari*. Presenter Johnny Morris of *Animal Magic* was our hero, and on the programme he was often a zookeeper projecting imagined voices of the various animals he cared for. His conversations with them were hilarious. I was intrigued by the chats he had with a huge gorilla. For me, a ring-tailed lemur called Dotty was the main attraction; she was always keen to take another grape from her keeper. It made Alan and me giggle when she politely took one from his extended hand. I longed to have a ring-tailed lemur too. Due to *Animal Magic*, I quickly learnt to recognise many exotic animals and birds, and on wet days lost myself in books with photographs of wonderful creatures.

Daktari is Swahili for 'the doctor'; that programme was set in Africa and centred on Dr Tracy and his daughter Paula, who protected animals from poachers and rescued various ailing birds and beasts. They had an animal orphanage. As I wanted to be a vet, Alan and I acted out dramatic animal rescues. He was the dashing Dr Tracy, and I was Paula, whilst Penny, our yellow Labrador, was their famous pet, Clarence the cross-eyed lion.

When I was alone, Penny also sometimes became Yellow Dog

Dingo from Rudyard Kipling's *Just So Stories*, another favourite of the books that Uncle Archie read to me. She was very obliging and, being a greedy dog, was happy to go along with anything providing there was a titbit involved. When she came with me through the woods on my expeditions and I found dead things, she'd let the side down by rolling in them and then we'd both get a row when we got home. I had a large toy monkey that we used for Judy, *Daktari's* chatty chimpanzee. We had pots of red poster paint for the blood transfusions that we carried out on our imaginary patients, and bamboo canes stuck onto toy building blocks as our walkie-talkies; we ran around the woods and garden frantically searching for ailing wildlife. We sometimes found needy fledglings, once or twice a road-casualty hedgehog, and tried to save them. Mum helped too, and was especially good with the hedgehogs.

Once, we found an abandoned pigeon squab that looked like a dodo. 'Pigeons are difficult baby birds to rear,' said Mum, 'because the babies need special milk made in their mothers' crops and they feed by putting their funny little bills straight into their mothers' throats.'

There were other excursions, such as when Alan and I sneaked over a tall iron-spiked fence at the manor house close by, and into an ancient orchard to steal apples belonging to Lord Leverhulme. Once, we were almost caught and a woman yelled at us as we fled in a panic. We were in such a hurry to get back over the wicked pronged fence that my bright-blue knickers snagged and ripped right off, and I had to race home without them. They were still hanging there next morning like a little tattered flag, but I dared not go and retrieve them.

*

When I was in my teens, and long after my parents had parted company, my mother laughingly told me that during the early years of their marriage, she and my father were nicknamed 'the two PBs' – the pompous bugger and the promiscuous bitch. It's not the greatest accolade applied to a couple, is it? As far as I can understand, and from numerous photographs and anecdotes relating to those early years, they were in fact incredibly popular. They were a flamboyant pair who loved parties, and were both renowned for their wit and devilish sense of humour. Mum made an impression wherever she went – she was sexy, flirtatious and colourful, she dressed with style, and men found her irresistible with her red hair and exuberant twinkle. She had a gap between her front teeth through which she could whistle so loudly and efficiently that it could make even the most disobedient fleeing dog skid to an immediate halt. It had a similar effect on people too. Particularly men. Mum was effervescent, and game for anything. When I was a small child, she was always kind. She let me spend most of my time outside, as she had done during her own childhood. And this suited me just fine.

Men said that Mum looked just as sexy in her old gardening clothes as she did when dressed for a special occasion. She was athletic, loved swimming and tennis, and had learnt to ride bareback with the local gypsies on a carthorse called Blossom, whose back was so broad you could have played patience on it. In many aspects Mum was fearless, but she hated flying and boats, and was a dreadful back-seat driver.

My grandmother told me that Mum was a very naughty child. One of her early school reports read: 'Anne is a born leader, it's just a pity that she leads in the wrong direction.' That particular comment came after she had taken her school friends out onto the roof through an attic window and waved at the headmistress, who was standing below in a state of anxious rage.

Mum was passionate about animals. When I was very young, we visited the exotic Harrods pet shop, in Knightsbridge, where we almost succumbed to the charms of an armadillo. The poor thing was utterly miserable and dejected in a wire cage. I was desperate for Mum to buy it, but it came with a hefty price tag. For the rest of her life, we frequently spoke of that little creature that had been stolen from a remote part of wild South America, only to be brought back to this country to be put up for sale in a fashionable London emporium. We always wondered what happened to it.

'I longed to buy it,' Mum said, 'not only because it was gorgeous but also so we could look after it and give it a nice home. But it really was way out of our budget. I have regretted it ever since and get miserable even thinking about it.'

Both my parents were involved in raising money for the World Wildlife Fund. I remember how aware they were even during the 1960s of the parlous state of the natural world. They would be deeply concerned, saddened and shocked if they knew how serious the situation has since become.

Mum adored my father, though she was advised not to marry him as his family had a history of alcoholism. Mum went ahead anyway. She had the stubbornness and determination of a jaded donkey that has worked a tourist beach all its life and is sick of demands made by horrid little children. If she disagreed with something, she wouldn't budge; like a donkey, she would dig her toes in. Indeed, she probably was promiscuous. Reflecting back on it all now that both my parents are long gone, I think she had good reason.

Dad – 'the pompous bugger' – had delusions of grandeur. If he had been a duke or an earl, he would have been happy. He loved double-barrelled names, as well as titles. Mum always joked about it. In 1950 he changed the family name by deed poll so that he and his brother, Archie, became 'Munro-Clark' instead of just plain 'Munro'. Clark was part of their mother's name. It was an odd thing to do. He was always adamant that people employ his full appellation. He was indeed pompous at times, sometimes so much so that it made me cringe.

But Dad was also exceedingly charming and had impeccable manners. His wit and humour were equally as sharp as Mum's, and he loved practical joking – he had caught out all his close friends with his innovative trickery. These jokes were always humorously entertaining and never designed to hurt. Some were complex and involved considerable planning. Many were played out over the telephone. He loved the phone and used to infuriate my mother by ringing someone shortly before a meal, and then spending hours engaged in conversation. Dinner went cold.

Dad loved tweed – Harris tweed especially. He loved perfectly crisp shirts from London's smart Savile Row. He loved cufflinks, and endless changes of socks – the latter because he had sweaty feet and athlete's foot. Our bathmats seemed ever to be liberally sprinkled with a snowy dusting of foot potions. Even though they had little money, he insisted on having his best clothes made by 'his tailor', as he grandly put it. He dressed immaculately, and in the perfect garb for whatever he happened to be doing at any given moment – even digging the garden – though he usually tried to extricate himself from that.

Dad was highly skilled in the art of manipulation and avoidance and could make an excuse to get out of anything he didn't like doing. He had avoided National Service because he said he had 'flat feet', and then of course there was the athlete's foot. He hated moving furniture and evaded any suggestion that he might lend someone a hand to move, say, a bed, or a sofa, and instead instantly made reference to his bad back. He would then go in search of a copy of Yellow Pages to find a firm of furniture removers. However, he could out-walk almost anyone, particularly if it involved hills and mountains, flat feet and bad back long forgotten. He loved shooting and deer stalking, but at school, though bright and academic, Dad had never been any good at ball games. He was a serious bookworm and read avidly. All the time. He also always knelt at the foot of the bed every night and put his hands together to say silent prayers. I found this fascinating.

Dad loved gourmet food, and he loved bitter black chocolate, strong tea, and even stronger coffee. Sometimes it seemed like liquid toffee. It was usually lavishly sprinkled with saccharine instead of sugar. 'If I had sugar too, I would be even fatter.' He loved to eat double cream straight from the pot. 'I cannot resist it,' he would say, dipping a teaspoon straight into a carton laced liberally with soft brown sugar. Thick yellow Devonshire clotted cream made him childlike.

Both my parents spent a lifetime battling with weight issues. I grew up thinking that saccharine actually kept you slim. I even tried eating it straight from the container. It was disgusting. Dad frequently won his weight battles and went through trim phases. Relapse, however, was guaranteed. He had a highly addictive personality.

Mum, conversely, totally lost control of her increasing buoyancy. She always blamed me: 'It's your fault entirely, I was quite thin until I got pregnant, and piled it all on then.'

Early photographs prove that this was not entirely accurate. Mum was never a sylph – she was simply not made that way. Dad also loved fine port, French wine, champagne, whisky, gin and brandy, indeed anything alcoholic. Unfortunately. Dad loved it far too much.

The two PBs – Anne and David Munro-Clark – rented part of a rambling house from Lord Leverhulme on the Wirral peninsula. It was a beautiful sandstone pile riddled with damp and dry rot and surrounded by a wild, rampaging garden; a maze of azaleas and rhododendrons formed dark, exciting tunnels for dens and exploration, and in spring a green slimy pond overflowed with frogs and toads. The house had a leaky conservatory that housed flowers and peaches. In the other half of the house lived a wonderful eccentric family who became my parents' long-standing close friends. Their daughter, Heather, was made my godmother when she was only eleven years old. This was an act of genius on the part of my parents as she has always been the greatest support throughout my life.

Builders were tackling the dry rot while we lived there and, typically, left their scaffold and shambles up the sweeping staircase whilst vanishing off to do other jobs. One of them had scrawled, 'THE POPE FOR PRIME MINISTER' on the crumbling plaster. Venturing up and down was a hazardous obstacle course. Early one Sunday morning, I found Dad suspended over one of the lower rails of the scaffold like a battered scarecrow, in a semi-rigor state, with a shoeless foot in a bucket of hardened cement and fag ends. He was snoring loudly and dribbling whilst repeating, 'Poor show, poor show,' over and over again. He didn't resemble the Dad I knew. I felt scared and beetled back to bed.

Years later Mum told me that she had given up trying to manoeuvre him in his inebriated state and had said, 'Fuck it', and just left him to get on with it.

Dad was exceedingly well read. He went to Cambridge, and though my mother was no academic and never passed any exams, it was there that they met one another and fell in love. She had been invited for a weekend and had tagged along to yet another drunken soirée where Dad was apparently both intoxicating and intoxicated. She soon became part of his Cambridge set.

Now they are both gone, and I can no longer ask them what happened next, I have to imagine so much of their story, and there is a gap I am unclear about. However, later, Dad, having studied law, decided not to take it any further because he unexpectedly inherited a timber business in Liverpool from an elderly uncle. Part of their business was supplying coffin oak, and on one occasion a Jewish undertaker took him into the back of his premises to show him a beautiful young woman perfectly made up and lying in her coffin. This really upset Dad, who realised that he was in totally the wrong profession. He didn't like it anyway. With the business, he also inherited two elderly gentlemen who worked in the office, filling ledgers in with ink quills in perfect copperplate writing. They became victims of one of his many practical jokes, on this occasion, more cruel than usual. He put stink bombs in their room so that each blamed the other for having rotten guts.

*

Our lives were filled with animals. We had another gluttonous golden Labrador, Jane, who was Penny's mother, and later two spaniels and numerous other dogs, and a ginger Persian cat called Oswald Bull – named after Miss Bull, his eccentric breeder. He got knots in his fur and suffered from incontinence. He piddled on my parents' eiderdown so that the red dye ran onto the sheets, leaving a pink, immovable stain. 'That's Ossie's piddle patch,' Mum announced each time she hung the sheets on the line.

Mum, who had always been fascinated with parrots (perhaps that's why I am called Polly), had an African grey with a nasty cough for which, despite extensive, expensive veterinary investigations, no reason could be found. We later discovered that the parrot's previous owner had been a chain smoker and coughed uncontrollably every morning.

Jane and Penny were dreadful scavengers and often bumbled off on their own little expeditions. For some weeks they came home stinking appallingly and had to be bathed. Eventually, the source of the vile stench was unveiled. A policeman called in to see my parents and told them that a dead tramp had been found in a nearby ditch and wanted to know if they had ever seen him before. This caused much upset. The dogs were in disgrace – they had found him first. The golden duo also regularly raided Lord and Lady Leverhulme's bins, something my parents found embarrassing.

'Ah! Theirs must be a far better class of rubbish,' Dad commented grandly. He liked living in close proximity to a lord. His middle-class family were never wealthy, but it didn't stop his aspirations.

I had a square chestnut Shetland pony called Peggy that I had been given for my sixth birthday. Peggy was over thirty and knew all about children and how best to handle them, having done the rounds locally. She was a besom. She dented my confidence and regularly bucked me off into the nettles, or placed her sharp little hoof deliberately over my foot, leaving it raw and bruised. She was an awful biter too, but such Thelwellian ponies were part of a character-building package that for a tomboy like me included copious amounts of tree-climbing, den-building and nature absorption.

Dad's brother Archie, who was a schoolmaster, had a flat in part of our rented house. I became hopelessly overexcited when I saw his little car coming up the drive returning for his school holidays. He loved children and always brought wonderful books to read to me. He gave me the complete set of Hugh Lofting's *Dr Doolittle*. I used to dream of being able to talk to animals as the doctor did. These stories unfolded a vast world full of fauna that formed a mantra for my life.

Archie was more down-to-earth than Dad, and far less conscious of his appearance. Whilst Dad loved looking smart and dapper, Archie was more casual, though having spent two years in the Royal Navy he could be just as immaculately turned out when the need arose. He was the seventh generation of the family to go to sea and though he almost stayed on, he decided instead to pursue an academic career; after graduating from Cambridge he took a post at a boys' prep school in the south of England. This became his lifelong career. He was a supreme communicator with people of all ages. Well-read, like Dad, he taught English, History and Games, and also wrote and produced the school plays.

Being a schoolmaster meant fantastic long holidays, and paid accommodation in term time. When he came back to stay with us, Archie and Dad sometimes smoked fat cigars together and sat up long into the night talking. In the morning the tarry aroma lingered amid the unwashed whisky glasses on the kitchen draining board.

Archie was always laughing. He'd laugh on long after a joke had passed. The sound reverberated around a room so that even if you didn't understand the reason for all the hilarity, it was infectious. He was always laughing at himself too. I liked that.

Mum, Dad and Archie were very close and clearly enjoyed doing things together. I remember now that they were together for much of the school holidays. Though Dad also read to me, he was often absent, and Archie filled the gap. At the time I never questioned this. It was simply the way it was. Perhaps Dad was working late.

My finest early childhood memories are those of Mum's mother, my grandmother, Bo. She was a treasure. A plain-speaking Yorkshirewoman, she was the kindest person I have ever met. There was nothing complicated about Bo; she was perfectly at one with herself and everyone else, and she too had a fabulous sense of humour. She and I shared the same birthday, and were as close as identical twins. She frequently fetched me from school, and I stayed with her in her lovely low, white cottage in the village of Heswall in Cheshire. The walls were thick and uneven, the stairs creaked, and there was a damp stain spreading over the bathroom wall that looked like a map of Africa. She would put an electric wall heater on whilst she ran my bath, and the room would fill with a dense blanket of steam. 'Is there anyone in here?' she'd laugh as she came in to check. The steam made the paint peel.

Bo had a blue budgerigar, Charlie, who was very talkative. 'Why do you buy such small packets of birdseed for him?' my grandfather asked her. 'It's so much cheaper to buy large ones.'

Without a moment's hesitation she replied, 'He is so old I am worried that if I buy a big packet, it may tempt fate and he will die, so I daren't.' She was a very generous person, but Charlie meant a great deal to her.

My grandfather's name was Wilfred – Wilf – but he had always been nicknamed Fitte. 'Fitte's bloody awkward,' Mum would say.

I never saw that side of him. Their relationship had always been volatile. When she was a child her strong will drove her father to distraction and, as it had become even stronger over the years, they did indeed seem to have a problem getting on with one another. There were frequent clashes. I once overheard Mum saying – 'My father prefers Polly to me.' She sounded hurt.

Fitte's mother was said to have been erratic, with a lashing tongue that was reputed to cut you in half. She was from a large Irish family in County Tipperary, and her grandparents were tinkers. I loved it when Fitte told me stories about them after he'd had a few glasses of sherry in the evenings. They sounded dramatic, colourful, wild, unruly, and so exciting. When I thought back on this years later, I often found myself hoping that I might have inherited some of their genes, rather than a collection of alcoholic ones from the other side of the family, for both Dad's parents had serious drink problems. This sad fact was frequently rattled out as part of the conversation.

'You come from a line of bloody drinkers,' Mum would say.

It didn't sound a great prospect, though at the time I didn't understand what it really meant.

Fitte was a quiet, shy man with a sense of humour so dry it would have served as kindling. Like Bo, he was very generous. He had been a market gardener and still kept a beautiful garden lush with vegetables and bordered by dozens of cheerful polyanthus. The sweet little tomatoes from his greenhouse picked straight from the plant, tasting of sunshine, were something we relished.

Bo once said the only religion that mattered was being kind. She also told me that you should always tell people what you think of them with regard to love, and treat them as if today might be the last day you saw them. Once, when she was very old, there was a knock at the door and a man pushed his way forward, saying, 'I have come to tell you that Jesus has risen from the dead!'

Without hesitation, Bo replied, 'Right, I had better go and put the kettle on straight away.' And then she politely shut the door.

Bo was fun and, like Archie, she was always laughing. She had slim legs and a big bosom, and she wore corsets and stockings, something I found intriguing as she hooked herself into an odd rigid garment that she said helped hold her tummy in. She was a huggable person, overflowing with warmth; everything felt right when I was with her.

We used to go straight to the local bakers from school and collect iced buns, or chocolate eclairs for tea. One day whilst we were waiting to pay, I asked, 'Was your grandmother an Ancient Briton?' as we were studying them at school.

Everyone in the shop laughed. 'I'm not *that* old,' I heard her tell them.

Bo was a skilled bridge player, and was closely involved in the local club where she was in great demand as a partner. She often had bridge afternoons with sumptuous afternoon teas, and then 'a spot of sherry', or a glass or two of Gin and French. Those tea parties lasted well on into the evenings. She was an integral part of village life, and everyone adored her.

Both my grandparents were heavy smokers. Mum laughingly told them, 'You two will puff yourselves to death if you don't stop.' However, they had a goal to acquire more cigarette coupons so they could obtain toys and games for me, and garden tools out of the cigarette company's catalogue; they must have had a marathon smoke in order to secure enough coupons for a wonderful shiny bike with stabilisers, but they did it.

My grandparents loved the birds in their garden. We would watch them bathing in a stone birdbath, or feasting on all the things Bo put out for them. We loved the starlings best because they were cheeky, and their antics and mimicry made us laugh. One in particular could

perfectly imitate a curlew, whilst another was a buzzard imperson-
ator, and several had perfected the cries of herring gulls. Then there
was one champion that could whistle like Bo's cheeky milkman.
She referred to them as the 'star-spangled starlings' due to their iridescent rainbow plumage. When the sun shone on them, I thought
their colours resembled oil spilt on a puddle: purples, mauves, blues
and yellows – pure perfection! Fitte had a passion for the robins that
followed him around when he was digging. He always kept a few
titbits in his shirt pocket.

The best thing about grandparents is that good ones have time.
Both Bo and Fitte listened to all my chatter. They believed in me
and were always encouraging. At times children need to be taken
seriously. Ours was a relationship like no other. My grandparents
were earthy country people, and everyone respected them both.

2

West of the Sun

During the 1960s, my parents found Cheshire's increasing urbanisa-
tion a threat. Dad hated the timber business and was trying to sell
it. They had reached a point where they wanted to have a complete
change. Though the Wirral peninsula was beautiful, the roads were
becoming busier every day and the landscape scarred by sprawling
development.

As our house was only rented for a nominal rate, my parents had
bought a tumbledown cottage called Ogof in the mountains in
North Wales. It was in an isolated situation near a remote, unmech-
anised hill farm. Sometimes we went to the farm to help the Jones
family – two brothers and their wives and children. At milking time,
in the afternoon, we would often help them bring in the cows, and
in summer extra hands were always much appreciated to help with
hay making. I remember the steaming cowshed where they kept
half a dozen cows. Their hot, sweet breath hung in thin clouds that
danced slowly upwards, among sparkling dust specks and weak sunlight that poured through the small window.

'Taste this,' said one of the brothers, passing me a small enamel
mug of milk that he had dunked into a metal bucket as he rhythmically milked their house cow. It was frothy and creamy. Everyone
laughed because I had a milk moustache on my top lip.

I was playing in the garden with the dogs when I encountered my
first adder. A passing buzzard had perhaps dropped it. When I saw
it, I assumed that our dogs had pinched a very similar-sized rubber
snake I had that we frequently used as a prop in our *Daktari* safari
adventures. I went to reclaim it. Then it wriggled and swiftly moved

towards the old wall that surrounded the garden. Mum shouted urgently from the window and told me to leave it alone. She rushed out waving a tea towel. She seemed worried. There was urgency in her raised voice.

Once the adder had vanished, she explained that this was Britain's only poisonous snake, and I must never touch one again. 'They are lovely, beautiful reptiles but you really don't want to be bitten. Sometimes dogs die of adder bites, Pol, so please do take care and if you see one again, you promise me you will leave it alone, won't you?'

When Mum told me to leave something alone, I never questioned her. She had always taught me to look into birds' nests and take note of their beautiful eggs, but never to touch them or take any. Mum knew about nature and how important it was to have respect for it. Like the tawny owl, the adder fascinated me. Grey, black and terracotta markings patterned its body, and its head had distinctive Vs on it. I found some adder pictures in one of my books. I wished there had been an opportunity to look at it really closely. Perhaps most surprisingly, it hadn't looked slimy. So why did people always refer to snakes in this way?

In 1966, when I was six years old, we were to spend Christmas at Ogof, and in the lead-up whilst visiting Father Christmas in a soulless department store in Liverpool, I became terribly anxious in case he might not know where I was going to be. The shop was hot and stuffy, frantic with shoppers, as we made our way to the grotto, a tented den at the back of the toy department with a sad-looking plush reindeer standing at the entrance. Its eyes were too big. I knew reindeer did not have lashes that long as I had seen them in my books. I was also sure their noses weren't red. This one had half of a red ping-pong ball stuck onto the end of its snout.

Inside the grotto Father Christmas sat bursting forth from his crimson suit. I sat on his capacious knee and explained my worrying predicament. 'You see,' I said, 'I'm not going to be at home this Christmas and I want to make sure you know where to come. You don't even have my address do you?'

He listened intently as part of his beard began to peel away from his fat, round flushed face.

'We are going to be in Wales, and this is the address: Ogof Llechwyenn, Penrhyndeudraeth, Gwynedd, Merionethshire, North Wales.' I slowly spelled it all out for him to make sure he was left in no doubt.

He looked at me curiously, every stitch of his red outfit doing its duty and his white beard now quite adrift. Then he exclaimed in broad Liverpudlian, 'Flippin' 'eck, chook, thare's a mouthful!'

Ogof was a beautiful place nestled deep in mountainous landscape. The surrounding hills were the domain of buzzard and wild goat. Sometimes I could smell the goats. The billies had a ripe, sickly smell that I didn't like. We occasionally saw choughs, crimson legs and bills cherry bright against a cloudless sky, their teasing, chuckling calls echoing over the valley. High above the cottage, hidden in the hills, there were eerie caves with dripping ferns fringing dark entrances that gaped like the toothless mouths of old men. Sometimes we would walk up and shine a torch inside, but Mum and Dad never let me go in. The area was latticed with old slate workings, and many of them were collapsing. Dogs had been lost, and once a boy had gone missing too. He was never found.

One morning some gamekeepers with aggressive, scarred, rough-haired terriers passed the cottage. They had been out looking for foxes and had a very young injured badger cub in a bloodstained game bag. My mother was talking to them over the garden gate, and by the time the conversation was over she had persuaded them to part with the tiny cub. This was my first experience of hand-rearing a wild mammal. We took it home with us when we left Ogof after the weekend. Sadly, though Mum did her best, keeping the cub warm on hot water bottles, and feeding it every few hours with puppy milk from one of my doll's bottles, it skirted precariously on the edge of life for a week, and then died suddenly. Mum said that the dogs had probably caused irreparable internal damage, and told me that it had succumbed to peritonitis, and severe stress brought on by separation from its mother and the other cubs. By the time I was having breakfast, Mum had already been out into the garden and buried it. When she told me, I was beside myself with a sadness I had never before experienced. It burnt deep inside and made butterflies race in my stomach, and with them also came fear – a fear that was new to me. I cried so much I had to miss school. However, I quickly learnt that if you love animals you must also learn to accept the devastation of their departures. That first close proximity to death lingered long.

Most years, Mum and Dad had holidays in Scotland and went deer stalking every autumn. They had always wanted to move north and return to their roots. By the time I was nearly seven, they were planning to leave Cheshire and to sell Ogof; they were looking for an alternative lifestyle. Dad no longer wanted to commute back and forth to Liverpool, and in a flash of inspiration they thought of running a hotel together instead.

We went to view two West Highland hotels, travelling by sleeper with the car from Crewe to Inverness. This was a service called Motorail that ran for a short time for long-distance travellers. Watching Dad drive onto the train's special deck added excitement to the trip. I loved the sleeping compartment that I shared with Mum, with its crisp white sheets and delicious little packets of biscuits brought with the morning tea by the steward at some ungodly hour.

'Make sure you aim straight, Pol,' giggled Mum after she had squatted over the porcelain potty full of piddle and then posted it back into its cupboard, delivering its contents onto the railway line.

Going on the sleeper was an adventure as it rocketed along rhythmically covering the miles. 'I'm not going to sleep, I want to watch the lights as we flash past,' I announced, peering under the window blind. But I was soon overcome with tiredness.

At Inverness we drove on north, heading through a world of wild, sweeping grandeur, where vast sprawling lochs fringed by russet and gold reeds and bogs perfectly mirrored the mountain drama. When I saw Stac Pollaidh (pronounced Polly) for the first time, on our way to Achiltibuie, it filled me with excitement, for not only did it have my name, it looked like a giant's castle straight out of a Grimm fairy tale, its grey grizzled battlements and turrets honed from sheer rock. Its craggy, giddying top wisped with low cloud like smoke coming from a secret hidden chimney on its castellated bastion. Just a couple of years later whilst on a fishing holiday, Uncle Archie took me to the summit. Stac Pollaidh was one of the first mountains I ever climbed, and I have been joyously climbing mountains ever since.

At the Summer Isles Hotel, the owner proudly showed us around, with great emphasis put upon the importance of fine fare despite the remoteness of the location. We were taken into the larder and shown an enormous cheese bell.

'This is where we always have a perfectly ripe vintage Stilton, a vital part of any good menu,' he announced, lifting off the lid.

'So important to accompany a glass of exquisite vintage port,' said Dad, smacking his lips and putting on an exaggerated grandiose tone. Dad was passionate about strong cheese, and quite a connoisseur.

Atop the reeking cheese, a small, immaculate brown mouse sat cleaning its whiskers. The lid was firmly put down again as our host glossed over this minor cartoon-scenario setback. We laughed about it for days.

However, instead of the Summer Isles, my parents chose the Kilchoan Hotel, in Ardnamurchan, on the Sound of Mull. The mouse nearly swayed their decision.

We were embarking on an adventure, and I was filled with excitement, but worried that I'd miss Bo and Fitte who were staying on in Cheshire. On the other hand, I had seen so many pictures of red deer, wildcats and eagles in my books that the thought of perhaps being able to see them for real filled me with glee. And I hated my dull school and hoped that perhaps my new one might be better. And then to live really close to the sea might mean I could see whales and dolphins.

Moving house is chaotic. Months of planning and packing result in eternal cardboard boxes and piles of miscellaneous belongings that fail somehow to warrant a place in the bin, the local charity shop or the new abode. When a move involves a complete change of occupation, a totally different lifestyle, and a far-flung location, bravery also plays a part. My parents were fortunate that the timber business sold quickly, and someone had also bought Ogof. Whilst they packed up and made interminable plans, I spent time with Bo.

Our departure from Cheshire in November of 1967 in a long-wheelbase Land Rover crammed with luggage, dogs, a parrot and a cat, was fraught. On the eve of our departure, there was a deafening thunderstorm that terrified me and made the dogs howl eerily. Rain fell like a monsoon and bounced violently off the house and out-buildings, and a large chunk of the jackdaws' nesting chimney came crashing down. In the morning it lay smashed in the middle of the yard. It had narrowly missed our packed Land Rover.

As we drove up the increasingly busy roads, I saw the vast smoking heaps of burning cattle on many farms, grim evidence of the dreaded foot-and-mouth disease. It was at its peak, tragically taking a heavy toll on herds all over Britain, particularly in the rich dairying counties of Cheshire and Lancashire. The memory of those grotesque pyres, animals piled high with legs akimbo, and the acrid stench of death, remains vivid. It seemed worse than a nightmare. In some cases, farmers had lost a lifetime's work as Ministry of Agriculture vets moved into their farms and felled their beasts with humane killers, often within a matter of hours. It would not be brought under control until the summer of 1968, by which time some 400,000 farm animals had been culled.

We broke our journey at a hotel near Lockerbie, where an ailing hedgehog joined the travelling menagerie and spent the night recuperating in a frilly pink en-suite bathroom noisily consuming dog meat. The dogs were glued to the scene. They peered curiously, their heads on one side, whining quietly. Next day, Glencoe was austere and brooding, its vertiginous ridges and peaks swathed in veils of muslin; from the car window I saw Ossian's Cave appear fleetingly through breaks in the mist. None of this was anything like Cheshire's soft, green, rolling land. I was intoxicated.

Once the two turntable car ferries had plied their way laboriously against the currents of Loch Leven and Loch Linnhe, we were finally on the Ardnamurchan peninsula. Today, only one ferry operates, for a large bridge spans the water at Ballachulish, but the drive to Kilchoan is still like none other. The road has been vastly upgraded and, though still twisty, long and narrow, seems fantastic compared to its predecessor of the 1960s. Back then it was single track, with grass growing up the middle for almost fifty miles, punctuated with switchbacks, hairpin bends, sheer drops into Loch Sunart and the Sound of Mull, and miles of deep, glutinous peat hags. It wends its way through some of the most dramatic scenery of the British Isles, through Atlantic oak woods of stunted hazel, rowan and birch cloaked in lacy grey-green lichens, mosses, liverworts and polypody ferns. Dozens of racing burns dance off the hillsides in a mad dash to the sea. This is Britain's unique rainforest. Seals haul themselves out onto barnacle-blistered skerries, filling the air with their melancholy Hebridean pibrochs, and herons, serious drab-clad clerics, stand patiently watching in almost every bay.

Though we arrived at our new home unscathed, the same could not be said for the furniture removers, who found the journey from Cheshire to Kilchoan harrowing. Their high vehicle was too cumbersome and unwieldy for the road and was harangued by an early equinox gale. Close encounters between the lorry and the peat hags and the viciously overhanging rocks left it in need of a respray, and there had been two punctures. When they literally fell into the hotel bar hours after their predicted arrival time, the drivers too were in dire need of rehabilitation. Jangled nerves had left them with an unquenchable thirst.

As my mother aptly put it, 'It took them almost a week to get over both the journey, and their excessive thirst.'

From their busy base in urban England, little could have prepared them for the tortuous single-track road where dozing sheep lie immovably cudding on the potholed tarmac, and red deer leap out of the gloaming into the path of passing vehicles.

Later that night in the public bar, a broad Liverpudlian voice asked, 'What on Earth made them want to move to a godforsaken dump like this in the first place?'

When the weather is settled and high pressure lies over the west, there is no better place on Earth; views stretch across the Sound of Mull to Morven and the islands Rum, Eigg, Muck, Canna, Coll, Tiree and Skye, and, on the clearest days, Barra and the Uists. But the peninsula is also a savage, hard-bitten, rocky landscape, famed for its extraordinary geology, almost an island itself. Ardnamurchan has exceedingly high rainfall and gales of often hurricane force. In January 2016 a friend recorded a wind speed of 111 mph from his house near Ockle on the peninsula's north coast.

The ceilidh that developed in the public bar the night that our furniture arrived in Kilchoan, as the removal men salved their frayed nerves in the wake of their hair-raising encounter with Ardnamurchan's highway, was simply the first of many. As our new life unfolded and we became involved in the village, I grew to love my conversations with the colourful characters; their tales inspired me and gave me a glorious insight into their lives. The Kilchoan Hotel, like the rest of the village, had no mains electricity. The crofters and villagers had tilley lamps and gaslights, whilst the hotel was run off an asthmatic generator that coughed and spluttered before frequently plunging our visitors back into the Dark Ages.

When my father's father, Roy Munro, a retired naval captain, first tackled the fifty miles of single-track road down the peninsula during the late 1960s, he said, 'It's like the surface of the bloody moon, you must be mad.' The weather was abysmal, and he was unlucky, for during his entire visit he could see no further than his nose and had to walk everywhere bent double.

If you want to live in such a remote place, a sea-girt exposed hunk of rock stuck out into the Atlantic, it is said that you must first experience a winter. If you can tolerate that, then perhaps you may survive. Locals say that holidaymakers charmed by a week of perfect weather have no conception of how miserable it can be when the rain goes on for months on end and gales lay waste to almost everything; then there is the gloom, the darkness, the melancholy, and loneliness. And also, the midges. Ah, but in winter *they* are gone.

Whilst my mother and I adored Kilchoan, my father did not. He was very lonely indeed in winter with no one to talk to and seemed to take to his bed frequently. Though I did not know it at the time, he was drinking incessantly.

My parents certainly can have had little idea either of how that life would be dominated by the elements. I giggle to myself when I remember that my mother's newly positioned greenhouse took off in a squall, last seen heading out to sea, en route towards the island of Coll. As in the Hebrides, caravans and sheds must be battened down if they are to withstand the erratic temperament of the gusts rampaging in off the Atlantic.

Gigantic waves frequently lash the 36-metre-tall lighthouse perched precariously on the bastion of rock at the famous Ardnamurchan Point, the most westerly point on mainland Britain. Standing sentinel since 1849, it is a fine example of Alan Stevenson's design skills. When there is a particularly violent storm, this is the place to watch in awe as the Atlantic boils and fumes like a mighty, malevolent maelstrom.

The farm animals of Ardnamurchan Estate and the local crofts became of constant interest to me. The estate had a pedigree fold of Highland cattle and a herd of hardy, woolly Galloways that thrived on the poor grazing and withstood the abuse the climate constantly hurled at them. There was an Aberdeen Angus bull and a couple of Herefords too. I loved biking over to the farm steading to see if there were bulls in the pens inside. Sometimes they stood placidly waiting for food, damp curly coats steaming, their breath smelling of hay and cattle cake. Or I could put my small hands through the bars and scratch a huge flank, though I was not meant to in case they got trapped. They recognised me and often lowed a soft greeting. Despite their size they seemed gentle. I, in turn, was always gentle with them.

There was a feed room at the back of the steading lined with cobwebby rosettes and certificates with turned-up corners, written in italics with ink that had bled in the dampness. Most of the rosettes were red. And best of all was a large wooden box with tiered layers inside, full of medicines, lotions and potions to make cattle and sheep gleam, odd-looking gadgets for grooming and beautifying, amid rusting tins of hoof and linseed oil, and curry combs and brushes. When various members of the Boot family (founders of the famous chemist chain) had owned the estate, their livestock had been shown all around Scotland, and the bloodlines of both their pedigree Highland and Galloway cattle folds were still revered.

The bulls intrigued me. Some had such vast pendulous pink testicles they almost hit the ground and swayed back and forth when they walked. Sometimes the bulls were inflicted with warble fly, a common parasitic problem for cattle and deer that damages their skin and often leads to a serious loss of condition. One of the farm men showed me how the large larval grub would burst out of the animal's leathery skin, leaving a pit like a mini volcano.

I wasn't really meant to be so close to the bulls, but I loved them, and no one ever tried to stop me. I took the three young sons of some visitors up to see them once, but the bulls were out in the field by the shore. We took a shortcut to the beach through their midst, and suddenly I noticed that they were looking explosive. The Aberdeen Angus put his great head down low and pawed at the ground, and then he bellowed in a threatening manner. Within seconds all five bulls were hurtling towards us. I ran as fast as my short legs would carry me but saw to my horror that the boys, being older and faster, were now yards ahead. With a thundering of hooves and a cascade of mud, the bulls shot past me as, breathless, I realised that I was now running behind them. The bulls were revelling in the escapade, bucking and farting, and spraying the air with loose green dung. The excitement was having a most laxative effect on them. I never saw three boys leap over a barbed-wire fence so fast. One of them left the seat of his breeks hanging droopily attached to the fence. Once the ordeal was over, we rolled on the ground laughing, helpless with relief.

Though we were largely cut off from the outside world, village life was never boring. People came and went. 'Vic Pictures' brought wobbly black-and-white films to the village hall several times a year.

Once the films were finished, another ceilidh might develop. By degrees, the hall would fill as people appeared carrying great platefuls of food and takeaway bottles in brown paper bags. When it rained the bag bottoms dropped out – all the more reason to consume the contents in haste. The previously damp, bare hall pulsated with activity: a baby in a carrycot swaddled in blankets; a collie that had slunk in dozing under a chair with one eye open, hoping for a fallen scone; Gillespie from the Post Office with his squeezebox; fiddlers, singers and children struggling to play a new instrument, or sing a song they had been practising for the Gaelic Mod; the smell of sweat and perfume, soup and strong liquor. Grannies danced with one another or tiny children, whilst the menfolk sat in a line, arms folded, refusing to budge till mellowed by drams. Only then would they take to the floor.

As we escaped outside for a breath of fresh air between dances, the rasping calls of the corncrake drifted up from the flag iris beds close by. And I stood transfixed, just listening to both the corncrakes and, even more magical, the sound of drumming snipe, a sound that never fails to send a frisson of ethereal excitement through my veins.

The other children soon went in and never seemed so interested in the wildlife around us: 'Och the midges are biting and she's chust standing there, come on let's go back in and leave her, she's cuckoo, she's away wi' the birds again.' They laughed and disappeared.

Then a couple might waltz out amorously arm-in-arm, giggling, and disappear around the back.

Travelling salesmen frequently came to the village too, and Peter, an Indian from Glasgow, brought a large selection of porous 'waterproof' rainwear and other clothing in various unsuitable pastel shades, much to the delight of the repressed shoppers.

Lizzie kept a tearoom and helped in the hotel. She came in every weekend to do the washing-up and sometimes helped out with waitressing. Her flock of Blackface sheep wandered around the village munching any colourful blooms that raised their pretty heads. She took all the scraps from the hotel for her beloved hens, the eggs of which had quite the deepest orange yolks imaginable. It must have been their seaweed diet, for they scratched on the shore too. She hated the great black-backed gulls that stole their food. Once, I saw her sneaking up on one with a huge shovel as it was feeding, oblivious, and then she felled it, killing it with one almighty blow. I was shocked, but I still loved her and her tearoom. It was also a favourite haunt on a wet day for many of the tourists. All her delicious home baking was priced at 1s 6d, for the defunct till that she had acquired from the hotel had jammed at this price.

Christmas in Ardnamurchan was still little celebrated in the 1960s. My mother looked out that first Christmas morning and watched the hearse filing down to the pier to catch the Mull ferry. Funerals even took place on Christmas Day. New Year was a different matter, cause for the utmost celebration. Once, the public bar was shut on Hogmanay; Mum loaded up the Land Rover with the hotel staff and anyone else keen to join in, and drove out to Ardnamurchan lighthouse. Here we joined the resident light keepers and their families for a spectacular ceilidh. At midnight, the New Year was ushered in over the radio as Gaelic songs were sung and stories exchanged with other light keepers in even lonelier Hebridean outposts: Barra Head, Hyskeir, the Uists, the Butt of Lewis, Skerryvore. Many of the other light keepers would be spending the time with only one another for company in their basic accommodation, their wives and children far away on the mainland. These Hogmanay airwave communications were their only link to the outside world, the only means of making this time of year special, instead of simply another day.

Ardnamurchan lighthouse had suitable accommodation for its keepers to have their families with them. The keepers' wives prepared an extensive feast, vital blotting paper to sop up the copious libations of whisky. After many hours of song and merriment, the return journey was hazardous; drink-driving largely ignored, as it was during this era in many remote parts of the country. Vehicles frequently went into hag and ditch, but the landings were usually soft, and fortunately no one was hurt, though a few vehicles were never the same again. And a long walk home had a sobering effect, with everyone ready for bacon and eggs, more singing and eternal merrymaking. New dents and scratches were added to our Land Rover, and its side steps, like its occupants, appeared to have a drunken list following these excursions.

Hogmanay celebrations continued long into January. My father was seldom a part of this. Two or three times I saw him in an advanced drunken state, and at primary school, I overheard the boys saying, 'David Clark is a boozer.' They always dropped the Munro part of his name, ironic given it was his real name.

One morning one of them said, 'Your Dad is an alky, but then so is mine.'

I thought for a minute, and replied, 'What's an alky?'

There was a long silence before my informer replied, 'Addicted to the bottle, and my mum keeps on telling my dad that he's one.'

I remained largely oblivious to the alcoholic turmoil that must have been percolating between my mother and father. I was, happily, too busy exploring. I only heard them have a serious argument once. That was when we lived in Cheshire. Mum always had a radio on, and Dad hated this and was always turning it off. He couldn't bear background music or radio chat. 'It's a lot of bloody tosh,' he would say. One hot day Mum was in the garden weeding on her hands and knees with the radio at her side. Dad appeared and switched it off. Mum stood up immediately, picked up the radio and flung it with all her strength so that it landed on the paving stones and smashed into tiny pieces that bounced and rattled across like gunshot.

The next day when he came home from work, Dad was carrying a smart new model – a state-of-the-art red Roberts. It looked expensive. After that he stopped turning it off.

I loved the sea. I loved wild storms, the wilder the better, and I loved watching the waves and trying to count them. I was beginning to learn how inquisitive the seals were, particularly if one of our dogs was with me on the shore. They would come close, and snort and I could see the salty droplets coating their thick whiskers.

On calm summer evenings I sometimes went out in a little boat to fish with DL, a local man known simply by his initials. Or instead, I would go with another elderly local character, and we'd fish for silvery mackerel with darrows sending out the weighted, feathery lines into the dark depths, and hauling them in laden with writhing fish. In the late evenings, phosphorescence mysteriously shone back at us like fairy lights from the vortex below.

'That's the mermaids lighting our way,' said my companion as he loaded the bottom of the boat with the next quivering batch of fish and fumbled about trying to re-light a small, soggy cigar.

The fish wriggled around my bare feet in a pool of salty water that was tinged with pinky blood as we despatched each in turn with a quick thump on the head with a piece of shaped wood known as a priest. I took some of our catch home and Betty, the hotel cook, or Mum, fried the gleaming fish with butter and oatmeal.

I was so excited when I saw my first orca – a killer whale – close to Ardnamurchan Point whilst we were trolling for mackerel that I nearly fell out of the boat. There were basking sharks too; they drifted randomly close to the surface with their great mouths gaping wide as they filtered the nutrient rich water for plankton. We could almost reach out and touch them. Sometimes dolphins and porpoises followed curiously in our wake, treating us to fine displays of their lissom acrobatics. They were so beautiful that they made a lump come to my throat. They still do.

There were often spontaneous boat trips over to Mull, and if the weather was obliging several small boats would take off across the Sound to the annual Tobermory Games. The return whisky-fuelled voyages were fraught with snags, dodgy engines, bad weather, or poor navigational skills. DL took his boat, the *Edith*, over to the Games, but on one notorious occasion he had consumed so much that getting himself back in the boat and homeward bound proved challenging. Tobermory harbour was like a packed car park, boats lined up and moored in rows. Though he miraculously managed to reach his waiting vessel without falling into the sea, once aboard DL steered her straight into the bows of a prestigious naval frigate moored further out in the bay. Feeling a small thump, the smartly uniformed captain appeared on the bridge clutching a mug of tea. He was red with wrath. Poor DL, lost in an alcoholic haze, thought he had landed in some French port and exclaimed, 'un petit garçon, un petit garçon', over and over again.

DL had two boats, both of which were held together with thick sticky tar. The *Nelly*, too, fished the waters round Kilchoan village, but visitors treated to one of his sightseeing trips along the coast sometimes had to row ashore when the rotten old engine conked out.

DL was a frequent customer in the public bar. Worried about his growing baldness he saw a newspaper advert for a state-of-the-art gentleman's wig – a Crown Topper – newly on the market. However, in telling all his friends about his purchase, he referred to it as a 'Town Cropper'. I could often earn extra pocket money by washing glasses behind the bar or sweeping up. Once, I thought there was a dozing cat under the seats in a corner by the fire. It was the Town Cropper. It was duly returned to DL, but no one came to claim the grinning false teeth with their electric pink plastic gums that I found there beneath a crisp packet.

The wonderful childhood that had begun in rural Cheshire became even better here. However, at school, to begin with, I was bullied. I had a different accent and was called a Sassenach. Some of the boys and two girls in particular made the start hell and did nothing to reassure me that school was a good place. But I enjoyed our sporadic Gaelic lessons and really loved our sweet teacher, Mary Cameron, and I quickly made two special friends. We sought our entertainment outwith school, knee deep in the rich rock pools around Kilchoan's varied shoreline.

On bright days, Miss Cameron, who taught at Kilchoan Primary for over thirty years, might suggest a foray to the rock pools at Mingary Pier. This, like the trips to the pond to collect frogspawn, stoked my lifelong love for 'guddling', catching small trout by hand, something we also did as children. It can also be used to describe the hours we spent turning over stones in rock pools, marvelling at our discoveries: deep red anemones, starfish, brittle stars, cushion stars, prickly purple and green sea urchins, scuttling little fish with clear fins of fine gauze, and squat lobsters. Intriguing hermit crabs, flamboyant one minute, were overcome with shyness the next, as they popped back into their borrowed shells in a flash. The vibrant colours of algae and weed, the roughness of rocks decorated with grey barnacles, and the pimples of limpets clinging on tighter than superglue – these perfect miniature marine gardens filled me with blissful delight. All was absorbed and stored. Tins and wooden boxes housed the riches I brought home: a gull's mottled eggshell, dried sedges, a mermaid's purse, shells of mother-of-pearl, and tiny yellow and orange periwinkles, as well as minuscule crabs, cowries and gull pellets. Once thoroughly examined in minute detail, the living treasures were returned to their pools.

When they were gathering the sheep, I joined the shepherds at the fank. The wiry Blackface ewes jostled and panicked, jumping in the air randomly, trying to avoid the worming gun, vaccination needle or foot-trimming shears. The men worked quickly and efficiently. Gaelic oaths and jokes that I didn't always understand kept every- one's spirits up when the weather closed in and another shower blew in off the Sound of Mull. Once all the ewes had been dealt with, they were duly marked with coloured keel, divided into a particular group and then the gates were opened. They'd race out through the mud and leap gymnastically through the gateway as the collies snapped eagerly at their heels.

Later in the summer it was time for clipping. The big shed at the farm steadings was cleared ready for days of hard labour. It was a gathering of people too as everyone came to assist, armed with their hand shears and sharpening stones, as well as advice and help for those young shepherds less adept. A rhythmic clack, clack of shears added a metallic ringing to the loud and furious bleating of ewes and lambs temporarily separated from one another. Women arrived with plates laden with sandwiches and home baking, flasks of sweet tea and bottles of lemonade, and set up camp in a far corner. My job, along with some of the other children, was to roll fleeces and jump in the woolsacks suspended from the beams to pack the wool down inside. By the end of those long days we reeked of sheep, and our hands and faces were coated in oily lanolin and sore from gorse prickles and brambles caught up in the fleeces.

The Ardnamurchan Estate farm manager, John Maxwell, was a real ally, someone I admired from the first moment I met him. He wore large, turned-up-toe tackety boots and khaki shorts in summer, and always a low-brimmed trilby. Eventually the last tups would be relieved of their weighty woollens, the shed cleared again, the wool and dags swept away, and more food would appear as if by magic. Then there would be a ceilidh that continued far into the night as a toenail of moon sent ghostly shadows to silver the backs of the newly clipped ewes, and John's fine fiddle-playing kept clumsy working footwear jigging until the small hours.

When one of our Galloway cows became mired in a deep bog, I went with John and watched as they pulled the poor terrified beast out with ropes tied to the tractor, having first poured a bottle of gin down her throat to warm her up. She came out with a glugging, sucking noise and a gut-wrenching roar of misery, and then stood shivering and wobbly whilst we rubbed her down with straw wisps, and I fretted that she would die. Other rescues involved arduous digs to free battle-scarred terriers from subterranean fox cairns.

Hugh MacNally, the estate stalker, brother of the famous stalker and naturalist Lea MacNally from Torridon, had the stride of an antelope and my short legs struggled to keep up. His voice was so soft that, if the wind was not in the right direction, his gentle, informative commentary was blown away far across the Sound of Mull. Like his brother Lea, he had an encyclopaedic knowledge of deer. During the stalking season we strode all day across the open hill on Ben Hiant and I listened avidly to his deer stories and learnt the best places to find them, the places where they sheltered depending on the wind's direction, and I learnt too that there was always a watchful old hind keeping guard, ready to warn the herd of approaching threats. After we had eaten our sandwiches, we might doze briefly in the autumn sunshine amid the roars of the rutting stags, with the Sound of Mull shimmering, liquid mercury far below, a golden eagle drifting over the ridge, its great wings outstretched, circling higher and higher until it was the size of a dust mote, and then vanished.

Then there was Lulu – the first of a long line of adored pet sheep. The hotel had a large, blowsy sheep-pruned garden. Sheep wandered randomly around the village, for most crofters had pet lambs and were always eager to find someone to relieve them of the burden. Alan McLachlan – pier master, crofter, gravedigger, fireman and general factotum – brought her to me because he had heard how much I loved animals. 'This is for you,' he said, lifting a sodden lamb from the back of his Reliant Robin, in which he frequently transported a large Blackface tup. She bleated in a plaintive, miserable little voice – she had a yellow backside sodden with scour, and she smelt terrible. In fact, she was not very attractive at all.

I reached my hands out to her and engulfed the small thin body as she cried pitifully, and then she began sucking on my ear lobe and nuzzling into my neck. There was no going back.

'I'm just away in for a dram,' said the wily Alan before I had a moment to renege on my new charge. He vanished into the hotel bar leaving me with a bag of milk and a bottle.

I rushed into the kitchen to find Mum and show her the latest member of the family. 'I am going to call her Lulu,' I said without a moment's hesitation as I put my new companion down on the freshly washed floor.

Lulu bleated loudly and then piddled spectacularly, sending a hot wave of steaming urine splashing everywhere, and adding a new scent to vie with that of floor disinfectant. Given her diminutive size, it was quite surprising how much there was.

'Well named, I should say,' laughed Betty the cook.

Like most of her kind, my pot-bellied Blackface waif survived and was soon greedily devouring an endless round of milk feeds. Mum became as attached to her as I was, but I knew that Lulu was really mine.

When a visiting photojournalist from a Glasgow daily newspaper came to stay, Lulu enchanted him. And so did my mother. He took numerous pictures of her going up the stairs carrying the guests' morning tea trays with Lulu at her heels. The pictures appeared in the paper and briefly boosted hotel visitor numbers. Other forays up the stairs were, however, less appreciated, and new arrivals might find ominous trails of black currants leading to their rooms.

With school being right next door to the hotel, it was easy for Lulu to follow me there every day. She waited for us to emerge at playtime, and as she got bigger she became a real nuisance, barging and shoving in her keenness to steal biscuits or cakes. The boys teased her and tried to teach her to box with her head, but when she did, they sneered and kicked her and that made me cry. I tried to defend her but then the boys began to bully me again. I wished I could stop Lulu coming with me, but I was her best friend and she was definitely mine; she would have followed me anywhere.

The district nurse also had a pet lamb, named Paddy. The two lambs, now getting very large and fat due to far too many biscuits, wandered about the village devouring any efforts to create floral displays. They were a menace, and neither had they any respect whatsoever for the numerous skulking collies that tried to round them up. Paddy and Lulu, when provoked, turned round and charged at them like two Spanish fighting bulls. Once, someone imprisoned the pair in the gents' outside lavatory adjacent to the public bar. Being shut in had a most laxative effect, and the subsequent skittery mess was even streaked up the walls. Later someone scrawled 'Paddy loves Lulu' on the walls, adding to the rest of the graffiti.

Acquiring fresh produce for the hotel had always proved difficult. It was a long haul from Glasgow Fruit Market and, by the time the goods had either come by boat via Tobermory on the small passenger ferry, the *Loch Nell*, or via the road, they were often somewhat limp, like the lorry drivers.

Despite their reputation, sheep are far from stupid. Lulu found that by scratching herself against the feed store door, it would eventually open. She once devoured an entire sack of Savoy cabbages. And those also had a laxative effect, mostly around the hotel doorways. This was definitely unappreciated.

A tray of fresh peaches, viewed as a rare treat, was Lulu's next casualty. She and Betty, the cook, fell out spectacularly the day that peach melba was grandly added to the menu. Lulu had reached the peaches first and devoured every single one. To further upset the irate cook, Lulu had spat a stone neatly back into the shaped cardboard holder where once there had lain a blushing prize. Betty was apoplectic and chased Lulu up the road with a carving knife. Tiny Betty, as broad as she was tall, wore long lacy bloomers. I could see the lace drooping down below her overalls as she toddled furiously up the road in hot pursuit of the peach thief.

Soon after that, Lulu stuck her head into a newly made vat of Betty's cooling marmalade and left wool all over the sticky contents. Then when she also devoured a tray of sugar-sprinkled shortbread, Betty threatened to put roast lamb on the menu. And I think she meant it.

Once children had finished at the primary school, they were sent away to weekly board in a hostel in Oban or Fort William, where the nearest high schools were. But when I was nine, and after only two years at Kilchoan Primary School, Mum announced with no preamble, 'We think it's now time for you to go to a new school.'

Panic set in. Why was I being sent away so early? My stomach began to churn. I didn't want to go away. I didn't want to leave Mum; and now at last the boys had stopped teasing me and I was part of the gang.

'We will come over to see you. You will really like it as it's a nice school.'

How did she know I would really like it? I hated all school, and now I wanted to run away to avoid going.

In the holidays we went to Perth and spent a night in a hotel there so we could go and buy a school uniform. The shop assistant was starchy, with a tape measure round her neck that stuck out over the top of her enormous frontispiece. She didn't laugh much, told me to stand still and stop fidgeting, and kept on adding more and more supposedly necessary items to an endless list. Mum shrugged; she had to pay the bill. It wasn't going to be like Kilchoan School, where we wore whatever we liked. Some of the clothes were scratchy. There was also a list of all the other things we would need in addition to clothing.

Dad had gone away on a business trip. I wondered where he was. I had been worrying about him as I had seen him very drunk again and had heard him crying like a child. Was this why I was being sent away? I didn't want to go far away and be stuck in what sounded like a horrible all-girls school without the animals. What about Lulu? I also had my spaniel, Flo, who was always ready for an adventure and came everywhere with me too.

Rumours were going around that the surrounding estate had been bought by 'two scrappies [scrap merchants] from Perth'. The bush telegraph in a small community frequently misconstrues the story. Kilchoan, like most villages, is a place where everyone knows what you have done before you have contemplated doing it, and if they don't, they will make it up anyway. The so-called 'scrappies' were nothing of the kind.

George Ferguson – better known as Geordie – had bought Ardnamurchan Estate in partnership with a close friend and business partner. They intended to rear livestock in the west to fatten on his farm on the richer agricultural eastern side of the country. He and his family would come to Mingary House for holidays, though would remain based elsewhere.

Dad was increasingly away 'on business'. Geordie was in Kilchoan for long periods by himself and whilst work was being done to his house, he would stay at Kilchoan Hotel. There he met Knickerbocker Glory or Annie Ruadh (Red Annie). It doesn't take long in a small community before you are given a nickname. My mother's attractive, vivacious personality, red hair and habit of wearing plus-fours had earned her the two apt appellations.

3

The Spell is Broken

Soon after the sickening announcement that I was to be sent away to Butterstone House School, near Dunkeld, I was summoned to see Mum in the sitting room. I wondered why she wanted me so urgently. The only other time this had happened was when I was trying out cigarettes with some friends and we were caught by one of the hotel staff. On that occasion I had entered the sitting room in trepidation, but Mum had casually said, 'I hear you have been smoking. Is it true?'

I knew with Mum there was no point in wasting effort by lying. 'Yes,' I said, 'I only wanted to see what it was like.'

She smiled at me. 'Well, why don't you have another one? Here you are, Pol, you can try as many as you like. Don't bother hiding in future.'

She passed me a packet but I turned away, full of shame. I already thought that cigarettes had the most revolting taste and hated them from the first puff. I was certainly not going to try it again. I shook my head.

Mum laughed and said, 'Well, next time you fancy a cigarette just let me know and I will get you one.'

This time I had not been doing anything I wasn't meant to, so I wondered why she wanted me to go and see her 'immediately'. She was sitting on the sofa with the dogs at her feet. She had been crying. I could tell by her eyes. And she looked pale.

'Dad has had to leave, and I am so, so sorry, Pol, but he won't be coming back here other than to pack up his things. Life here really doesn't suit him.'

The Spell is Broken

I wanted to know where Dad had gone. Mum said that he was ill and had gone away for some special treatment. A hot feeling filled my head and then I felt waves of giddiness as if I was about to faint. 'Why won't he be coming back, why?'

She made me sit beside her and then she hugged me. 'I am so sorry, it's very hard to explain to you, but he has to move away as we cannot live together any more. It's not that we don't love each other, but we don't love each other in the way we used to.'

What on Earth did that mean? My mouth went dry, I felt confused, even a little sick. 'Does that mean you might stop loving me too? What will happen to Dad? Where is he going?' Poor Mum, all these questions.

'No, I will be staying here. Of course I love you. I am not going anywhere.' She started to cry but quickly pulled herself together. 'Dad is very ill indeed and he has to go away for proper treatment. It is difficult to explain to you but he really can't live here any more. He is very unhappy here.'

When I started to cry she swiftly took the situation under control and was effusively sympathetic in her reassurance.

This news was so sudden. There were so many questions, all without proper answers. How could anyone stop loving someone in the way they had before? I didn't understand this at all. My spaniel Flo was lying in a sodden heap steaming by the peat fire. She quickly got up and wagged her way over to me. She licked my hands and then she jumped up on the sofa beside me and put her head on my knees, whimpering. Mum didn't say a word to her. Nor did she try to push her off the sofa, where she was not supposed to be, especially in such a sodden state.

We sat there in silence for a few minutes before Mum got up to make some tea. I had noticed that recently she seemed to be drinking a lot of tea. 'Everything will sort itself out in time. Both Dad and I still love you more than anything and, when he's better, you can go and stay with him.'

It all looked so simple in her eyes. In mine, it did not.

Mystery surrounded the situation. No one would explain and the hotel staff, who I regarded as my friends, were all talking in whispers. It was only a matter of days after Dad had gone that I went into my parents' bedroom and found Geordie, the new owner of the Ardnamurchan Estate, who I had only met a couple of times when he was staying in the hotel, sitting up in bed with my mother, drinking more bloody tea. She explained that now she loved Geordie and we were going to be living with him instead. I felt very embarrassed and rushed out. Once again it seemed so simple to her. Adults were peculiar.

This situation was becoming ever more complex. Over the coming weeks, Mum continually told me how lovely and kind Geordie was.

'He has bought the hotel from Dad, and either he and I will run it together, or we will find a manager. We won't live in the hotel any more and will be moving to Mingary House next to the farm. You will love being there, so much nicer than living in the hotel and it's going to be a really beautiful house once all the work is done. We will paint your room yellow.'

More panic. 'Will Lulu be able to come too?' Why did adults see things in such simple terms? Yellow?

Though it was probably as amicable as these miserable events ever are, I soon found out that Dad was devastated. Though he never, ever maligned my mother at any point, over the coming years he constantly broke down and cried about how much he missed her. However, he appeared to behave impeccably and was, according to Mum, agreeable to the various deals that had been struck between them. There were no slanging matches, and I never heard either of my parents miscalling the other. Ever. This is a rare thing. I will always be grateful to them both for that fact.

Was Dad's going away also the reason for me being sent off too? We were both going to leave. It was years before I fully appreciated that they must have thought it would be better if I weren't around witnessing the unhappy developments.

The dreadful day of my departure came around all too quickly. Though it was in an outstandingly beautiful location, in Perthshire, I hated the new school from the beginning, and was acutely homesick.

I had an awful engulfing butterflies sensation, the feeling of dread and fear mixed together, and a mounting stomach-ache, waves of panic and nausea. I was bullied again and didn't seem to fit in. This time it was because I had picked up a West Highland accent.

I do remember one ghastly episode when my father drove Mum and me to meet Geordie at the Ballachulish Hotel. We were going away for a couple of weeks – this was so that Dad could move all his belongings out. It was intended to minimise the upheaval for all of us, but me in particular. I made a scene and insisted that if we were leaving, I had to take Flo too. I didn't want to be separated from her as well as Dad. She was a cheery, tail-wagging dog eager to join in everything. She loved swimming and it was hard to keep her out of the burn or the sea, so her shaggy liver-and-white coat was always sticky with mud and sand or had extra dark patches from wallowing in peat hags. She lived outside in the kennel and didn't have good manners. She was a thief, and she frequently grabbed hens, with fatal consequences for them. To make it worse, she was not very well house-trained. My mother certainly did not want to take her to stay in a smart hotel where she would be sure to disgrace herself. However, I apparently made such a fuss that she capitulated, and Flo came with us.

The drive was awful, as Dad was steamed up like a rampant bull. Mum shrieked at him to slow down. He did seem to be going far too fast. Every time he slammed the brakes on hard when another car appeared around a corner on the single-track road, all the Land Rover seat backs banged down, and then banged back up again as he accelerated away after each car passed. It made Mum and me jump.

'For Christ's sake, David, will you slow down?' Mum was now angry.

Dad took no notice.

When we arrived at the hotel, Mum, Dad and Geordie had a meeting and I was sent out to play in the garden with Flo. I didn't mind because I was always happy to be outside exploring instead of listening to the waffle of boring grown-ups. When I came back in, Dad had gone.

Despite having been outside for a long time, Flo squatted in the hall and produced a huge turd, planting it neatly underneath the tall leather-fronted reception desk. It resembled a giant walnut whip with a little curl at its summit. Behind the desk sat a frosty old woman. She couldn't have seen Flo's misdemeanour unless she had stood up and leant over the high barricade. However, unless her sense of smell had been seriously impaired, she must surely have noticed the unmistakable aroma that filtered through the building.

Mum and Geordie laughed when I ran in to tell them what had happened. Geordie got up, sauntered past the aged receptionist, and politely said 'good morning' and then went into the dining room and stole some red napkins from out of the glasses on the tables. He then crawled on his hands and knees in front of the desk so the old crone couldn't see over. Luckily, the heap was fairly solid. He grabbed it in the napkins and then crawled back to the dining room. He then stood up and proceeded to saunter past again, said good morning to the old bat a second time, went out of the front door, and threw the contents into the hedge outside. He then winked at me as I was standing by the door with Flo on the lead.

This was an episode that endeared my future stepfather to me. I could see he was full of fun. I could also see he was very kind. Though we laughed about it, Flo was indeed in disgrace. We stayed for a week in a hotel in Angus where she was an absolute pest. She did the bum trick on the cream-coloured carpets, leaving amber streaks, and she jumped on the beds, leaving muddy paw marks and copious amounts of hair. She also succeeded in partially preparing a hen for the oven, leaving it almost totally bald, though happily on this occasion not dead. Importantly, however, she was of great solace to me, which is, I suppose, why they agreed she could come.

Meanwhile, Dad was moving out. His departure was an upheaval as great as the expedition north but plagued by setbacks. The furniture lorry taking his belongings south crashed in Glencoe, ruining many treasured items. It was a while before I saw him again but I wrote to him several times a week. When he did come up to my new school he seemed unhappy and worried. Even as a child I picked up that on occasions there was something pathetic about him. He was either in perfect control, witty, loud and authoritative or, perhaps when he was battling to keep off drink, would seem edgy and concerned.

The first time I went south to stay with him in the holidays, I was nine. He was living in a little flat in London where I made him pancakes every day for tea, cooked over a camping gas ring. In the daytime, we had exciting visits to the Natural History Museum and to see a matinee ballet of *The Tales of Beatrix Potter*.

Holidays in Ardnamurchan were very different. Mum was usually busy in the hotel so I was once again blissfully free. Sometimes Geordie's son Malcolm was with us, though he was four years older than me so didn't think much to having a girl around. Geordie's daughter Mary, who is two years older than me, did not come into our new life until much later on as a rift had developed following her parents' divorce. Malcolm was keen on farming and in his holidays was either out with the farm manager, John Maxwell, or fishing and stalking with Hugh MacNally. Geordie had generously bought me a pony called Gingerbread Man, and I spent my time grooming and riding him. Flo would come with us on all-day wildlife adventures.

By this time, we had moved out of the hotel and into Mingary House. From there I often rode along the track on the shore, and left Ginger grazing whilst I went into the ancient stunted oak wood that sprawled up Ben Hiant's westerly flanks to explore and look for eagles and wildcats. I watched seals and otters and lay in the bracken listening to buzzards and ravens. Oddly, Flo was always very obedient on these excursions and stuck to me like a leech. Lulu had come to Mingary too but was unpopular because she was eating Mum's new garden, and Mum was threatening to move her into the fields with the other sheep.

I dreaded the return to Butterstone. Freedom gone, I had to adjust to a world of 'ladylike' behaviour and prickly clothes, a cape for church visits, and a hard straw boater in summer. And then there was sharing a dormitory with a lot of spoilt, bitchy little girls. Several of them were bullies and continued to tease me due to my

West Highland accent. It was such a contrast to the peace of home, where, as I opened my bedroom curtains, my first view was of the ruin of Mingary Castle and the glorious Sound of Mull. There were frequently otters on the shore below. Often there were porpoises in the bay.

At Butterstone we were sent to bed when wide awake, and woken up when fast asleep; in the morning we donned the two pairs of regimental knickers – a thin pair beneath and a voluminous grey woollen pair on top. Then after queuing to wash behind our ears in a cracked basin with verdigris taps, we trooped down to breakfast. The toast was rubberised and the butter slightly rancid, the teachers strict, the lessons uninspiring.

It wasn't all bad, because at break time and during the weekends the surrounding ancient woodland revealed its secrets. We made extensive dens, and I built a hiding place where I could watch birds, the elf-like red squirrels with their big ear tufts and exotic acrobatic displays. I was besotted by the squirrels. Then there were wide-eyed spotty fallow deer that came out to graze in the early mornings and at dusk. We didn't have fallow deer in Ardnamurchan. A pair of wrens had made their perfect nest in a chicken-mesh fence and were using one of the honeycomb shapes as the entrance. The nest was domed and constructed with softly fading green moss. I learnt that it was actually the cock bird that was the nest builder, and he made several different bowers so that the hen could choose the one she liked best. Each of his creations was a work of art. When eight little wrens began to appear at the nest's doorway, I raced eagerly out of lessons to go and watch them. Like avian mice, the babies gaped little beaks wide open, begging for a ceaseless supply of food. I also learnt that wrens never came to feed on our bird tables and mainly ate live insects.

Though the strict, and often pointless, rules meant we were not allowed to take in any extra food for ourselves, we were permitted to take packets of wild bird food back to school. Bird nuts, however, had been banned for we occasionally became so hungry that we ate them ourselves. Sometimes I felt so famished that I even ate the birdseed. It blew up in my stomach and gave me a pain, and then I had to go to matron. She was a dragon. Mum received a sharp letter from the headmistress instructing her not to let me bring birdseed any more either. The birds would have gone hungry, so I secreted pieces of soggy toast up my sleeves to take out. It was inedible as far as I was concerned.

School food was grim: the nauseating aroma of overcooked cabbage reminded me of the fermentations of a steaming cow pat or, worse still, the stench of a dead cow with a gas-filled gut; I had seen plenty in Ardnamurchan. Then there was the disgusting habit of boiling the life out of yellow smoked haddock in milk, and its dreadful lingering stink; worst of all was the revoltingly slimy chicken fricassée accompanied by rice in a solid grey ball. And haggis. We all hated the idea of what was in it, mostly grease with gristly bits and unmentionable animal parts. I stuffed tissues in my pocket, asked for a small helping and then tried to dump the hellish stuff onto my knee straight into the tissues. Often, I was caught or, worse still, forgot it in my pocket and it made a repugnant mess on my skirt. If we were found out, we had to eat another helping. School food put me off certain dishes for life. It still brings back repulsive memories.

We had a rotund and bossy Scottish dancing teacher whom I loathed. She clearly loathed me equally, perhaps because it took me so long to learn to *pas de basque*. She had flat feet (probably from doing too much *pas de basque*) and a big arse that stuck out like a tray. She also had BO. We had to perform in Perth City Hall in a competition and my kilt fell off midway through a reel, revealing what we called LTBs – 'lastic top and bottoms' – capacious, thick, grey knickers that would have served as fine contraceptives a little further down the line. For now, some aspects of sex remained a mystery, although I had seen the cows and sheep, and other animals and birds, mating and giving birth back home. I knew how things worked, but certainly had no idea that sex might happen other than for procreation.

We had riding once a week and counted the days till our cheery teacher, Pat, arrived. Some girls had their own ponies, though to begin with Ginger stayed at home. As soon as Pat appeared, we followed her out to the fields to catch the ponies, and those of us who were good riders were allowed to ride bareback to the manège where we tied them all up.

We loved the grooming, and so did the ponies for it soothed their tickles. The atmosphere filled with clouds of dried mud and dust, and we could hide our faces in the ponies' long manes and breathe in their sweet, distinctive aroma. There were shrieks as someone had their toes stood on, more shrieks when a pony refused to pick its feet up to have them cleaned, and cries of 'Oh yukky!' when the ponies dumped large dollops of steaming dung, splattering a small groom in the process. And there were always yells of 'Help, he's so fat I can't do up the girth. Please can you help me, Pat?'

Pat whizzed round us all and patiently dealt with everyone's particular problem. 'Goodness, Seagull, you have piled on the beef. You'll have to go in the starvation paddock this week.' Seagull was a particular favourite, a gentle grey pony that whinnied softly when we went to catch him.

Time with Pat made us forget the parts of boarding school we didn't like; we made calendars with pictures of our ponies with Pat, and ticked off the days until she arrived again. Sometimes after someone had been bucked off or bolted with, she got aboard and quickly reminded the culprit exactly who was in charge. A few rounds of the field with Pat at the helm amid puffing and blowing, and a meek mount could then be returned to its eager jockey. Even equine egos had to be deflated on occasion.

Eventually, I was allowed to take Ginger to Butterstone with me, and a guinea pig called Winifred. Winifred was a saviour.

Ah, Winifred! I had been to London to stay with Dad in the holidays, and I had travelled south on the plane to Heathrow with a label around my neck as an 'unaccompanied minor'. When it was time for him to take me back, he arranged for us to have tea on the way with friends who lived close to the airport and had two daughters my age. Whilst Dad was busy chatting to the mother, the girls took me to see their baby guinea pigs. There was one still without a new home, an adorable purring ginger-and-white female. By the time we had to leave, I had struck up a deal and swapped a precious box of coloured crayons for the guinea pig. I announced that she was coming back to Scotland with me. Poor Dad! The children's smart mother was clearly thrilled to be shot of the last baby. She dashed off to the nearby pet shop to acquire a travelling box before Dad could change his mind.

Dad, meanwhile, was on the telephone to the airline, instructing them rather pompously, and with much authority, that his unaccompanied daughter now had a travelling companion. I am not sure quite how he managed to cut through all the red tape associated with a globetrotting guinea pig, but once we arrived at Heathrow Airport he had turned on the charm and was sweetly persuasive. A glamorous mini-skirted hostess wearing a stockade of mascara came out from behind the scenes and whisked off Winifred and me – as with Lulu, I had had no hesitation in naming my baby guinea pig. Soon we were airborne.

When Mum arrived to pick me up, the tiny, terrified Winifred in her box emerged from the hold on the carousel with all the suitcases. She seemed none the worse for her jet-setting and lived for eight years. I suspect that guinea pig cost Dad a fortune, but she was worth every penny because I loved her with all my heart and, like so many of the animals that have been part of my life, she was a great source of comfort and security during a difficult time.

I saw little of either Mum or Dad during those gloomy years at Butterstone, though sometimes one or other would come to take me out. Dad's planned visits often fell through at the last minute and I would be summoned by the headmistress to be told he was ill – again. I missed both him and Mum dreadfully, and I really missed my grandmother Bo, though she wrote wonderful letters with poems she compiled for me about two mice:

There met two mice at Scarborough beside the rushing sea,
the one from Market Harborough, the other from Dundee.

Their antics and adventures kept the pair of us amused for months.

I wrote back in turn and told her that sometimes I took Winifred to church with us, hidden under my cape. Once, Winifred escaped in Dunkeld Cathedral, and we only narrowly managed to catch her again before she dashed from under the pew and right down the aisle. We'd had to feign terrible coughing fits to cover up Winifred's indignant squeaks after her escape bid had been foiled. I stopped taking her after that. It was too risky. The other downside was that she filled up my pockets with what we called 'liquorice torpedoes', as well as horrible wet patches.

Bo appreciated that story; she hated me being away as much as I did. Though I saw her little we rang each other often and wrote letters every week.

Then Dad did come to take me out. He arrived smelling of whisky and was behaving in an exaggerated manner, verbose and long-winded, and I felt very embarrassed by him, particularly when he said good morning to the headmistress over and over again. Eventually, after much pomp but no circumstance, we got into his car.

Dad immediately announced, 'Let's have a decent lunch, Pol. I know you hate school food, so let's go and get something really good. How about a big rare steak, mmm?'

We left the school in a swirl of gravel and went straight to a hotel he had already chosen in Dunkeld.

At the hotel, Dad asked for the wine menu and after protracted deliberations ordered a bottle of claret. I asked for roast chicken. Soon the bottle was empty. He ordered a large glass of brandy. He was now being even more erratic, slurring his words, and I could see waves of emotion like tsunamis welling up in his dark brown eyes. I was dreading him talking about Mum. He really wasn't fit to drive. I was worried he was going to start crying and would talk about how much he was missing her, something he said every time we met. Lunch was long, and afterwards he consumed black coffee on an industrial scale.

On our way back to school he kept stopping the car pretending he needed a pee, but I could see him behind the trees swigging out of a whisky bottle that he had in his bulging tweed jacket pocket.

It's a narrow, twisting road from Dunkeld to Butterstone, fringed by trees and lochs, a place where deer frequently cross in front of cars, and after heavy rains the lochs rise and lap close to the road. I thought he might even drive straight in. As I had feared, he was now drunk and maudlin.

When he took me up to the dormitory, he saw the framed picture on my chest of drawers of Mum with the dogs. He picked it up and collapsed on the bed, weeping like a child. I didn't know what to say to him.

'I miss her so much,' he repeated over and over again. I hugged him hard, and then we both cried.

We went downstairs and met the headmistress in the hallway. She asked if we had had a good day. Then she saw that I was distraught and my father was drunk. She asked him into her study and suggested I wait outside.

I could hear muffled talking, and then I heard Dad crying again. Then it sounded as if the headmistress was on the telephone, something about a room for the night. Confusion raged in my head; I couldn't bear him to go.

He emerged eventually and she shook his hand. 'It was so nice to see you again, David,' she said and looked directly at me with a very warm smile. All the austerity that usually surrounded her had evaporated like steam. 'Now please drive carefully and I will ring the hotel in Dunkeld shortly to check you have arrived safely.'

With that, she hugged him, and we followed him to the front door, where she firmly took my hand. She then led me into the study and shut the door quietly behind us. 'It appears poor Dad is not very well today so I have arranged for him to spend the night in a nice hotel in Dunkeld for this evening.'

I didn't know or understand alcoholism then – I am not sure I do now – but back then I had no idea that Dad was so ill mentally and that he was struggling. However, I had started to accept that there was indeed something seriously wrong.

Next day I had to take my common entrance exam – Butterstone was only for primary-school-aged children – and failed dismally.

I had been awake all night crying. I think I would have failed it regardless, so this is not an excuse. It was probably just as well, as it was for a strict convent in the south of England. My mother certainly wasn't religious, though Dad was, but it did seem an odd choice – and why so far away?

I worried often about Dad and wrote to him incessantly, asking him to send me more stamps so I could write more. All my letters told him to take care of himself and to get better soon, and to stop worrying. Some of them told him I was enjoying school – I didn't want to worry him and tell him I hated it. He seemed to be so anxious. I wanted to reassure him. I needed to reassure him.

During holidays with my father in the south, things didn't always go well. Sometimes we stayed with my Uncle Archie and his wife, and their burgeoning family at the school where Archie worked. They had four small children and I always enjoyed helping with them. They were mucky and full of devilment, but they were happy, healthy country children who loved me in turn. They appeared at dawn with their sodden nappies leaking through to the pyjamas, their arms full of books, and piled into bed with me. I had to sit up, prop us all up on pillows and read to them despite the steam and overpowering smell of urine.

On other occasions, we stayed with Dad's various lovers, few of whom I liked. In the New Forest, I was taken hunting for the first time by a particularly horsey girlfriend. Buxom, with dyed jet-black hair, she sometimes dressed in thigh-length boots and wore leather trousers. One wild night she and Dad fell out and he shook me awake saying we were leaving. Wearing pyjamas and an extra jersey, I was bundled into the car, and he took off at speed into a world of blackness and rain. He was very drunk and rambled madly whilst slewing the car through narrow lanes. I was cold and terrified, but after an erratic half-hour we returned, and his girlfriend led me back to my bed with a mug of cocoa.

As soon as I was home in Scotland, I told Mum about the incident. She was livid. This meant that it was now almost impossible for her to let me go and stay with my father. And that, in turn, had repercussions. I felt so guilty, for it was I who had told her about the incident.

If I thought Butterstone was awful, at least it was in a beautiful wooded location surrounded by glorious wildlife. The next boarding school was far worse. In Ascot, not the highly academic convent originally planned due to the common entrance failure, it seemed we were not allowed to do anything normal. There were no animals about and there was no wildlife other than a few shabby birds that looked as fed up as I was. I thought incessantly of Ardnamurchan and longed to be home again.

Rules were rigidly strict, most utterly pointless: for example, we were only allowed to wash our hair once a fortnight. For any teenage girl with explosive hormones, spots and self-esteem issues, this was torture. We sneaked into the biology labs and washed our hair under the cold tap, with someone keeping guard at the door. But if our wet hair revealed our sin, there would be a severe punishment.

'How dare you wash your hair? You know you are not allowed to. Go straight away to see matron and she will punish you,' roared the fierce games teacher when she once discovered me trying to hide beside a depressing straggle of rhododendrons, looking as if I had been out in a monsoon.

Lessons were austere too, though I think had I stayed on, my academic achievements might have been more impressive. I loved games, art and English but otherwise hated the place. I constantly told my parents, but they never seemed to listen.

The atmosphere at school worsened when a rapist managed to shin up a drainpipe and broke into one of the rooms to attack two sixth-formers. After that disaster, which hit the national press, our movements were even more restricted and we were all scared stiff, especially as there seemed to be a man behind every bush – usually a policeman. Our imaginations were vivid.

I did have an English Literature teacher, Mrs Armstrong, whose lessons were an inspiration. She was obese, looked about a hundred, and had mad, pure white hair. She limped in, swathed in marquee-style garments. She was always weighed down with books with little pieces of blue card sticking out of them. She never wore stockings, had swollen ankles the colour of pastry, and feet that spilt out of her badly fitting shoes. She waddled like an Aylesbury duck and, like an Aylesbury duck, she was delightful.

I loved poetry – it seemed to fit the confused emotions that were stewing in my head. Often, I would stay behind, if the next event was lunch, and chat to Mrs Armstrong for a little while, merely risking a row for being late. It always proved worth it. She gave me lots of books of poems about nature and wildlife, and once she took me out for tea to her ramshackle cottage in Windsor Great Park. There were shelves and shelves sagging with the sheer weight of the dusty tomes. There were mountains of books all over the floor, organised by subject. The natural history heap toppled at a precarious angle, and often a book clunked dustily to the carpet and lay with pages temptingly open. Everything was decorated with cobwebs, but on the table was a large, crisp white cloth and a beautiful crazed ceramic jug of blue and yellow flowers. I wanted to stay there indefinitely and never return to that ghastly school. She had made egg sandwiches with too much black pepper and we both coughed between poetry readings. It made us laugh.

I told Mrs Armstrong that I thought it was odd that talking after lights out was punished with the forced learning of various poems. She thought it was outrageous; it was the first time I saw her getting cross, but she did not have the clout to influence whoever decided this was a good punishment. I never dared complain to the teachers that had the idea for as far as I was concerned it was a pleasure, and it was due to this that I have always revelled in the work of such poets as Kipling, Tennyson, Keats, Clare, Stevenson, Lear and Browning. For most of the other pupils, it only made them dislike what should have been joyous. And another thing: it certainly didn't stop me talking.

During term time I saw even less of my parents now, but far more of Archie. He was always incredibly loving and loyal towards me; at this stage we spoke a little about Dad's problem and, though it was referred to simply as 'Dad is ill again' he knew that I was aware that my father was a serious alcoholic. I loved Archie very much. We were always close and there was an unspoken bond between us. I knew he cared deeply. He seemed to understand without ever saying so, and I longed to spend more time with him, hating it when he took me back to school again.

In the end, I ran away, planning to go home to Scotland. However, luck was not on my side as I met the headmistress on the station platform where she was picking up another pupil. I was marched straight back to school, and there was an ominous call home. The outcome was less worrying than I feared.

Now nearly fourteen years old, the next term, I was sent to Gordonstoun, an outward-bound school near Elgin on the Moray Firth. It was Geordie's idea. And that was a positive turning point. There, I learnt skills that would prove useful for the rest of my life, and I made friendships that have never faltered. There was plenty of sport, sailing and endless other outdoor activities. There were expeditions into the Torridon and Glen Affric hills, where we honed our capabilities on vertiginous wind-scoured ridges, and I discovered the thrill of hill walking, which has stayed with me ever since.

There were also week-long cruises on the school boat – twelve of us sailing around the west coast – and seamanship lessons in the fishing village near the school, where we learnt to sail cutters. During our allotted seamanship week, we cycled the few miles to the village after daily chapel and spent the mornings in a tarry boat shed dripping with nautical paraphernalia – life jackets, buoys, ropes and fascinating tackle and gear. It had an aromatic oily smell, long benches and a table where we were taken through dozens of useful lessons by either the commander or, better still, the first mate, Barney. We had to first learn nine knots. In my eagerness, I bungled the easiest one and got it back to front.

Everyone adored Barney. Long retired from the merchant navy, he had a West Country burr and a round, cheery red face like a Cox's orange pippin, caused by both the maritime climate and probably many libations of naval rum. He called us all 'my lovelies' and was a great tease. He could spot the slackers with ease and had an excellent way of dealing with them, merely giving them something challenging to do, and then praising them effusively. Though I was an academic non-achiever, I certainly put my heart and soul into anything to do with the great outdoors.

The staff seemed to treat us much better than they had at my previous school, and, as far as I was concerned, encouraged me in what I was good at rather than the endless list of things at which I was not. My aunt, Archie's wife, had given me my first camera, a Kodak Instamatic, for my eighth birthday and I was passionate about photography. Then Geordie kindly lent me a fabulous 35 mm camera and several lenses. Geordie was proving to be exceptionally understanding and generous and seemed very tuned in to encouraging my creative side. I was becoming increasingly fond of him. He was never pushy in his approach towards me, but he was quietly there from the start as a stable and supporting presence.

I became the school photographer and developed pictures in the darkroom. I also became editor of the school magazine, and for community service went to help a local vet, often getting called out to help with lambing and calving – more skills for life. I helped with spaying operations, shaving endless cats' tummies in readiness for the scalpel to terminate their gene spreading. The vet was a patient man and when he learnt how I hated maths he sometimes rang the school to ask if I could go immediately to an emergency call-out that oddly coincided with the hated lessons. However, it came with a proviso, as he also informed me that to be a vet I would, unfortunately, need maths. Though I still wanted to pursue this career more than anything else, it was pretty clear that my scientific prowess was badly lacking.

Dad had moved to Somerset to run a brewery-owned hotel on Exmoor. There were memorable occasions when he came north to take me out for a weekend. On wet days, we would picnic on the harbour wall, watching the herring gulls hanging in the air as the sticky salt spray battered on the car window. Afterwards, we'd drive to Inverness to root around bookshops. There were enormous teas to satiate my voracious appetite and then evenings spent in a cosy pub devouring the books we had bought or listening to one another's tales. My father always listened, except when he was drunk, but then who listens when they are drunk? I always forgave him. He could be off the drink for months or indeed years, and then a bout would be triggered and he would become seriously ill, often ending up in a hospital or a rehabilitation unit. Then I would have that call from Archie merely saying that Dad was ill again and wouldn't manage to come to see me.

Other outings with Dad were spent in the hills. We walked all day, stopping frequently to scan the landscape with our binoculars, spotting deer and birds of prey as we sat near the burns that trickled and bubbled therapeutically, or roared off the steep glens in full spate. We climbed Munros together. He could stand on the summit and tell me the names of all the surrounding mountains, having only first glanced at the map. This is how I like to remember Dad, but these interludes were all too short lived. Our partings were painful for both of us, and though I had the reputation of always being cheery, inside I was engulfed in sadness and increasing anxiety, wondering how he would be the next time – would he be sober? Increasingly, he was not.

I had not been at Gordonstoun long when my mother announced that they were selling both the estate and the hotel in Ardnamurchan. We were moving to a new farm in Angus. To say I was devastated is an understatement. I spent my last holiday in Ardnamurchan rising early and coming home late, taking picnics with me to eat during the day, or riding Ginger along the shore path. I couldn't believe they could even contemplate leaving such a life, such a place. It would mean more turmoil and upheavals. But there were financial reasons for their decision. Geordie had bought the estate always knowing it was for the short term. This was another thing I was yet to fully understand. I returned to school with a heavy heart, but thankfully Gordonstoun was a haven that, compared to the other schools I'd attended, was a very happy place.

Gordonstoun was a place where I could be myself. I began to learn my strengths and weaknesses, and also the importance of grasping opportunities. The school motto – *Plus est en vous,* 'There is more in you' – is an excellent ethos for life. The Gordonstoun philosophy involved self-discipline too. If you wanted to avoid doing things that were a part of the regime, such as exercise and extra projects and activities, it was fairly easy, but I quickly learnt that this was detrimental in the extreme. What was the point of having all this on a plate and trying to avoid it? And when it came to rules, most had to be stuck to, but some could be easily manipulated.

My all-consuming love for wildlife was growing daily, and during the cruises and expeditions I was able to indulge this passion and enthuse many of my friends. By the time I reached fifteen, I had a soulmate, Pete, whose family had an estate in Cumbria. It wasn't long before we felt so passionate about one another that it seemed to hurt. We met in every available spare moment, wrote each other long notes when we should have been studying, and went for circuitous walks in our free time. Favourite places were the local wind-honed beaches, Lossiemouth and Burghead – the headlands electric yellow with gorse, its coconut scent filling the salty air, high dunes fringed with marram grasses and studded with wildflowers. Ravens nested on the cliffs, and sometimes we saw peregrines. We could also watch dolphins and porpoises in the Moray Firth. Nature had a free hand over the extensive school grounds too, with wildflowers, skylarks over the Games pitches and the cries of curlews feeding on the surrounding fields.

Though there had been other minor fumblings with various characters at school previously, such as a little over-exposure with an Italian pupil in the darkroom and a shared sleeping bag on a frozen expedition to Nigg Bay, my relationship with Pete developed daily until we were consumed with one another. It was as much about our similar minds as the physical attraction. We were fit and sporty, our connection fuelled by shared interests and raging hormones, and we learnt about lovemaking through trial and little or no error. Luckily. We were so besotted with one another that we could end up in tears simply because we loved one another so much. Sex was banned at school and we avoided serious trouble, but by holiday time we were explosive. We spent half the holidays together; either I went to Cumbria or Pete came to Scotland.

By now Mum and Geordie were living in Angus. Though I remained deeply saddened that they had left the place I loved so much, the new farm was also beautiful. For Pete and me there was plenty to do, plenty of wildlife to absorb us and to learn about. There was a hill loch surrounded by creaking pine trees. Sometimes the wind whistled eerily through the branches, as mallard, teal and wigeon winged in at dawn and dusk. Close to the farm there were three ponds nestled in a sea of phragmites and reed mace. Moorhens with their broods of tiny babies with red wayward feathers on their comical heads puttered effortlessly in and out of the rushes, and then there were beautiful roe deer, with their dark eyes and white rumps, feeding on the lush growth close to the water's edge. Occasionally I saw otters too. The ponds were stocked with rainbow trout, but there were also a few wild brown trout. Whenever we caught these, we put them straight back in. We loaded up the small boat with a picnic and spent the day fishing, and perhaps in the evenings we might go up to the River North Esk to swim.

Back in Cumbria we rode on the fells and camped in a remote bothy where we had barbecues and watched the sun setting over Blencathra.

One holiday, Pete's furious father summoned us. Pete's report had arrived and the housemaster had written: 'If Peter paid as much attention to his work as he did to Polly, he would get straight As.'

Mine was equally affected by being in love. The Geography master was clearly used to dealing with teenage hormones. He wrote simply: 'We have been studying Africa this term, meanwhile Polly has been in other parts of the world.'

I loved Pete's parents and became very close to his mother. She must have driven Pete's two brothers and his father mad, as I could do no wrong. In fact, I almost walked on water in her eyes. This was probably largely because I always helped her with the eternal mountains of washing-up, and sided with her when the boys ganged up. It wasn't hard, as she was a long-suffering and incredibly kind person with a very big personality, and she was pleased to have another female in what had always been a male-dominated household.

Pete and I were not allowed to share a room. There were two staircases in the house, and I was always put at the far end of the corridor, near the main stairs, whilst Pete's room was at the other end. There were numerous squeaky floorboards between, and one particularly treacherous one, oddly right by his parents' room. One night Pete tried to creep along to see me. That damn floorboard announced his presence, and his father threw open his bedroom door and roared. So, to get over this minor setback, next night Pete went down the back stairs and then came up the main stairs. Ah, but this worked only until his father became aware there was something going on. He strategically placed several dining chairs on the upward route, and in the dark Pete didn't see them and they all went clattering down the highly polished wooden stairs. The noise woke everyone up and his father came rampaging out of his bedroom, angrily shouting.

So that scheme failed. His mother was always on our side and warned us if his father was close by. Much of it was bluster, and Pete's father became one of my closest friends.

Bo, by now, had moved to Scotland because Fitte was unwell, and Mum felt it would be better for them to be in a cottage close by on the new farm in Angus. For Bo, it was not a good move, as it was a cut-off, lonely place compared to the bustle of English village life that she was accustomed to. She found it impossible to integrate, particularly as we were several miles away from a village and she didn't drive. Fitte died shortly after the move, and for her sake Bo should have returned south again. But for me it was a dream. She and Pete loved one another too, and every day in the school holidays we visited her and enjoyed listening to all her stories. She kept busy making sticky cakes for us that sank in the middle.

Sadly, following a Geology expedition to the States to walk across the Grand Canyon at the end of our final year at Gordonstoun, Pete and I began to drift apart. Our schoolmates had always referred to us as 'the married couple'. He was planning to join the army. Our serious relationship happened several years too soon, and besides I would never, ever have made an army wife. We were basically just too young, though other school love affairs stuck the course. The split caused a pain like no other; I always felt I was largely to blame because I was so unsettled. We tried on a couple of occasions to get back together, but it was not going to happen. My diaries from that era are fuelled with pages of poetry and teenage dross, as well as self-doubts and anxiousness. Leaving Ardnamurchan and the incessant problems associated with Dad had merely played into this.

From early on I had wanted to be a vet but my lack of a scientific brain meant that was impossible. Then I also really wanted to be a photographer but needed Maths O-level to attain a place in college. There seemed to be endless hurdles, none of which I successfully climbed. What I was going to do now was unclear. Mum and Geordie were supportive and seemed to understand, and there was little pressure. I excelled in Art and English, or anything to do with wildlife and animals, and the rest was a pretty fair disaster.

4

Vive la France!

After I left Gordonstoun I had an opportunity to go to France for a few months with one of my school friends. What began as a three-month French course at L'Institut de Touraine, in Tours in the Loire Valley, led to a far longer sojourn. All the students spoke English and when we went out after formal classes, this meant there was no conversational French whatsoever. The college course was far too highbrow for me and I felt frustrated that, even after all the years of learning French at school, I was still not able to manage even the most basic conversation. It didn't seem as if being at the college was going to help either.

I lived in a large attractive house, Beauvoir, on the outskirts of the beautiful town, with the widowed Madame, who took in five students every year. The house was extraordinary, and smelt of a mixture of delicious expensive French scent and burnt food. Madame was glamorous, but not quite as glamorous as her sister, who lived in a grand house next door. At Beauvoir, we met an eclectic mix of other would-be Francophiles: two Americans and an old Etonian. This combination sometimes turned our stay into a hilarious farce. Only Paul, the Etonian, had a car, and he was constantly called upon to transport us around the district. We each had our own lavish room, but we ate all our meals together.

Unlike many French women, Madame was not a skilled cook. Her creations looked partially edible, but she got carried away, then forgot things and frazzled them, or added peculiar ingredients to the leftovers, and then reheated those. Despite the occasionally tired, shrivelled or charred offerings brought to the table, oddly the overall effect was still of fine French cuisine. This was to do with Madame herself, who could have added panache to a plate of prison porridge. Her lack of culinary skill mattered not in the least, for the general ambience of Beauvoir was so happy. And we quickly learnt to help her in the kitchen. At Christmas time, in her wild enthusiasm for the festive season, she went crazy with the silver spray paint – even the pork chops were sparkly. It was an extremely harmonious house; Madame was the queen bee and buzzed about doing her utmost to make our stay successful.

Madame was also a snob in the nicest possible sense of the word, and therefore loved anything to do with English, or indeed Scottish, grandeur. She had many titled French friends: counts and countesses plus several dukes. Paul, with his smooth Etonian voice, was a huge hit. I had a double-barrelled name and red hair and lived in the Highlands of Scotland; what's more, our new house was termed 'castle' simply because the Victorians had stuck turrets onto it. These were all things Madame considered grand.

After a few months, my father came to stay and played into this spectacularly. He was, as ever, well dressed in his immaculate Harris tweed, with his Lock's of London trilby placed at exactly the right forward-tilted angle. He was off the drink at that point, though had wine with Madame, luckily with no ill effects. They were incorrigible together, both name-dropping and outrageously pompous. They seemed to know so many of the same people. Madame thought my father was 'magnifique, et si charmant', and of course he was, being under such a spotlight. When he wrote her a polite, effusive and engaging thank-you letter after his stay, he was raised to a pedestal. At one point I really thought that the pair might get together.

Madame was always perfectly turned out. Before she surfaced in the mornings she etched two surprised eyebrows onto her tanned, Gallic-skinned face, and made herself up beautifully. Her 94-year-old mother also lived in the house, but we never saw her, for she was bedridden and kept behind several closed doors. There was a constant stream of relations, who arrived in a cloud of floral scent, or were accompanied by the woody notes of Havana cigars, frantically kissing one another on both cheeks and 'bonjour'ing – as we referred to it. They would then add that we were all 'mignon' or 'charmant' or, if we were really lucky, both, and then with doleful faces, they would say that 'la vie est si terrible'. This last because the elderly matriarch was supposedly about to die within hours . . . She didn't; she lingered on for many weeks.

Ironically, the way Madame's relations behaved and looked made it quite blatant that their lives were anything but terrible. Paul would comment dryly that all this drama added to the value we students were extricating from our time in Tours. He, in turn, was the epitome of an urban English gent, dressed in an immaculate Barbour and carrying a black umbrella under his arm. An Englishman through and through, he stuck out like the proverbial sore thumb. Once, we went to Paris by bus to see a play with several other English people we didn't know. Paul was unimpressed by their behaviour and loudness.

On the return journey, he suddenly commented, 'Oh my God, these ghastly English people *are* letting the side down; someone's written "NEWCASTLE UNITED" on the window.'

At the weekends, Madame did her bit for the local tourism industry by taking us to a few of the Loire's many chateaux to do 'the tour'. However, she only came in with us once and from then on stayed in her car for what she referred to as a 'petit dodo', where she proceeded to snore elegantly in the passenger seat, her dark pencilled-in eyebrows rising up and down rhythmically. Looking after students must have been very wearing, but the money was good.

The chateaux and their gardens were glorious outside, but after struggling around the interiors of the first few with dismally long-winded and boring guides, and accompanied by frenetic, canned harpsichord music, we decided we couldn't stand it any more. We would wait until our chaperone had nodded off (this usually took only a few minutes) and then we nipped into the nearest brasserie or café instead. It also worked out cheaper than paying for the tour.

Once or twice we were caught out, like the time when Madame asked about tapestries and we said, 'Bien sûr, ils étaient magnifiques.'

It turned out that the particular chateau she was asking about didn't have any.

Madame was no fool. She knew what we were at. Her eyebrows rose astonishingly high, and she frowned and then giggled. I suppose she just accepted she was doing her best and it was up to us if we wasted our parents' hard-earned cash and chose to ignore the wealth of French heritage she was endeavouring to show us.

I loved France and I loved the French. I loved the food, the weather, the atmosphere, and I loved the small-scale agriculture and smallholdings where many rural dwellers were totally self-sufficient. People appeared to be more in touch with the land and less homogenised, as was increasingly the case back home. They appeared to live more naturally. However, I found canned thrush or lark in the French supermarkets abhorrent. And then there was foie gras – poor bloody geese forced to eat until their livers nearly burst. It was so sickly too.

Two of us picked grapes for a week. Instead of tea breaks, an elderly man with nicotine-brown teeth wandered about with a barrel strapped to his back and a tin cup tied on. I naively thought it was some non-alcoholic juice to quench our thirst, but it was wine as rough as the sea in a storm-force gale. I quickly became tiddled and almost snipped the hand of the picker on the opposite side of the vine, mistaking it for grapes.

At lunch, we gathered in a long barn with a trestle table laden with *pain de campagne* and wide, white porcelain bowls, knives, forks and spoons, and earthenware mugs. Two elderly women with faces the texture and colour of walnuts came round with a large pot of succulent, earthy rabbit stew. The cheese that followed was delicious, waltzing off the board with its overpowering smell. And as if that was not enough, vast apple pies then appeared. After several more glasses of the homebrew, picking grapes would become even more of a challenge. We were all rendered useless, but it was quite usual to have a 'petit dodo' under some wizened fruit trees before picking resumed a couple of hours later.

Then one day I met a charming French artist friend of Madame.

Dominique had come to take Paul the Etonian out riding in the local countryside. He asked if I would like to go too. I was over-effusive in my acceptance as I missed riding very much. A letter to my father describes events:

> We arrived in a remote area in the country and drove into a muddy farmyard. Four horses were poking their heads over the stable doors. There were hens everywhere, naturally clucking in French, and two goats sticking their heads through holes obviously chewed by dogs in the bottom of the stable doors. On opening the house door out flew a whirlwind of noise, hair and colour. This consisted of two cocker spaniels, two black cocker spaniel puppies, a fat lumbering basset hound tripping over its sail-like lugs, a vast Great Dane, a greyhound, and a beautiful Gordon setter. The house is absolutely charming with four rooms. After a fantastic ride (Paul nearly fell off and looked very precarious), we had tea in the sitting room that has a stone floor and an enormous open fire with hams and strings of sausages hanging above. The walls are covered with old prints of animals, the mantelpiece laden with bronze dogs. The tea was delicious, and I had two purring cats on my knee, whilst seven dogs were stretched out on sofas. Dominique also showed us his naive paintings, though most were at an exhibition in Paris. They are stunning and he is brilliant. He has no hot water, loo or shower but his house is spotless and one could honestly eat straight off the stone floor. The kitchen where we later had dinner with some of his French friends (who suddenly appeared out of the blue) is equally fantastic. Walls are lined with oak shelving and an oak dresser and there are rows and rows of colourful homemade things in jars, as well as beautiful old plates and crockery. A ginger cat was sitting on the dresser too amid a sea of very shiny green glasses.

I was clearly impressed. Paul, however, was not too keen on the riding as he was a total beginner and admitted on our way back that he found it terrifying.

I continued to go and fell in love with the menagerie. And Dominique. He had a fat, woolly black ram called Amin Baba and a feisty stallion called Assan, and this unlikely duo shared a stable. As both were at the peak of their testosterone levels, there were temperament issues. I had to keep my wits about me to avoid getting bitten or butted, and ended up suffering both afflictions.

As Dominique's English was limited it made it imperative that I learned French. As I love to talk I was finding it frustrating not being able to join in, and even more frustrating that I could not tell people the names of birds when most of the French people I met did not know what they were. I managed to find a French bird book in a shop in Tours that was identical to my English version. One night I sat up pencilling in all the English names. I could then tell people that a wren in French was a *troglodyte mignon*, a flycatcher, a *gobemouche*, and a *circaète jean-le-blanc* was a short-toed snake eagle.

By this time I had finished the course at the Institut, and I had been looking after two rather spoilt children in the daytime and babysitting at night to earn some extra money. My application to an arts college to study photography in London had been turned down for a second time simply because I did not have O-level Maths. I had taken it at school four times and must be one of the few people on Earth who became worse every time. At the last attempt, I had failed spectacularly. I suppose if you are going to fail, there is no point in doing it half-heartedly. Therefore it seemed to matter not that I stayed on in France and I took full advantage of my time there until I decided what I was going to do next.

There were some peasant farmers living close to Dominique's: Gaby and Madeleine. They had a troop of thirty milking goats and grazed them down the roadside verges. Their farm was extremely old-fashioned even for that era. I remember going with Dominique the day they were killing the pig and can still hear the squeals now. I was surprised how little was wasted as everyone got stuck into butchering and boiling the various pieces in huge bubbling vats over open fires in the yard. There was much clucking of hens and quacking of ducks, all of which probably ended their happy days in the same pot. Legs and various joints were tied with string and hung from the rafters to smoke, having first been soaked in brine. Gaby always wore a greasy, grey flat cap at a drunken angle, and had a permanent filterless Gauloise sticking from his mouth, lodged securely in a tight gap between various missing teeth, which looked like a row of condemned houses. Rough wine and his cigarettes had darkly stained the sparse remnants. Both their accents were as thick as sludge so that I struggled to understand; they found it very amusing and teased me incessantly. Their white goats were gentle animals that enjoyed attention, and I, in turn, loved helping with them and watching as Madeleine made cheese from their milk. She also had a large black-and-tan dog that escorted her everywhere to stop the goats from straying. However, like its owners, it didn't speak any English whatsoever and struggled with my French accent, looking totally blank when called. It would run off immediately in the opposite direction with a bemused expression.

Gaby collected adders and drew off their venom to send to a lab for medical purposes. I couldn't believe that he would walk through the same dry, crackling undergrowth where I had been only a short time earlier, and seen nothing, and return slung about with several writhing snakes. He had a long, forked stick and wore a thick leather belt around his bib and brace to which they were attached.

I was now almost twenty and I travelled back and forth between Scotland and France doing various odd jobs that included teaching English to French students back home, and looking after various French children in France. I still wanted to work as a photographer, or with animals, and was searching for anything appropriate. Dominique came to Scotland too, and, as most French people I'd met seem to be, was inspired greatly by the dramatic scenery.

Meanwhile, things with Dad were deteriorating. Running his brewery-leased hotel alone on Exmoor was a struggle, largely because the staff took advantage of his inebriation. His drinking sessions were becoming more frequent, and he was becoming more and more unstable. He was also becoming more argumentative than I had ever known him to be and was beginning to blame everyone else for his major problems. Following another pleading, sad telephone call in which he begged me to come and help him, I took the fateful decision to leave France and help him at the hotel. I felt sure that, if I were there all the time with him, the drinking would stop. He was delighted.

Mum, understandably, was not. 'You are a bloody little fool, you are so stubborn, for God's sake leave him to get on with it.' She knew it would end badly.

Unfortunately, I took no notice and decided, if anyone could sort Dad out, I could.

5

Exmoor

Parts of Exmoor are as beautiful and rugged in their own way as Ardnamurchan. However, the wild red deer that live on the moor and in the rich oak woodlands hugging the steep valleys are many times larger due to the lush feeding. They have impressive racks of antlers, often with numerous points, unlike the smaller stags found on impoverished hill ground. There was one special wood close to the village where twisted oak trees provided a sheltered place for the stags to lie up. Often filled with low mist caught between land and sea it lingered teasingly and sometimes remained when the mist had cleared elsewhere. This added to the mysterious aura of this hidden dell. I loved Exmoor's creatures, both wild and domesticated: the distinctive Exmoor horn sheep and Exmoor ponies that lived out on the moor, foxes and badgers, and the abundant bird life.

It is also unsurpassed riding country – miles and miles over rugged moorland through dense oak woods on a latticework of tracks and paths. Hunting was still an integral part of rural life on Exmoor, stag hunting in particular. My father had bought himself a horse, a superb weight-bearing Irish cob. Due to his hogged mane and rounded outline, Dad nicknamed him Chaucer, as he resembled a horse from the cover of *The Canterbury Tales*, but everyone else called him by his proper name, Rory. Dad kept him at livery and hunted regularly.

Rory was a wise beast. He looked after Dad, who was often plastered by the time he had partaken of the contents of several hip flasks, and probably half a bottle or more, before he had left the house. The local farmers knew the pair of them well and joked that

Rory was not very athletic, and certainly never to be seen jumping the area's bogs, ditches and occasional low walls. However, when I rode him he almost flew; this amused them too. The reason was purely the weight difference, and I think the poor, clever horse also knew that if he went into orbit, Dad was likely to do the same. I found it astonishing that Dad never did fall off. I was sure this was only due to the sagacious and sensitive nature of his mount.

However, Rory did have one vice – he couldn't bear pigs. Close to the stables where he was kept at livery was a pen of weaners. I took Dad to the yard for a day's hunting and was standing chatting with the father and son who owned the stables whilst he got ready. Dad was embarrassingly pompous and loquacious as he prepared for his day out. He had been drinking. His long black boots were gleaming, his battered bowler hat brushed up and smart again. As he fussed about, he was supping large amounts of tea from a huge flask he kept in the back of the car. He always left the teabags in so that by the end of the day, it was darker and thicker than tar. The preamble that led up to him actually getting aboard was taking a very long time. My father was never very supple, and always used a mounting block, but even that on some occasions took a lot of effort. Rory was raring to be off, and was beginning to fidget. Like the rest of us he too was getting bored with waiting. He started to paw the cobbled yard and shuffled from one leg to another so that Dad had to have another go at hoisting himself aboard. A winch would have been most helpful. Finally, with much puffing and blowing and several failed attempts, the pilot was up. He doffed his hat to a beautiful woman who trotted up the road on a shining bay cob, and then began to wave at the three of us waiting patiently in the yard. He thanked us over-effusively, and repeated numerous times that we would see him again at the end of a long day out with the hounds. And then off he trotted.

Meanwhile the two men began to laugh and said to me in broad Exmoor accents, 'Ye just wait 'ere a coupla moments and ye will see what 'appens next.'

There was the rhythmic thrum of newly shod hooves on tarmac,

and the view of Dad's back as he waved regally like the queen from
one of her limousines. He had clearly forgotten about the pigs. But
Rory hadn't.

My two companions led me to a gap in the wall. 'Come on over
'ere, maid, ye'll get a far better view from 'ere.'

We waited and watched as Dad trotted casually up the road. The
sun was shining. The sky was benign. And so were the pigs. They
calmly snuffled and grubbed close to the fence, emitting the occasional soft appreciative grunt. On Dad and Rory trotted. Suddenly,
without any warning, Rory slammed the brakes on and skidded violently, turning 360 degrees in a millisecond. Dad lost both stirrups
and was thrown forward into a most undignified heap. He was now
flailing his arms around his mount's prickly, hogged neck. His hat
was over one eye, and he had lost the aplomb of a few moments
earlier. He was still in this sack of potatoes pose when Rory came
skidding back into the yard, sparks flying from his hooves.

'Sod those pigs!' said Dad, pulling himself back up with great
effort into an upright position. His hat was still askew and his face
puce and scratched from coming into contact with Rory's bristly
mane. The three of us had to control our laughter.

Alcoholics should not be in charge of hotels but all too frequently
are. I knew that, and so did everyone else. However, what I did
not know was that Dad had other problems, probably connected
to the drinking. Mentally, he was battling with himself in several
directions though I had still to discover more about this. I worked
hard trying to stop him from the numerous perils that tempted him
at every turn. And failed dismally. The more I helped in the hotel,
the harder he leant on me.

The hotel was not doing well. Some of the kitchen staff were
dishonest. They secreted much of the produce away under their
clothing when they left at night. I would go to the freezer to get
food out for a guest's dinner and find empty boxes, yet I knew orders
had only recently come in. Dad hadn't noticed. I could sum it up by
saying that they were taking their work home with them. That is the
polite way of putting it. As we relied on them so heavily, and had so

many other problems to deal with, it was better to be there and put a stop to it that way rather than confront them and cause an almighty row with accusations of stealing. I tried to be everywhere at once. Though the petty pilfering stopped, the bar takings went down. Various bar staff were giving their mates too many free drinks. But that stopped too, due to the long, smoky hours that I spent behind the bar trying to keep my eye on the situation. Often the till was a little out when we counted the money each night. But that had a less sinister reason – it was due to my maths. Or should I say the lack of?

On the one hand, the public bar could be a lively, cheery place full of local farmers. Some of them were passionate about ferreting, and occasionally I would go out with them too. Nets were pegged over holes, and the plump Exmoor rabbits would thunder out in an eruption of surprising velocity. Someone waited poised by each entrance to grab the fleeing rabbit before its weight pulled the net pegs out. Often the sheer force of the petrified rabbit's exodus led to escape. Once caught, their necks had to be quickly wrung. The men were very good at this, but I struggled, as some of the buck rabbits were surprisingly strong, so I passed the largest kicking rabbits straight on to those who could do it faster. On occasion a ferret might lie up and stay underground and have to be dug out – this caused cursing and head scratching, and ears were put to the ground to listen for subterranean thumps as a rabbit charged about with a ferret at its heels. Sometimes there was merely an ominous silence. Perhaps the ferret had killed a young rabbit and had its knife and fork out – a bad habit that caused more swearing and joking. Then a sweet little innocent ferret's face would reappear, curiously peeping from a hole further away with blood on its nose. When its owner went to pick it up, it might nip him.

'Li'l bastard, I'll kill ee for doing that,' the owner would exclaim as he grabbed his ferret and sucked at a blood-dripping bite.

After a productive day out, there might be a rabbit-skinning competition in the bar. Some of the men were astoundingly fast.

At other times the public bar was not a nice place. Flirting and smiling, I suppose I'd be lying if I said I didn't sometimes enjoy the attention and the lewd comments. The boozy bar-propping regulars boosted my shaky morale. However, having seen enough of Dad and his drunkenness, I was aware that people are often increasingly revolting in this state. I was fast becoming an expert on degrees of drunkenness. I became adept at recognising the stages and various behaviour patterns that befell the intoxicated. Some men became more and more pleasant and generous, and then fell asleep like peaceful babies. Many were amorous. Drink often brings a shy person out of his shell, allowing him the freedom to say all those things he has often thought but never dared voice. It was amusing at times and sometimes surprising. Many of the comments referred to what they'd truly love to do to me, and to the other women that came and went. The perils of brewer's droop appeared not to be a consideration. Other drunks became pleasant, then violently argumentative, and then snored loudly, bottom jaw falling open and exuding a disgusting bubble of spittle.

Luckily, they were not my drunks, but my father was, and he was now drinking all the time. It was becoming unbearable: the lies, the devious behaviour, his edginess and rudeness, his fussing and flapping, and the blame he laid on me, his latest girlfriend and the staff. Every day there was another issue to deal with.

'Where the hell were you this morning when I needed you?' he shouted pompously when I had vanished off to help clean the bedrooms, or was working in the kitchen, or restocking the bar

For some reason I felt unable to let go, and in my naivety continued to think I could help him. In retrospect I only had myself to blame for what lay ahead.

Though the drunks in the bar, like my father, were often horrible to deal with, some of the village boys who came in were very attractive. One in particular eyed me from across the dartboard and bought me drinks that I always put down the sink or gave away. Being drunk myself was not an option. We were physically attracted to one another but had absolutely nothing else in common. We had brief, furtive encounters when he would come over to my room once the bar was shut and everyone had left. My father strongly disapproved. Later there were others that he disapproved of too. I had similar feelings about many of his numerous girlfriends.

*

March 1980, and it's another frantically busy day in the hotel. Dad has been drunk for days, and his behaviour is becoming more erratic and unpleasant. I have been to see the local doctor but feel even more despondent than before. Rather than suggesting practical ways to help my father, he was cold and unsympathetic and has suggested that the only way now is for Dad to go into a proper rehabilitation centre – again. The doctor also hasn't listened to my concerns about my own increasingly anxious state and has instead fobbed me off with some nerve-calming pills – Librium – but I don't like the idea of taking them because I am worried they will fog my judgement. However, every time Dad and I have another dispute, my stomach churns so badly that a sharp pain comes on and I have to go and lie down because it makes me feel like fainting.

Since leaving France, Dominique, my artist friend, and I have remained in close contact, and I have received a letter from him in which he writes: 'I'm afraid for your position in Somerset and your troubles with your father, and I ask if you can continue there. Somerset may be as beautiful as parts of Scotland but it's not a way of life for you. Please leave and come back to France.'

So why am I still here, still battling with Dad and his own battle with the bottle? I am beginning to have fears for myself too, and a mounting feeling of hopelessness.

Today, however, Dad has briefly sobered up. He has lost a bunch of hotel keys. The office has been ransacked, papers lie in chaotic heaps, and the filing cabinet doors are yawning open, folders strewn all over the desks. Dad has been blaming me for losing them, and is now in such a state that he will probably go and have another drink at any moment. I try to avert disaster and scuttle off, tail between my legs, to make him a bucket-sized mug of black coffee, loading it with unhealthy amounts of brown sugar. He has the shakes, and as I hand it to him, it slops on the papers on the desk and makes a new map all over them.

'Fuck, fuck, fuck, where are those bloody keys?' he says taking a large swig at the coffee. He then goes through a loaded armoury of blame: 'Sick And Tired of being surrounded by incompetents and incompetence. Fed Up To The Back Teeth with bloody inefficiency. At My Wits' End. Where the hell have you put them, Polly?'

He never, ever calls me Polly – always Pol, always has done. This is a very bad sign. His sighing is now brewing up to gale force and he is fast becoming as cross as a bag of weasels. He looks hellish, and I feel like giving him a smack on the face to silence all this blame. He is driving me mad. The coffee has all gone and he is now slumped over the desk, head in hands grumbling under his breath.

'Shall I go round to the cottage and see if they are in any of your pockets there?' I suggest gingerly.

The groaning stops momentarily. 'I suppose I may have left them in my tweed jacket pocket, all these idiots that surround me are making me crazy.'

I rush out, relieved for the escape onto the street if only for a few brief minutes. The shops are busy, an old lady carrying a basket limps on ahead of me, a cat races across the road, and a dog barks from an open window. Once at his little house down a narrow alley off the main street, I race upstairs to his wardrobe.

After much fumbling about in his various jacket pockets, the keys remain elusive. Knowing that he was out hunting yesterday, I eventually feel the hard metal of the bunch of keys in his riding coat pocket.

Something in the bottom corner of the wardrobe catches my eye. There is a large heap of magazines – nothing particularly unusual in porn mags, but on top there is a projector and some videos, and a heap of boxes underneath. I open them and wish I hadn't – after all it's none of my business. On closer inspection I see that these contain maids' uniforms, black leather outfits, and there are some whips as well as handcuffs. I open some of the magazines and see they all relate to bondage and flagellation. The video covers reveal more of the same.

A physical feeling of nausea chokes me. I am well aware that different things please different people, so why does this fill me with such horror and revulsion? Why? This is my father. Is that why? I even feel a little scared, yet none of this affects me – well, not directly. My thoughts are confused and wildly irrational, and now they drift back to the horrible ex-girlfriend with her thigh-length boots.

I take the keys downstairs and sit quietly on the faded green-buttoned chair at the window. A blackbird is pulling at worms on the grass outside. An irritable fly buzzes in the top corner of the window. After a few minutes I leave, quietly closing the cottage door behind me, knowing another door has opened on a new concern. I return to the hotel and, without looking at him, I hand Dad his keys.

6

Skeletons out of the Cupboard

The contents of the cupboard shocked and shook me. I didn't want to face my father. I couldn't face my father. He disgusted me. I took to the woods, wandering aimlessly in the mist sweeping in off the sea, and sat under curled oaks with my back against the fissured bark of one particular wind-bent tree whilst my confused mind ran back and forth over and over a morass of mental and emotional mayhem that seemed to have no meaning. There's something so solid and reassuring about an oak tree. I was in turmoil and nothing seemed right. Deer came into the wood to shelter close by as I sat there wondering, thinking about everything, and nothing. The wind lamented in the branches as milky filaments of sea mist poured over the landscape as if to help blot out my bewildered conflict. By the time I had sat for a while amid the pungent aroma of deer, watching their quiet cudding through my binoculars, I felt ready to go back to the hotel. But I felt like a nervous dog that couldn't look its owner in the eye.

I worked hard, continuing with the mundane chores, but I avoided being with Dad, keeping him at arm's length at all times. He did not even seem to notice that I was avoiding him, but then he was drinking almost without cease.

I was due to meet Mum in London later that same week, as she had planned a special outing for the two of us – a couple of nights in the Basil Street Hotel, a wonderfully old-fashioned place in Knightsbridge. We were going to see a comedy play and do various things together. I caught the train from Taunton to London. When I arrived at the hotel Mum was already there. She was on sparkling form. I was determined not to spoil this treat with any of my petty turmoil. However, in my mind the revelations in Dad's wardrobe and the unbalanced thoughts that surrounded that day had burgeoned out of all proportion. I had worked myself up into a state.

We went out for dinner and enjoyed the play, which left us sore from so much laughing. However, I felt uneasy. If only I could put my own concerns to the back of my bloody overactive mind, we would be having a wonderful time. It was impossible though, and next morning as we were having breakfast in our room, I told Mum what I had found. We never did go out to see the sights and instead spent the day holed up, discussing the situation amid copious trays of room service tea, and various delicacies that we barely touched.

What my mother told me was extremely sad and explained a great many things. It also explained why my parents' marriage had failed. As if living with my father's drinking problem for more than eighteen years had not been reason enough for her to leave him, it transpired that Dad had always been totally impotent. Totally? How could he be impotent if he was my father? I listened in an ever more confused state, not pursuing this question until later. Perhaps I didn't dare to ask, but I also wanted to let her speak without interruption. She was deeply sympathetic about the shock I had had and told me there had been years of soul-searching and that she had had various love affairs, as she had not been able to go along with the type of sex that turned Dad on. When she did, it never led to intercourse. She said that she had one affair in particular soon after they were first married. It was intense and when she found herself expecting a baby, she had to have an abortion. Poor, troubled Dad had been understanding and did not blame either my mother or the third party.

I thought about it in that hotel room surrounded by grandeur and silver teapots. I looked up to the massive windows with their brocade curtains and filament of net, and saw a fat spider tying its victim in a gossamer thread. There was a desperate fizzing hum. It was not going well for the fly.

A lump rose to my throat. I felt no blame towards Mum but there was an overriding sadness and understanding of the frustrations she

must have endured, as well as those suffered by my father. To be
married to someone in an unconsummated relationship, and for that
person to be constantly drunk – it was not hard to see how she had
fallen into someone else's bed. I knew from countless photographs
how very beautiful she had always been. My head swam. Butterflies
danced a crazed ballet in my stomach. It was impossible to absorb. I
looked up. The fly's struggle was over. The spider had won.

Mum and I discussed Dad's drinking. She told me that she and
my father had always been the greatest of friends. It was their shared
sense of humour in particular that had kept them together. They
had so much in common, and had always laughed. This made the
situation all the more pathetic. She told me that the family doctor, a
friend of Bo, had said that it would be better if her daughter didn't
marry Dad. He had said (though he probably should not have done
so) that the family had a history of dreadful, complex alcohol-
related issues.

'I really loved him you know,' Mum said, 'and I always will.'

Her story, like mine, is probably inaccurate when relating to the
fine detail – memory is not wholly reliable, and its loss is a human
strategy for damage limitation – but the gist of it was true enough.
And it broke my heart. During their marriage, my parents had been
to see a psychiatrist about both the drinking and the impotence. It
turned out that Dad had been favoured by an intense and difficult
alcoholic mother and had what the psychiatrist described as a fairly
classic Oedipus complex. He had also shared his mother's bed as
a child – for far too long. Mum explained that though it all must
appear shocking to me, Dad was never a violent person. He was not a
danger to anyone. Dad was a good person. He simply had problems.

What my mother revealed that day in the hotel bedroom caused
an earthquake inside my head, with tremors that continued until
the end of her life. It was something I didn't want to address, yet
it returned to taunt me over and over again. I was not sure she had
told me the truth, for on the one hand she had said Dad was always
impotent, and on the other that he was indeed my father. It really
didn't make sense.

Against all advice and after a short break back home with Mum and Geordie in Scotland on the farm in Angus, I returned to Somerset. Here I had what I now see as a rebellion, continuing to have flings with various willing partners. Many years later I began to wonder if part of my promiscuity was because I, in turn, felt confused about the love my parents had for me. At the time, however, I found it a powerful drug. It provided me with a temporary morale boost and comfort – probably for all the wrong reasons.

Pete had left a huge void, and I thought of him on an almost daily basis. And I felt incredibly lonely. I had lost my soulmate as well as my perfect lover. I worked harder than ever but kept Dad at arm's length. Hard work, an ethos that has continued throughout my life, was a convenient escape from my numerous problems. Keeping busy meant I did not have to face myself, and had less time to face Dad too. An even better escape came in taking to the woods and fields where I lost myself in nature's endless revelations. Riding Rory for hours over the moors and down through the steep oak glades, splashing through the streams and rivers, became a drug. I loved Rory, his smell, his gentle nature, his willingness to please and his quiet understanding.

Meanwhile Dad was deteriorating. Looking back over that depressing era, I was rudderless, and so was he. What I had discovered about him merely made it all worse. I felt swamped by sadness and became anxious and edgy, and started to have terrible night sweats. Dealing with Dad was dire, and the local doctor continued to be unhelpful. I went to see him on numerous occasions but hated his supercilious, patronising approach to alcoholism – I later discovered that he was a serious drinker himself.

Eventually the doctor washed his hands of Dad. He once again put him on some strong drugs as well as sleeping tablets, and told me, and Dad's latest girlfriend, that there was little more he could do except to recommend he went in for a major rehabilitation spell. Dad refused to accept he needed to go away. It would take another crisis before we were at that stage.

It came sooner than expected. I found him one afternoon lying face down in a pool of blood and had to ring for an ambulance. He had knocked himself unconscious; the blood was merely a nosebleed but it terrified me.

Three days later he returned from hospital looking dapper in an immaculate three-piece suit. 'Hello, hello, hello, how have you all been whilst I have been away?' he said, behaving as if he had returned from a business trip. To the disbelieving addict, denial is a river in Egypt.

Once again the old pattern resumed – it seemed as if Dad's girlfriend and I were the fools. He looked 'splendid' whilst we were worn out: punctured, defeated. At Our Wits' End.

It was not all black. Numerous humorous interludes were a vital part of survival. One day I was laying tables in the dining room that backed onto the office. I heard Dad shouting down the telephone in an exaggerated, plummy English accent. He was trying to give someone, who was clearly hard of hearing, his name and address, and it went on and on and on: 'No, M-U-N-R-O, not M-U-N-R-O-E, hyphen, C-L-A-R-K', and then the address. He must have repeated it about twenty times, and I was giggling to myself. About a week later a letter arrived addressed to Mr David Munro-Python-Clark. The sender clearly had an excellent sense of humour.

Another episode involved the AA inspector – not Alcoholics Anonymous, but the Automobile Association; it is unfortunate that both use the same initials, particularly as drink-driving is such a horrendous subject. For years we had been trying to acquire another star for the hotel to upgrade it to a meagre two-star hostelry. Each time it had been turned down due to minor issues. The first was that the inspector came in the dead of winter and there were no fresh vegetables. The second was because he felt that even in winter there should be fresh flowers or plants about, and reported that the place needed a more feminine touch. Dad's latest girlfriend Kate and I had endeavoured to sort these details out, so that when there was a surprise call announcing that an inspector would be paying us a visit the very next day – the way these ghastly things work – we raced about, determined to get one or even two more stars, and really felt they were deserved. So much had improved.

Dad was like champagne that had been violently shaken. When the cork came off, he was going to explode. The impending visit was the cork, the strain too much. That morning, as I had feared, he took to the bottle. Now we were doomed. Then the cook went off sick, and our usual waitress was also off with the same bug. We decided to try to keep drunken Dad in his room and not let him come anywhere near the inspector; that way we felt sure we could cope.

When the prophet of doom arrived, I realised it was the same grumpy bastard who had been so fussy before. My precarious optimism began to crumble. I showed him to an immaculately spotless room, and took him a tray of tea and shortbread. Before dinner he sat in the lounge bar by a roaring log fire, amid a froth of foliage. The place looked like Kew Gardens – greenery everywhere, and we had an excellent selection of fresh food on the menu. He had some tonic 'with three lumps of ice and a slice of lime please'.

No bloody lime, not on Exmoor in the middle of winter. Lemon had to do.

He tutted and shook his head. He then ordered a bottle of one of our most expensive French red wines to go with his steak. 'Make sure it is at exactly the right temperature, please.'

All went swimmingly, with Kate at the cooker and me acting as waitress. I was pulled up for delivering food from the wrong side, but otherwise the inspector seemed benign, even smiling patronisingly and inscrutably like the Sphinx at one point. There was a little too much gelatine in the fish mousse, and I noticed him having trouble with his false teeth. They revolved around in washing machine action. They were clearly a very poor fit. By now I was paranoid. He asked to have his coffee in the lounge bar, and was wiping his downturned mouth on a huge stiff white napkin when I heard heavy footfalls on the stairs.

The beast was abroad. There was a panic in the kitchen whilst we tried, without success, to lure Dad away from the dining room. My father was on a mission and as immovable as the Rock of Gibraltar. Indeed, I now felt like one of its notorious monkeys. He waltzed in reeking of whisky and, in theatrically grandiose mode, told the surprised gentleman that he was going to fetch him a glass of particularly fine brandy – 'on the house'. I stood in the doorway with a waitressing cloth over my arm wishing I could strangle him with it. Dad lurched out, hiccupping. He reappeared shortly, bearing a small tray with not one, but two huge brandy balloons containing the beautiful amber nectar. He then pulled up another chair at the inspector's table and started to talk to him – utter rubbish it was too. He went on about the provenance of the brandy, and then put his elbow on the table, leaning so heavily that I thought it would topple over.

I went over to them and with a forced smile said, 'There's a telephone call for you, Dad. You need to come and speak, as it appears to be quite pressing.'

At this he waved me aside and slurred, 'Pressing, pressing, oh for God's sake, Pol, tell the buggers that I will ring them back. Pol, I have important business to attend to here with my dear friend. This brandy and this charming gentleman are also pressing.'

I cringed and retreated. A few minutes later I returned and tried once more, unsuccessfully, to extricate him.

Dad took a huge swig of brandy and tried to put his elbow back on the table for support, 'Cheers, my good man, cheers, your very, very good health. It's lovely to see you, jolly good show, what ho!' But his elbow missed the table spectacularly and as it did so he let out an equally spectacular fart. It ricocheted off the wall, followed by a trio of genteel squeaks.

I rushed into the kitchen to inform his girlfriend of this latest catastrophe, and the pair of us collapsed, pouring ourselves huge glasses of cooking wine as she shrieked, 'Oh, fuck it!' weak with manic laughter.

The inspector left before breakfast next day. From then on, our solo star was extinguished. The skies above the hotel remained dark.

I had begun to notice that the tablets that the doctor had given me to help with my growing anxiety had in fact made me feel worse. It was as if all my senses had been filed down and I had no sharpness, and little ability to rationalise. Thankfully, I do not clearly remember all the incidents leading to the next disastrous event, but what I do remember is that Dad and I had a dreadful row whilst he was very drunk.

He had come out of his room and was in an appalling, repulsive state. I was standing at the top of the stairs and he was angry, very angry indeed. He could barely stand, and rocked from foot to foot like a sailor on a rough sea, clutching at the banisters for support. He accused me of causing all his problems: everything had got worse because of me; I was the reason for his utter misery. I felt drunk myself just inhaling his breath – it was so fume-laden it was inflammable. I stepped back to avoid it, and at that moment he did something he had never, ever done before. He took a swing at me. His flailing arm caught me on the shoulder, and I slipped and fell backwards down the stairs. I managed to save myself, though was severely bruised. Now I had had enough.

Dad stood at the top of the stairs, glowering wildly at me as I gathered myself up, hurting everywhere.

I couldn't speak to Mum about this, because I knew she would be furious and demand I leave immediately. She had been getting angry with me already for staying on. And anyway, I didn't trust her any more. I didn't believe she had told me the truth. Now I could no longer communicate with my father either. I left the hotel and went to the cottage.

I knew Dad was taking sleeping tablets. There was a nearly full bottle in the bathroom. I took it down from the shelf and also took a hip flask of brandy that he had left on the hall table. I walked through the village and up to the oak wood, my heart racing. It was all too much – too much. Mum wouldn't understand. I wanted out, to leave Dad to get on with his bloody miserable existence. I clearly remember that the deer were there, and there was a thick sea mist. It was a very cold day.

I had never felt hatred for either of my parents until that point.

Now I hated Dad, and I hated Mum too. I hated her because I did not believe her about the paternity issue. I hated him totally and I wanted to escape from the whole shambolic mess. I had set Dad up to fail because I had put expectations on him that he was totally incapable of meeting. He was sick, and though I had hoped I could help him, I now finally accepted that it was impossible. Alcoholism pulls everyone into the quagmire. All this was coupled with the feeling of having no one I could rely on, and the instability of my own relationships. Everything felt out of proportion in my head. I was not thinking clearly. I could not deal with any of it a moment longer.

There was the distinctive, strong aroma of the red deer that I loved so much. I could see their comforting blurred shapes coming and going through the curvaceous sylvan architecture of those ethereal stunted oak trees. There was comfort in that. I sat down with my back against one of my favourite trees, and I remember, too, thinking what a dreadful waste it all was as I swallowed the horrible pills, washing them down with brandy – something I also hated.

Then all I remember is that the deer seemed to engulf me. They came so close. I could smell their breath now, a mixture of grassy cud and leaf litter. There were two large stags, animals I had seen several times. Animals I knew. They remained aloof at the edge of the group. And then a curtain of grey mist blotted them all out. I still wonder if they really did come so close. Perhaps I imagined it.

Through a white haze and with an evil buzzing sound in my head, I saw Mum's face. She was crying. Geordie was there too. They had flown down from Scotland and were now at the hospital bedside. I was still unsure where I was or what had happened, but as that dreadful awakening unfolded, I realised that I had now shattered their lives with my actions, and I felt deeply ashamed. I had the worst headache I could have imagined, and I felt even more desperate knowing that this thoughtless episode would negatively affect us all.

I never found out who found me. I didn't think anyone knew where I went, deep in the oak wood. Clearly someone did, and I will always be hugely grateful, but at that moment I did not feel gratitude; I knew I had made everything far worse. Then I realised it was Mother's Day.

We returned to Scotland. I was not allowed to communicate with Dad. Our family doctor, who knew me well, was understanding and sympathetic, and after long sessions together she sent me to talk to an equally sympathetic psychologist. And since that nightmare time, I have never, ever taken any form of antidepressant or nerve-calming drug and instead take to the hills, for that is where I find the peace and solace that I need.

Mum and Geordie were outstanding in the immediate aftermath, but knowing what I had done to them, and to Bo, especially to Bo, was something that engulfed me with sadness and guilt – more bloody guilt. And there was so little I could do to rectify it. I think for years Mum blamed herself, for she raised the subject often, and said it was all her fault.

Then Mum began to use it as a weapon and frequently dragged it up: 'You have no idea what you have done to me. You have ruined my life with your selfish actions. And on Mother's Day too. You are so bloody ungrateful for all I have always done for you. You are so lucky that Geordie accepts you, because you are really just an appendage.'

That last comment stuck. Outbursts like this simply led to more misery, and became more frequent, particularly on one occasion when I asked her once again if Dad really was my father. 'How could he be, you told me that he was impotent? Impotence doesn't just vanish does it?' I said accusingly.

Her sympathy vanished too, and instead there was real venom. This made things even harder for us both because she reminded me about what I had done, over and over and over again, and I was desperate to forget it. It was a spear that she relentlessly jabbed me with, and it increasingly began to make tensions develop between us.

After this monumental upset, it was nearly two years before I saw Dad again. We had an emotional reunion in a hotel in Perth, both grateful to put the past behind us and move on from what had been a fiendish period in our lives. He had been off drink for some time and seemed well, but I could see how much my attempted suicide had affected him too. I knew he felt wholly responsible. Rather than hate him, I loved him more, but equally I knew that he was a sick man, and our meeting filled me with concern for what might happen next. I worried incessantly about his drink-driving and had nightmares that he might kill some innocent person with his nocturnal drunken drives. I became obsessed by it.

7

Monkey Business

Mum and Geordie had married quietly on their own while I was still at school, aged eleven, however, it was not until six years later that Mary, Geordie's daughter came for her first brief visit. I liked her instantly. Like her father, she was extremely generous, and like him, she too was warm and big-hearted. She had been affected by the instabilities surrounding her parents' marriage break-up and had stayed with her mother, whereas her brother, Malcolm, had chosen to spend most of his time with us in Ardnamurchan. In early adulthood Malcolm's life was fraught, and once he left school and university he had issues with addiction of various kinds.

Alcohol-associated problems surrounded us. While I was working out my next steps after my time in Exmoor, I remember Malcolm went for treatment to a renowned rehabilitation centre in a castle in the Scottish Borders, and Mum, Geordie and I visited and had to join in various group-therapy sessions. We sat around in a wide circle clutching mugs of tea and toying with soggy biscuits. We were supposed to talk through the problems we encountered when dealing with our nearest and dearest and their drinking issues. Some people were in tears; others were matter-of-fact. Several were angry, rage held in for years and now unleashed in a torrent. Mum and Geordie contributed nothing. They sat in silence. Geordie was frowning and shaking his head. This was not the way either of them operated; the idea of talking about it openly filled them both with horror.

My father being uppermost in my thoughts, I was longing to add something. I wanted to tell people how I felt about him despite his drinking, but how it, in turn, made me feel. I wanted to sympathise with them. Instead, I thought it best to keep quiet. I didn't want to embarrass Mum and Geordie. We nodded and smiled and tried to look animated or concerned, particularly as another person set free their innermost thoughts and the group leader stretched out to them with a box of tissues. And more tea. The tissues were an important prop and were regularly passed around, more sugar was added to the tea and the phrase 'in denial' dominated nearly every heartbreaking revelation. It felt surreal, as if I had been here before. The establishment also dealt with serious drug abusers. The pathos of the troubled souls, and, even worse, that of their distraught families forced to deal with it but pulled down in the process, was desperately sad.

After the last session, we went to find Malcolm to say goodbye. He was ashen, sitting trying to read, his hands shaking violently. We hugged him and promised we would be back soon.

'Thank God that's over,' said Geordie as he reached for a cigarette before we got into the car.

The driveway was long, fringed on both sides with mature trees, a map and compass needed to negotiate the deep potholes. It was starting to rain. Raindrops splashed like massive tears into brown puddles on the pitted tarmac.

When we reached the main road Geordie announced, 'Christ, I need a bloody drink after that ordeal!' Then both he and Mum began to laugh as the tension and worry of that difficult afternoon came to the surface like a rash of teenage acne. We found the nearest pub, where he and Mum each had a large brandy. Life is full of ironies.

Tragically, Malcolm would die young, afflicted by various health issues and throat cancer in 2001. He was just forty-four.

*

In 1979, once I had more or less recovered from my time with Dad at the hotel, I took a job in London as a photographer working in a ghastly department store in Oxford Street. The organisation was called Pleasure Portraits. It was no pleasure. There was a studio set-up and a range of pull-down backdrops – a clichéd fluffy cloud, plain black or white, and a selection of fake sunsets – and customers chose the one they wanted. All I had to do was press the shutter. It was nothing like the photography I was used to, and there was nothing to satisfy my increasingly creative soul. I was filling endless notebooks with poems and descriptive writing, and taking more and more pictures of children, animals, flowers and landscapes.

During my short stay in London, I lodged with my godmother Heather and her husband Will. Heather and her family had been our neighbours when we lived in Cheshire. Despite loving being with them, I hated London. It was a lonely place, doubly lonely because I felt that it was not a world in which I would ever belong. I was out of place. London simply highlighted to me how tough people's lives seemed, and fuelled me with a longing to return to Scotland.

After work or during lunchtime, I found myself lured to pet shops to speak to the puppies, kittens and guinea pigs in their cages, or chatting to the pigeons in the park. I missed contact with animals terribly. The pigeons kept me amused, and they also amused a couple of dejected elderly characters that came daily to feed them. We became friends as we sat together and talked about nothing in particular. There were also pigeons that went to work each day, for every morning when I caught the Tube from Putney into Earl's Court I watched as one waddled onto the train and rode a few stops, and then got out again. It did this most mornings. I recognised it as the same pigeon by the ring on its leg and its distinctive grey and pied plumage, though I never saw it making the return trip – perhaps it flew. There it would be again the next day with the rest of the jostling commuters; it just didn't have a briefcase.

Several of my school friends lived and worked close by, and we sometimes met up for an evening, but I then had a long trek back to Heather's alone on the Tube, often late at night. The underground was frightening and full of drug addicts and drunks, many aggressive and others with wild looks in their eyes, haunted and mad, their fragility clearly visible. A couple of times someone followed me almost to the gate of the house and I felt intimidated. I was sometimes terrified. Yet being alone, even in savage weather in remote places, has never given me that feeling. Heather did her best to make my stay happy, but London was not for me.

I had finally accepted that even had I gone to a crammer and tried to attain the qualifications I needed to be a vet, I just did not have the academic prowess required, and due to the infuriating lack of a maths qualification, photography college was also out. Then I saw an advert for a job overseeing all animal husbandry at a privately owned zoo in Northamptonshire. I had had few dealings with exotic animals but my enthusiasm convinced them. The pay was almost non-existent, but the work was fascinating and there were even opportunities to become involved in the veterinary side. Animals and birds of all kinds surrounded me. I was finally doing something I loved.

On my arrival, the zoo's owner said, 'Kalli will show you around.' I waited, expecting a girl or woman, and then shortly a small black-and-tan collie mongrel appeared. 'Here she is.'

It was indeed the dog that took me around the park, stopping at every cage and pen with much tail-wagging and a gentle aura of excitement. When we approached one large enclosure, two lions rushed to the door, their huge bodies straining against the wire whilst they purred like enormous domestic cats. The magnificent animals had come to the zoo as tiny orphan cubs to be hand-reared when they were only a few weeks old. Kalli had begun to lactate and had suckled them for several months, nurturing them as her own. This had given the orphans the best possible chance of survival. Often Kalli went in with them, and they rubbed themselves affectionately against her, pushing her over with their great bulk. She was minute by comparison, but their gentleness and respect for her was extraordinary to witness. It was a relationship I found fascinating.

Kalli herself had arrived at the zoo by accident. The zoo owner's daughter had been sent into the local pet shop to buy some vital parrot food and emerged instead with a small puppy under her arm. This was Kalli. She cost £3.

Kalli also suckled two orphan puma cubs. She had previously suckled other big-cat cubs too. She was an extraordinary dog, a dog with a presence that set her apart.

I was given the task of taking Kalli and the little pumas to the BBC television studios in Bristol to appear on *Animal Magic*. My childhood hero Johnny Morris was still presenting it. He was very amusing and told me why he had plasters on his fingers. The *Animal Magic* studio had a large glass-fronted cage – high-rise living for hamsters, made specially so that they could be viewed racing up and down inside, and you could see into different chambers and their sleeping compartments too. However, Johnny had taken one of the hamsters out to have a closer inspection, and it had bitten him in several places. Weeks later when the programme was shown, the plasters were clearly visible.

Another of my roles involved looking after school parties. There was an elderly capuchin monkey who had been rescued from a miserable existence tied to a barrel organ in a London marketplace. Understandably, he had temperament issues and either loved you or hated you. He was not averse to biting or pulling hair venomously if he felt you were a threat to him. Luckily, he liked me. Visiting children adored him, as he came up close to the wire and chattered to them and made funny faces that made them laugh, and then of course when he heard their giggling he played up to them even more.

However, he had a bad habit and masturbated in front of his spectators; it was awkward trying to explain when they demanded to know, 'Why's he doing that?'

The best response seemed to be the simplest. 'He does that because he likes it.' And that triggered more laughing.

There were numerous parrots: macaws, cockatoos and parakeets, a mynah bird, and also a giant hornbill. At dawn the sounds of a tropical rainforest mingled amongst the glorious dawn chorus of English woodland. The hornbill had an accident and badly damaged his lower mandible, and in a very delicate operation, under the guidance of our excellent vet, it was put back in place with superglue. This proved efficacious, and the bird made a full recovery.

A pair of eagle owls bred every year but anyone going in to feed them had to don a helmet and goggles, as they were fearless when protecting their young and would have quickly sunk huge talons into an intruder's head or face. A grey seal called Magnolia lived in a murky lake at the bottom of the extensive property. Unfortunately, she had devoured most of the lake's other occupants, including a pair of rare geese. The zoo's owner was renowned for her skills of hand-rearing wild mammals and had also raised a pair of Arctic foxes. When they moulted in spring, they resembled little burst pillows with wisps of loose fur sticking out in all directions as their thick white pelts changed into sleek grey-brown ones for summer. There was a red deer hind called Polly. She loved being brushed.

A constant influx of wildlife arrived too. A special wildlife hospital area had been created and brimmed with hedgehogs, barn, tawny and little owls, kestrels and buzzards, and an assortment of deer and small birds. The area's busy roads accounted for creatures we could do little with, but equally there were many successes.

Badgers and foxes were often brought in. The badgers were particularly difficult. One night a sow was brought in. She had been hit by a car and was very badly injured, though appeared to have no visibly broken bones. She lay comatose with blood trickling from her nose, her breathing laboured. Her grey coat was spiky like combed wire, with henna highlights added to it. We carried her carefully to a pen with a concrete floor and a suspended heat lamp, and after giving her a series of jags including an anti-inflammatory, and some rehydration therapy, left her motionless and barely breathing on a soft bed. As dawn broke I rushed out expecting her to be dead. Instead, there was a neat hole in the concrete in a corner. Our patient had discharged herself.

Some casualties arrived in a feisty state, hissing, snapping, scratching and biting. I knew from the beginning that wild animals are not dangerous, but when in such a situation, terrified and badly hurt, or at a low ebb, they are merely defending themselves. When picking up certain patients, foxes, otters and badgers being a prime example, the situation had to be quickly assessed, the stress minimised. Too much hesitation and messing about and you are liable to receive a wicked bite. Deer in particular suffer from stress and can also inflict bad injuries with sharp hooves as well as antlers as they thrash about in sheer panic when captured. It is not always the injuries that are the greatest threat to the afflicted. Stress is the bigger killer by far. Blindfolding an animal and keeping it in the dark is important, and in the case of birds, transportation in dark boxes rather than wire cages.

I learnt much about wildlife rehabilitation and hand-rearing and loved every moment of it, though there were the inevitable heart-breaks. I would have stayed longer, but on little or no pay it was unworkable – yet I felt I had not only begun to really start learning but had also found something that I could do without qualifications.

I applied for a keeper's job at Edinburgh Zoo and was accepted for the role, but it was going to be another three months before the position was vacant and, rather than waste time, I found a short-term job working on a farm on Loch Melfort, south of Oban. The owners had bought a new farm in Auchterarder in Perthshire and needed someone to help them during their move to look after Blackface sheep, goats and Highland ponies, as well as domestic animals.

I loved the farm work and they asked if I would stay on to work for them full time at their new Perthshire farm. I accepted. Though the thought of working at Edinburgh Zoo was incredibly appealing, there was the problem of finding accommodation, which would doubtless have been expensive, and I really did not want to be city based. It seemed better to stay put.

My main role was as groom, preparing their fine Highland ponies for the showing season and over the summer months doing the rounds of competitions all over Scotland. The high point was the Highland Show – several punishing days of hard graft, little sleep and all-night partying. Stock attendants had their own boxes – a line of flimsy, ramshackle wooden huts with high partitions between each. People clambered in with one another in the night, and there were monumental boozing sessions amid hours of preparation, pol-ishing and mucking out before the various competitive classes.

One highly strung mare I was showing had a mind of her own and a terror of pipe bands. Pipe bands and shows go together. On this occasion I had painstakingly soothed her before entering the main ring for the auspicious ridden class and was leaning forward rubbing her ears and neck. However, she remained on a hair trigger and I was hoping that the pipe band wouldn't venture too close. I felt as if I was sitting on a jelly. A Highland pony breeder of repute, Cameron Ormiston, saw my jodhpur-clad backside as I was leaning forward and gave me an enormous tweak on the bum. I shrieked. The pony erupted, dumping me on the ground at the ringside in front of a large audience, and my mount shot into the ring without me.

It took about twenty-five years for me to get my own back on the old devil. Cameron was a real ladies' man. Revered in Highland pony circles, he had dozens of important old Highland pony bloodlines, and often had dealings with the royal family and their stud of Balmoral Highland ponies. Years later I wrote a book on Scotland's native farm animals and the people who kept them, and Cameron formed part of the chapter on the Highland pony. Artist Keith Brockie, who did the illustrations, included a portrait of him. We had an exhibition of the paintings at the Highland Show in 2001, and Cameron's picture was one of few unsold. On the first morning of the show Cameron's son's girlfriend bought it as a surprise Christmas present for him. We put a red sticker on it. Soon after that Princess Anne and an entourage of farming politicians came in to view the exhibition. And shortly after a gossipy woman from the Highland Pony Society came to the stand for a second visit. She noted the new red sticker and said, 'I see that Cameron's portrait has just been sold; who bought it?'

So, I said, 'If I tell you, will you absolutely promise me not to tell him or anyone else?'

Of course she agreed, saying her lips were sealed and that my secret was safe with her.

'Well,' I said, 'if you really do promise, I will tell you. It was Princess Anne.'

By lunchtime a rumour was going around the Highland pony

breeders that the Princess Royal had bought Cameron Ormiston's portrait. On the last night of the Highland Show there was a celebration barbecue. Spirits were high and Cameron was well-oiled.

He sidled up to me. 'Hello, honey,' he said as he pinched my bum and winked. Then he whispered, 'Is it true, honey, what I am hearing?'

'And what would that be?'

'Well, that the Princess Royal has bought my picture?'

I nodded and did a sign that my lips, too, were sealed.

Quick as a flash, he replied, 'Well, it doesn't surprise me in the least, as she has always been very, very fond of me.' And then he winked and pinched my bum again.

That was in June, and the joke ran on until Christmas when his son's girlfriend presented the picture to him.

When we next met, my bum got another large tweak, and he laughed and said, 'Aye, you're a wee besom, so you are. You really had me believing.'

I replied, 'It's payback for that day all those years ago when you had me ditched at the entrance of the main ring at the Highland Show.'

Whilst working on the farm in Auchterarder I met my future husband, Joe. I was twenty-two. He was working on a neighbouring farm and I stopped to chat to him one day whilst out riding. He was fencing along the roadside. He looked up, and his sapphire-blue eyes seemed even bluer twinkling out of his weather-beaten brown face. He was charming, with a smile that would have distracted a dedicatedly chaste nun. We talked until my pony got bored and started pawing the verge.

We began to meet regularly. Joe brought me unusual books to read and sent me poems and notes about the natural world, or deep philosophical quotes. He had a minivan and travelled around fencing and doing livestock-related jobs for local farmers. The first time he took me out, the steep road from the farm was sheet ice. The minivan traversed sideways and narrowly missed the burn at the bottom. It was an inauspicious start.

Joe was living temporarily with his father's mother – Grandma – until he could find alternative accommodation. He had been educated in England and had been to university to study agriculture but hadn't finished the course, and instead had come north to set up his own freelance farming business. Though Joe had grown up in England, he had also spent much time in Perthshire, where he had decided to settle.

Grandma was a soft, gentle soul, and having long been widowed had remarried in her eighties to a retired army colonel, nicknamed Rusky, who was as dry as the Sahara. He was no spring chicken at well into his nineties. He had a slow, shuffling gait and padded around wearing green velveteen slippers with emblems on their fronts, watching his step-grandson's comings and goings with an air of bemused curiosity.

It was Grandma's friend, Miss Douglas, their loyal octogenarian housekeeper, who told me many of the priceless stories that emerged from that particular household. They all found having Joe and his un-house-trained collie living with them a trial. Punctuality was not his strong point. Their own lives conversely ran like clockwork, or should have done. Joe was late for every meal, often didn't get up in the morning and was usually filthy dirty from his farm labours, bringing back boiler suits so plastered in muck that they stood up by themselves.

When the minivan finally broke down irretrievably, Joe announced he was off to the local car auctions to find another vehicle. He returned having bought nothing but a beautiful, ancient, pure wool Persian carpet. 'I couldn't resist it, it was a real bargain,' he said proudly.

Joe had laid the carpet out in the garage ready to clean it. Doddery old Rusky inquisitive as ever, shuffled out to see what vehicle had been acquired and instead found the carpet. At dinner that night, Rusky raised his wine glass to Joe and said with a twinkle, 'Thoroughly approve of your new mode of transport, boy.'

As well as working on the farm, I had started my own photography business, and was writing reports with photographs on various country events for a couple of magazines. I had moved out from living with the family into one of their cottages. It had previously been inhabited by an elderly German keeper and was a shambles. The worst remnant of his occupation was the vile gibbet surrounding the garden – a fence hung with pathetic bodies: stoats, weasels, foxes, rats, polecats, moles, several badgers and numerous hedgehogs. Sun-dried husks, these gruesome casualties scowled in a macabre fashion, skulls visible, patched with sporadic hair, yellowed skin stretched over wizened skeletons.

Once the cottage was cleared out, the victims of the keeper's killing fields cremated in a miserable ceremony, and the place painted, it turned into a delightful first home. The new arrangement worked well as the owners now only needed me part-time. I specialised in portraiture of children and animals, and had started photographing weddings.

Joe came for supper most nights. However, he frequently arrived hours late to find the food ruined, and it would make me cross until he flashed his charming smile, and all would be forgotten. Sometimes he picked wildflowers for me, but one day he turned up very late at the cottage and presented me with a pet lamb – Bean – she'd cost £2 at the market. He couldn't bear to see her with no buyer.

Bean was a difficult orphan because she wouldn't take to the teat and became more and more pot-bellied. She came everywhere with me and eventually, when she grew a little bigger, lived in the field next to the cottage with the ponies and loved chasing around with them. However, one day the horseplay became too vigorous, and her back leg got broken. We took her to the vet, who told us she should be put down, but we shrieked indignantly and asked him to put a plaster of Paris bandage on it. He shrugged and raised his eyebrows but did as bidden. The leg healed beautifully though was always slightly askew.

My mother was fast becoming more spoilt because dear, kind Geordie indulged her all the time, and she appeared to have lost her sense of values. She felt that money was vital to everything and as Joe didn't have any, she was unimpressed. I had been going to beautiful little Fasque Church nearby every weekend when I was at home. There, I could sit silently listening to the activities in the surrounding rookery. The birds' dark shapes appeared against the sunlit stained-glass windows and their caws and croaks sounded almost human. We sang a few hymns accompanied by the damp squeaky strains of the organ. The elderly Canon Gait and his wife were enchanting and I found the experience calming.

When I came home Mum said, 'Polly's got God, and she's also turning into a bloody socialist to boot.' This latter because I did not always now agree with her views all the time. 'Why the hell can't you pick someone who can support you, for God's sake, instead of that useless man?'

When Joe asked me to marry him and I told my parents, Geordie put on a very good show and said how pleased he was. Mum was reticent. I knew she was furious.

Later Mum said, 'I am very worried about you, and I really don't think this will work, you seem to have changed so much and I cannot understand you any longer.'

Joe and I were engaged for six months and the wedding date was set for Geordie's birthday, 10 September 1983. Dad was having a calm phase; he came to Scotland to spend a few days with us and helped with much of the planning. Mum and Geordie meanwhile had gone berserk in their ambitions and were organising a grandiose affair even though we had been adamant that this was not what we wanted. They were both being impossible. Their plans grew grander and grander. They were both also on strict diets that made them grumpy.

Meanwhile, in the lead-up to the wedding, I was busy photographing numerous big local weddings and relied on Joe to act as my assistant. Though it was stressful and very hard work, it was worth it as we could make decent money in a short space of time, and we really needed it. I often felt anxious before photographing a wedding because there is but one chance to capture an important moment and I feared my technical abilities would fail me under pressure. On numerous occasions when we needed to leave for these events, Joe went missing, did not show up as planned and put further pressure on me by keeping me waiting. Once, I was forced to go without him and had to ask the best man to help me. You cannot really turn up to someone's big day when you are the photographer, and say, 'Sorry I'm late.' It was fuel for arguments of grand proportions.

Later that summer I got a job working for *The Field* magazine, photographing the Game Fair, which that year was being held close by. Joe was to join us in a lunch invitation with the editor but didn't show up. I wasted hours looking for him.

When I told my best friend Clare about this and the pattern that was developing with the wedding jobs, she said, 'Do you really think you should be marrying him? It's not too late, you know.'

Dad was coming to give me away, but the afternoon before the wedding he rang in an inebriated state. I had no choice but to tell Mum, and she and Geordie agreed he had to be banned. Mum and I passed a sleepless night in tears over this latest development in the alcohol-fuelled saga. The wedding day dawned, sponsored by paracetamol and too much caffeine.

'That bloody man has ruined everything again; I am furious with him,' Mum looked pale as semolina. Both of us felt wrecked.

As ever Uncle Archie gave his support and was very sympathetic. He knew how disappointed I was. Geordie gave me away. On reflection, it was appropriate given that he had paid for the wedding, and it was really his party.

It was indeed a large, flamboyant wedding. The awful truth was that had I not been put under pressure with such a big, ostentatious occasion, I would have baled out. My mother knew this too, for cracks had already started to appear in my relationship with my future husband, but now I had to make the best of what lay ahead. As for the wedding itself, we barely knew half of the assembled guests.

Dad's behaviour cast a shadow on any prospects of nuptial bliss. That night, from a luxurious honeymoon suite in Edinburgh prior to flying abroad, I rang him. He was still drunk.

'Fuck off!' he said. 'Just go and fuck right off.'

I hung up.

Joe had taken on a full-time job as manager on a little hill farm near Auchterarder and once we were married we lived in an old house that went with the job. It had a panoramic view over Strathearn. It had room for a darkroom too. I gave up my part-time work on the farm where I had lived previously so that I could concentrate on my photography business and more writing, though instead did a great deal on the farm that had now become home.

We had a flock of cast Blackface ewes (sheep that have come off harder, higher hill farms and are moved to softer, low ground for the last years of their breeding life). We also had a few younger ewes and a herd of suckler (breeding) cows. And of course we had Bean. Suffolk tups were used on the ewes, and Joe acquired an impressive Suffolk cross Border Leicester tup called Spud.

During the late 1970s it was compulsory to dip all sheep twice annually. The government had inflicted this upon farmers and their unfortunate sheep as a means of keeping various diseases, including the highly contagious sheep scab, at bay. Laced with lethal organo-phosphates, the dip was noxious stuff and it was a hard, unpleasant job. We had to put Spud through the dipper last, as his largesse and subsequent splash, like that of a breaching whale, sent its filthy chemical contents far into the air, leaving the dipper empty. One of the Suffolk tups, named Moss, was an unpredictable character. If you didn't watch yourself, he would butt you over the feed troughs and send you flying into the mud. He got me once, and it really hurt. I learnt to be vigilant.

Visiting agricultural sales reps often appeared at the farm with time to waste, usually when we were up to our eyes in worming and jagging sheep in the fank, or were trying to calve a cow. They drove us mad, as it involved a long stop, and too much talking over the prowess of various new livestock-enhancing products, all of which cost a fortune. And Joe's employer was ever on a tight budget.

One morning we were doing sheep's pedicures and had brought the tups into the fank too. They had been fighting and some were hopping lame. They resembled prize boxers with bloody patches on their polled heads. They were in a pen by the first gate and looked an unsavoury crew. A sales rep we both disliked drove into the yard in a flashy new car. He was the worst of them all – pushy and patronising, and he always spoke down to us as if we were two stupid kids. Joe suggested we pretend we hadn't seen him and keep our heads down. This we did, but by now he had decided to come right into the fank to collar us. Luckily it was a windy morning and the sheep were making a racket, having been temporarily separated from their lambs. We had a valid excuse for not hearing his calls. I mumbled something about Moss being in the first pen, and Joe smiled in his melting, good-looking way and again told me to keep my head down. We giggled. We knew that the obese rep couldn't climb the gate. Instead he tried to open it, but it dropped on its hinges. He struggled through, and then turned his back to drag it shut. Moss was in the waiting room preparing for his assault. He took a few steps back to give himself a bit of extra run and began to scrape at the ground with a foreleg: a Spanish bull facing a toreador. Then he went for it, walloping our friend neatly in the middle of the arse. There was a yelp such as a terrier emits when rabbiting, and the silly man turned to face the tup and received a second bull's eye in the balls. After that episode, we saw far less of that particular rep. It was cruel, but it did the trick.

Joe and I veered between getting on well, to pulling in totally the opposite direction. Much of it was about time-keeping, and his hatred of early mornings. Rows were salved in bed.

Even though the farm was not particularly high, it was in an exposed position, north-facing and with the inevitable difficulties that come with such a situation. Winters could be long and treacherous; the road frequently blocked with snow and ice which, due to the way it drifted over the road, was hard to clear.

Some of the stubborn old cast ewes had come from far bleaker farms and were unused to trough feeding. They refused to come near and wouldn't eat even if the feed were taken closer to them, despite being heavily in lamb and extremely hungry. This made them at risk from one of many ovine afflictions, such as twin lamb disease, also called pregnancy toxaemia. Caused by a drop in blood glucose often triggered by the stress of being in lamb and being too thin, it can also be set off by the weather, or another underlying health issue. If caught in time treatment is usually efficacious. Then sometimes, just prior to lambing, the ewes would prolapse too. This is when a sheep puts out what looks like a red balloon from her vulva, and sometimes pushes out a bit of the rectum too. Old, slack muscles and big lambs cause this unpleasant occurrence. Putting back prolapses is something I hate, because no sooner have you got the wretched bits back inside the sheep, than the unfortunate animal strains because it must be most uncomfortable, and the bloody thing pops out again. We used to pin them back in with nappy pins, or stitch them, but then great care has to be taken when the ewe starts lambing as the stitches or pins must be swiftly removed. It always seemed to happen on fiendishly cold, wet days when the north wind had a bite to it and our hands were numb and useless. Eventually, as we replaced the old sheep with younger gimmers (two-year-old sheep), the problem seldom occurred.

Lambing time on any farm can be fraught, and though it can be the loveliest season, there were some miserable days too when, far from lambs happily skipping about amid the daily growing dawn chorus, the weather chucked more hell at us, the ewes went off their milk due to lack of grass and the chill biting winds, and we were occupied through every daylight hour sorting out maternity problems.

One disastrous year it poured for the entire month of April, and farmers in the area lost literally hundreds of lambs. We were bringing our own hypothermic creatures into the kitchen in desperation – the floor was wall-to-wall with lambs, Aga doors thrown wide open. We brought in extra heaters to try and thaw the sodden creatures out. We massaged them with warm towels, but many already had their heads set back in near-death posture and were impossible to revive. The vet showed me how to inject the lambs straight into the abdomen with warmed dextrose in the hope of reviving them more quickly. This often proved successful, but despite this intervention, the heap of our casualties grew. That year sheep farmers in our area were shattered by one of the worst lambing seasons on record – the carnage was depressing, to say nothing of the economic impact; it all seemed such a waste.

We worked very hard, and I loved it most of the time. I loved rising before dawn just as light was beginning to seep through the gap in the curtains. I hastily dressed and went straight out into the lambing fields to see how things were progressing. There were curlews and lapwings on the hill and snipe drumming over the wet areas, and the sweet arias of blackbird and thrush to accompany me. I have always loved daybreak and the peace and solitude of dawn. Joe, on the other hand, always found getting up impossible and was extremely uncommunicative and bad-tempered for the first few hours of the morning. He could stay up far into the small hours, which was something I found hard. Though I had noticed his moods from early on in our relationship I had naively believed that once we were settled and happy these would ease. I was wrong.

8

A Bitch of a Month

July 1984, and Joe and I have been married for less than a year. July is a bitch of a month. Sheep are laden with hot, heavy fleeces and are troubled, backsides butted into the air as lambs now bigger than themselves dive into the udder. Soon they will be clipped and the lambs will be off to market. Summer is the season when they are plagued with a motley crew of flies. All creatures have their place – but some are less appreciated. Blowflies, clegs and midges drive them crazy. I found a ewe infested with maggots yesterday, caused by the muggy weather. Hopefully I caught her in time, and she will recover from the shock of being almost eaten alive. Ticks seem a worse hazard this month. Hidden in tall bracken that is staging a takeover bid, they cling to any passing flesh; I have seen tiny house martins and swallows festooned with ticks – nothing is safe. Bloated, grey, perilous packages laden with infections that fall off the dogs, they exude dark, glutinous blood smears when squashed. July, and the undergrowth is a jungle. Mother Nature is overdressed, humidity merely exacerbating her tired, thunderous humour.

Mum and Dad are sitting in the garden by the hedge beside the farmyard. I hear laughter and joking. I ply them with coffee but keep my distance. Dad is upbeat even though Mum has been talking to him about the incidents that have led to this visit. She came because I am upset. And she is upset too. And I think she came because she wanted to see him. He is full of promises, pomposity and shite. It is as if he believes his own myth. I see red-haired Mum, still beautiful, hiding behind dark glasses and not much enjoying the sun, whilst Dad, with his dark skin, is nut brown and lapping it up. They appear oddly at ease, genuinely pleased to see one another, though it is years since they met. I don't think he ever stopped loving her. As I interrupt with more sustenance, I overhear them swapping notes about their continuous battles with weight loss, and various ailments associated with the ageing process. Both are laughing incessantly. They do seem happy; they share a history and a colourful sense of humour. When they parted company at the start of the 1970s, they independently booked into the same health farm, unbeknown to one another. A new chapter needed a trim new figure; stress and a pending divorce had taken their toll. However, it turned into a farce as they met accidentally in the health farm's hall, both bearing excess baggage. Dad, ever the gentleman, agreed it would be better to move on and swiftly did so. Both have regaled me with differing versions of the tale and view it as an enormous joke. Luckily.

Mum stays for lunch, and the three of us sit together around the kitchen table, driven in by flies and thundery showers. It is the first time we have been like this since I was a child; it feels odd, just my parents and me. I have a lump in my throat and can't eat. My stomach is knotting with spasms, as it has always done when I am worried or insecure, ever since childhood. Our mental health requires firm foundations, a stable home, grounding; these drink-related inter-ludes set me astray. I feel weighed down. Our local doctor came to see Dad earlier in the day and has put him on the drug Antabuse again. I see the tell-tale signs that he is feeling better and back in control. It is as if the car accident that has led to this moment never happened, and we are the idiots.

*

The previous day, when this latest fiasco began, Joe had been away to market all day. I was working in the fank, sorting ewes and lambs. I had gone into the kitchen to make myself some tea. The telephone rang and a strange female voice garbled a tale that made little sense. Something about someone having a horrendous brush with death and driving into a wall.

'I think I have your father with me, but I'm not sure of his name,' the voice continued.

Not sure of his name? What did that mean? There was drink involved. He was now in a hotel some twenty miles north of Callander, in a poor state. The woman seemed non-committal.

I began to ask questions. The voice trailed off; the phone went dead. Why did she cut me off like that?

I panicked. The telephone stayed silent; the woman didn't call again. With adrenaline fuelling my system, I tried to be rational and sought a map. Twenty miles north of Callander? Lochearnhead was a likely destination. I rang the police but they had no record of any incident. Hearing my distress, they promised to ring back. After what seemed an age, a policeman did call back. Dad had been traced to a hotel at Killin. He had written off both his car and a high wall. The car had already been towed away.

I spoke to a kind woman at the hotel who said that my father had ordered a taxi and had already left, and was on his way to me at the farm. She added, 'I am afraid he is paralytic, battered and bruised.'

My recall of this particular event, one of a long catalogue of similar incidents, may be flawed, since it was shortly to be clouded by far worse. Memory is unreliable.

When he arrived, Dad looked awful, but the effects of the drink were wearing off – he was obviously shocked following the crash. The taxi driver had dumped him as if he were manoeuvring a floppy, heavy woolsack. He then chucked Dad's leather cases and thermos flasks unceremoniously onto the drive whilst Dad fumbled for cash. The driver raised his eyebrows skywards whilst tutting, something I have always found exasperating. Once the cash was in his pudgy hand, he revved off at speed, as if Dad were a hand grenade on the point of explosion. I suppose he was.

We stood by the luggage in a haze of exhaust and alcohol fumes before staggering into the house. Tea, that salve for all problems, was the next priority, and then Dad (a solid, heavy man, who was as hard to steer as a supermarket trolley with a wonky wheel), tottered precariously upstairs to the spare room where I instructed him to sleep it off.

Dad was now benign and remorseful: 'I'm so sorry, so sorry, what the hell shall we do? Please forgive me, Pol.' At this point I could have asked him to take me to the moon and he would have tried – all part of the alcoholic pattern I was increasingly able to recognise. Like an obedient collie, he did as bidden.

Later, his explanation of the lead-up to the crash unfolded. My father, who, as I have mentioned before, was fascinated by deer and everything to do with them, including stalking, had been at a Red Deer Commission meeting on the Isle of Mull and then was heading back to stay with me for a few days before going south. He had been escalating the profits of the Caledonian MacBrayne bar on the car ferry en route back to Oban. A concerned traveller aboard had warned the Oban police, and there was a reception party waiting as the boat docked. Dad ricocheted like a wayward skittle towards his vehicle on the car deck. The police were waiting but Dad refused to take a breathalyser test. A doctor was bidden to take a blood sample. However, as Dad was not actually driving when the ferry docked, by some quirk of law he was able to argue that he was not therefore technically in charge of the car. Caledonian MacBrayne were still responsible for it at that point. This might have extricated him from a lifetime driving ban, something that he feared, for he had lost his licence already several times. The vehicle was removed from the ferry by one of the staff and left parked until Dad was fit to drive again.

However, next day whilst driving around Oban in a drunken stupor once more, he had sped up a one-way street, realised his error and backed out in a hurry. Straight into the parked car of the very doctor that he had seen the day before. The doctor was on a home visit. On hearing the bang and splintering of headlight glass, he rushed out to investigate, only to find a large dent in his car. This time the doctor had my father firmly by the balls. A life ban was now a certainty, though would not come into effect for some weeks. When Dad told me all this with pathetic honesty, we both laughed.

It seemed something you couldn't make up. I still giggle about it today. It makes a good story. Sadly, it was true.

This episode was the reason for my mother's visit that hot July day. I had called her to say that Dad was in serious trouble and she had come to support me. When I look back, I always think that she also genuinely wanted to see him.

After Mum left to return to her own home, Dad and I had another long talk. I told him he had to remain positive; we chatted over the prospects of him running a second-hand bookshop instead of a pub, and I told him how much both Archie and I loved him. We talked a great deal about his alcoholism, about how it was ruining his life, and mine, and we both cried. He admitted he didn't know how he could deal with it. It was not as if he hadn't tried, having been in some of the best drying-out establishments in the country, and on numerous occasions. I thought of all the hidden whisky bottles I had found in astonishing places.

Once, when I was staying at his cottage in Somerset, the loo wouldn't flush. I took off the cistern cover and found two full whisky bottles all at sea in the water, sailing around the ballcock. One day I spied a bottle down his riding boot, and bottles of various spirits kept cropping up endlessly in other bizarre places: the garden shed, the compost heap, under blankets in the linen cupboard, and often under the car seats – and always when he was supposed to be off the drink. He was a squirrel burying nuts, and forgot where he had hidden them. Another time, I had to collect his car from the police pound after he had been arrested for drink-driving on his way home from an Alcoholics Anonymous meeting. There was much clattering and the sound of clanking glass. There was a case full of bottles in the boot. There was a sad but also humorous irony to that episode: he had gone to the meeting in good faith, left it and got plastered outside the hall, and then proceeded to drive home. His slalom driving style had caused the police interception. I, meanwhile, was at the pub shutting up the bar and worrying about why he wasn't home.

On occasions, things with my father were so awful that we laughed, black humour papering over the misery. Alcohol had him by a ghastly stranglehold, and my struggles to help him had almost led to my own downfall. There was a simple fact: I was not able to cope with it.

Two days after Mum's visit, Dad had pulled himself round; that particular bout was at an end. He was back to his immaculate and perfectly dressed self, clean-shaven and polished, full of confidence and a little of the pomposity for which he was famous. This was the Dad that I loved. He was insistent on hiring a car to drive himself back to Somerset, via Liverpool, where he said he had business to attend to.

'Look, I am absolutely fine, there is no problem at all. I really do need to go to Liverpool and see about various business things and it would suit me far better to drive. Pol, I love you so much and I will be fine, so please stop worrying about me.'

I did so want him to go on the train instead. We argued gently round and round. But Dad won.

I was unhappy about his drive south as he seemed so frail, but he loved driving and it was clear following his pending drink-driving charge that he would not be doing it much longer. Ironically, he had completed various advanced driving courses and had a phase of driving flashy sporty vehicles with big headlights, open roofs and no leg room. The makes of car that a randy male friend once told me had the ability to take off at such speed from a standstill that a girl's knickers would be blown straight off, or so he probably hoped. However, this time a sedate car was hired from a garage at Stirling.

The morning I took him to collect it, the sky was pregnant with malevolent intent; gathering clouds like spreading bruises matched the way I was feeling: knackered. It was so humid that it felt as though the atmosphere was bearing down on us. I waited whilst he filled in various forms and then made him promise to ring me on the way and to keep me informed. I hugged him, and we said goodbye. The short drive back to the farm was blurred not by rain but by my crying. I felt hollow.

Next day there was a message on my answerphone thanking me

for everything. He sounded cheerful. He had got back home safely and added that he would ring again soon. But he didn't.

Two days later, on 9 July, the telephone rang at a quarter to seven in the morning. It was Archie. I was well used to him ringing me about Dad. After all, he was the one who had always turned up and taken me out for the weekends from school when poor Dad was comatose again. The words he spoke were plain and simple, yet taking them in was not.

'Pol, my dearest Pol, I have very, very bad news for you,' he said. 'I am so sorry, so very sad and sorry, but last night Dad shot himself.'

Silence – a long silence. 'Is he alright?' I asked. It did not seem to be my voice that asked this ridiculous question, yet somehow I was hoping.

'No, I am so, so sorry, Dad is dead.'

I felt numb and could not speak any more. I said so, and we hung up.

On hearing my tragic news, Joe, who was still in bed, shot out like a stone from a catapult. After a brief hug, he disappeared up the hill to check the sheep. And I did not see him again for much of that ghastly day. He simply could not cope with the emotions, and neither could I. But I really needed him. That absence put the first of many nails in the coffin of our marriage. Mum and Geordie were away south on a short holiday. I was unsure where. I left a message with my stepfather's office. Grandma, Joe's grandmother, who lived close by, soon appeared to keep me company since Joe felt unable to. Still I did not break down. It was too hard to absorb.

It was a relief to see Grandma's sweet, kind face, her trademark bonnet perched at a jaunty angle and her rosy, rouged cheeks, two large perfectly round spots. She was bearing a big bunch of wild-flowers mixed with some from her garden. I remember because there were foxgloves specially picked. She knew how much I loved wildflowers. She made tea and we sat and talked. Her unobtrusive presence had a wonderful calming effect, like the soothing hum of bees gathering nectar.

Bizarrely, I went to a hair appointment I had previously booked and even bluntly told the hairdresser what had happened – 'My father shot himself last night.'

She went pale and nearly nicked my ear.

I was in shock – freeze-framed into an icy coolness.

I then went to see another of my closest friends, Caroline, whose seven-year-old son had just had dangerous open-heart surgery, a life-threatening operation – as ever she was incredible, she knew so much about the struggles with Dad, and in turn the struggles I had with myself. Her kindness and sympathy were overwhelming, and we both wept for the terrible events of that fateful day.

Then I carried on much as usual. I remember other odd moments such as the fact that Grandma took me to Perth later in her red Mini Metro so we could do mundane things to keep us busy and stock up on food. I remember that she drove all the way in third gear. And I commented to her about how well the car went like this in the desperate hope that she would realise and change up, but she didn't and kept talking all the way without moving the gear stick once. We proceeded in a smog of fumes.

That date – 9 July – was a devastating smudge of indelible ink spreading fast onto crisp, pristine white linen, an oil spill wrecking all in its wake, a vast blot with no pattern sprawling on and on into densely blurred edges. And oblivion. Black was the colour: July is a bitch of a month.

Suicide. It leaves a gaping wound, an abyss laden with regret, sorrow, loss, hopelessness, and, perhaps worst of all, a hundred unanswered questions. And it leaves guilt, horrendous guilt, and what-ifs, and if-onlys. The telephone call that changed my life with a single shot, like the bullet that blew my father's head off, would have far-reaching repercussions.

When the police asked if I would go to Somerset to identify my father's body, I declined. It would be too much to bear. I had to strive to remember Dad in the times when we were happy. There were so many of those. Then his normality had filled me with relief and contentment. I had been too young and naive to realise that this was only temporary. That his foul demons would return again and again. Now I had to accept that this was the exit route that my father had chosen. He was fifty-four and I was twenty-three.

I went to the answerphone and without playing his final message again, I pressed delete.

A few days later Kate, his girlfriend, who had told him she would leave him if he lost his licence again, rang to speak to me. She told me in graphic detail that it took three people all morning to scrape my father off the walls of his cottage. This was an image that stuck with me worse than any other and, though I never saw her again, I came to loathe her for saying it, for it haunted me for years. However, it backed up my conviction that refusing to identify my father's body had definitely been the right decision. I knew that one of the worst problems with Dad was that he constantly put himself in situations he could not handle – and that, in turn, led to self-destruction. I knew that I must not fall into the same trap.

Joe made a fuss about the funeral date, saying that he had to make silage despite the fact that his employers had been hugely sympathetic and had come to the farm the morning I had heard the news. They had told me that they would get contractors in to help over this tragic period. But no, Joe insisted on being difficult and was little support. I understand now that he simply could not handle any of it. I was lucky that others stepped into the breach. My mother was always superb in a crisis and she and Geordie could not have been more supportive, and Bo, though increasingly frail and living at home with Mum and Geordie, was marvellous, enveloping me with her eternal warmth.

Due to the circumstances of Dad's departure, there was an inquest that extended the waiting time for his funeral. The trip to Somerset for the funeral was a test of emotional endurance, a marathon fuelled yet again by adrenaline. Geordie, who had long since become someone I loved and relied on, drove Archie, Joe and me to Exmoor. I was supposed to meet the solicitor and go to Dad's house to do an inventory of his belongings but despite being advised to do so, I decided against it. Kate would do it instead, but this too had consequences, since half his stuff mysteriously vanished. Belongings meant little to me, though, and following Kate's horrible graphically gory descriptions, I was terrified of what I might find. Even a small remaining blood smear would knock me sideways and remain with me forever. Dad's cottage was an enchanting little place and I wanted to remember it that way. There had been times that we had been so happy there. When he first bought it, it was in a rough state, and we had decided how to do it up together. Dad always did have good taste.

On the eve of the funeral, we had dinner in a local hotel. The food threatened to choke me. As we were having a drink beforehand, I saw a local newspaper on the table and in it read a short description of the events of Dad's death. This was the reality: finally, I was beginning to believe that it had indeed happened. It simply read: 'Ex publican David Munro-Clark found dead beside a shotgun and spent cartridge. There are no suspicious circumstances.'

Those eighteen words floored me, and I still have that cutting. For some inexplicable reason, I cannot throw it out. I know I should.

*

It's nearly the end of this grim month and I am feeling hollow, exhausted and listless. I really cannot be bothered to do anything. The events of the past weeks seem unimaginable. I still don't really believe that Dad is gone, that I won't ever see him again. I am standing at the window looking out over the field in front of the farm. Ewes and lambs are gathering around a bedraggled heap of feathers. Is it a dead bird? It looks like a young kestrel, and it looks exactly as I feel – utterly dejected and miserable. I wonder if it has flown into wires and crash-landed. I creep out quietly into the field to have a better look, half expecting it to fly away.

It is a kestrel. Its feathers are sodden. It lets me approach, and doesn't even bother to try to escape. It's tucked up, and its plumage is puffed out – this is a bad sign. I bend to lift it and carefully wrap it in the folds of my jersey. I take it into the kitchen for closer inspection. It looks uninjured. It's certainly thin but readily takes fresh meat straight from my hand. Later, I catch a mouse in the byre, and this too goes down rapidly. Why is it so tame? I can see that it is a young bird – a fledgling from this season. Perhaps its starved state is the only reason for its trusting behaviour. Sometimes with injured wildlife, birds and animals can seem tame but the truth is that they have gone so far down that they simply have no energy left to try to get away. Usually this supposedly trusting behaviour is the prelude to death.

It seems odd. I am unaware of any kestrels nesting particularly close, though have been watching a pair displaying on a crag on the Ochils behind the farm. After a few days, the little bird has recovered, but still remains fearless. It is content to perch on the back of a chair in the kitchen, bobbing its head while watching intently. Its dark eyes follow me as I prepare our meals, and it bobs its head again as it watches the small birds pass the windows.

The kestrel soon puts on weight and becomes stronger. One bright morning I endeavour to give it back its freedom. Like a boomerang it keeps coming straight back to me. I leave it perched on the garden fence for a few hours, and then come back and find it has flown around for a while but returned to the same spot, very close to where I first found it. In that position and seemingly so un-streetwise, it is vulnerable to predation by a cat. There's a pair of peregrines nesting high on the hill above the house too. It would make easy prey.

The kestrel is a mystery. I wonder, has it perhaps been hand-reared? Unlikely. I fit its slim, daffodil-coloured legs with soft leather jesses and begin to train it to perch properly on my gloved fist. I take it for long walks around the farm with the collies and teach it how to climb back onto my fist after it bates in fright. It doesn't take long for the bird to become even more trusting. I name it Sorrel but am still unsure of its sex. Juvenile kestrels have the same barred plumage as adult females, and young males do not develop their slate blue-grey head feather tinting and matching tail until after their first moult.

The ancient falconry tome, *The Boke of St Albans*, 1486, states:

> An eagle for an emperor, a gyrfalcon for a king
> a peregrine for a Prince, & a saker for a knight,

a merlin for a lady, a goshawk for a yeoman,
a sparrowhawk for a priest, & a kestrel for a knave.

A kestrel for a knave – so this little falcon was seen as worthless and certainly did not warrant the effort of falconry training according to the old book. Even so, kestrels are sometimes used for displays by falconry centres, but are seldom widely flown to the lure. Using basic falconry techniques gleaned from a more recent book on the subject, I am able to train my bird to return to me for small pieces of meat when I whistle, and I can let it fly free as I go around the farm. I am absorbed in my new charge, the pain of Dad's departure eased by its need for my constant attention, and its companionship. It seems to need me as much as I need it. It consumes me. It comes in the car, and it comes when I visit friends. By autumn, a bluish tinge begins to show as tail and head feathers alter gradually. My bird is a male.

I had read Barry Hines' classic novel *A Kestrel for a Knave* during my teens and read it again soon after Sorrel's arrival, for I'm interested in the relationship between the boy and the bird, and also want to see how he trained it. But the part where the bird is brutally killed is too much to bear. I'm shocked by the fact that even though I know it is coming, I'm devastated to read it again. Things are so raw; Sorrel is my vital crutch and I nurture him with all I have.

9

Fishwifery

We had been at the farm for less than two years when Joe's employers, who were past retiring age, sold it in 1985. We began searching for a little place of our own. Eventually we found a smallholding in Kincardineshire, close to Mum and Geordie. It only had twelve acres and was in an advanced state of decay. However, it also had a fish farm that was being sold as a going concern, providing rainbow trout to hotels and shops, as well as for restocking lochs and ponds for sport fishing. There was an extensive range of outbuildings; it had potential. We knew nothing about fish farming but we could learn. We could also have a small flock of breeding ewes and then buy in lambs for indoor fattening in the sheds. Being young, energetic and full of enthusiasm, we took it on knowing we were both going to have to work exceedingly hard.

The move from Auchterarder was not straightforward. We had accumulated enough animals to fill an ark. We had an Aberdeen Angus heifer calf, two collies and a terrier, a tabby cat, Sorrel the kestrel, Bean and various other sheep, as well as Spud the tup, given to us as a leaving present. He would be the founder of our new flock. There were also three pet lambs and a dozen quail as we hoped to sell quails' eggs to some of the hotels and restaurants that took our fish. However, our new cottage was being renovated and to begin with we stayed in a flat in Mum and Geordie's house.

First the heifer was transported in the luxury of a borrowed horsebox, and the next day we followed in convoy with the furniture van, in two vehicles laden to the roof with gear. My car was filled with the smaller animals, and our pick-up filled with sheep and Spud, whose great bulk dominated most of the back. Just to complicate the matter, I had stupidly put a rabbit that Parsley, our terrier, had killed, in my car too, to feed Sorrel. The three dogs could smell the deceased, and wouldn't leave the bag alone. Basil, our cat, grumbled in a basket on the front seat for the entire journey, making throaty growls of discontent. He jabbed his paw through the mesh, angrily trying to claw at anything. When we were well on the way and the menagerie was settled, he managed to turn the radio button with his extended paw and it came on suddenly so loud that I nearly drove off the road. Beside the three dogs on the back seat, a laundry basket housed the quail. The cock bird clearly found the movement of the car arousing and was amorously chortling to his hens. This temporarily took the dogs' minds off the rabbit as they peered through the weave of the basket, their heads coming almost unscrewed. Sorrel was in a small basket in the front footwell, and finally, taking up the rear in the boot were my three pet lambs. They settled immediately and having had the comfort of an extra bottle of milk lay down in a heap and peacefully chewed the cud. Sheep are not stupid.

It was another inauspicious start, but like all my moves with an ark-load of creatures, it involved regimental-style planning. The hilarity began before the first of the beasts was even loaded. Once the furniture and Joe's charges were aboard, I took the dogs up the hill behind the farm to allow them to complete final ablutions prior to departure. In my haste I tripped spectacularly, landing in a deep bog on top of a sharp rock. And though Joe and the lorry driver found it highly entertaining when I reappeared covered in mud, it was acutely painful and made sitting for the next week excruciating. Next day I could see from the mirror that I had definitely got my troubles behind me, for my backside was the colour of crushed brambles, with streaks of yellow spreading out in all directions like an angry sunset. And it was as tender as a prime fillet steak.

Our new home was an extraordinary spot. Set in a little glen, its few fields ran alongside the burn. The fish tanks were below the cottage; an ex-army ambulance was plumbed into the water supply, fitted with stainless-steel sinks and used as a gutting shed adjacent to the tanks. The place was infested with rats. They were enormous, fearless and opportunistic. They were even evident during the day, squealing gleefully as they raced in and out of a honeycomb of holes. They were thriving on spilt fish food laced with rich oils. This made their coats gleam as if they had been painted with varnish. They were so confident that when cornered they didn't hesitate to show us their yellow teeth. Parsley, who had been bred by a keeper and was a mixture of Lakeland, Cairn and Patterdale terriers, became a gold medallist in the ratters' Olympics. Using a long bamboo cane, I poked rats out from underneath various buildings, and she accounted for dozens, swiftly despatching each with a lightning-fast hit. Though the rat situation was a concern, Parsley clearly thought that ratting was good sport. And death came swift and furious – just one shake and the unfortunate beast was out of the game. Parsley, being an intelligent little dog, wasted no time once the task was done and raced in ready for the next one to explode from cover. But even she couldn't cope with the sheer numbers, and eventually we had to employ a professional hit squad to rid us of our rodent peril. All domestic animals were kept away from the farm until the plague had gone, as we were terrified of secondary poisoning. It was dire, but we had no choice.

The farm was a shambles. The baler twine of years was strewn everywhere and even seemed to be growing, embedded in the grass swards and poking out from banks and the small fringes of wood-land at the field margins. The fences were collapsing; the sheds were full of black polythene and barbed wire, empty chemical drums and massive rusting gates. Pools of old paint had spewed out of rusting cans and lay solid in a grey-white mass like giant gull shit, on the concrete shed floor. The priority was to remove the old wire and col-lapsing fence posts, and divide the fields into neat paddocks. Joe was an excellent fencer. We hired skips and filled them so fast that the skip company couldn't keep pace. It was exhausting but satisfying work, and we quickly saw results. And in between we learnt how to gut and package fish, freezing them ready for sale to the hotels. Once a week I took to the road and travelled over the hills across the

David (left) and Archie with their mother, Doris.

Mum with Penny and Jane, mother and daughter who regularly disgraced themselves because they loved rummaging in the neighbours' dustbins.

Mum and me on a holiday in the West of Ireland. Mum was mad on donkeys, but giving her one as a present years later proved disastrous.

Above. With Mum, Bo, Archie and friends, 1961.

Right. Dad and me on a beach in north Wales with Labrador Jane.

Above. The main building at Gordonstoun, on the Moray Firth coast. This was the only school where I was truly happy.

Left. Barney Robinson, the first mate, who taught us so much about seamanship at Gordonstoun and who was a wonderful, cheery character loved by all.

Pete fishing for rainbow trout on one of the ponds on our farm in Angus.

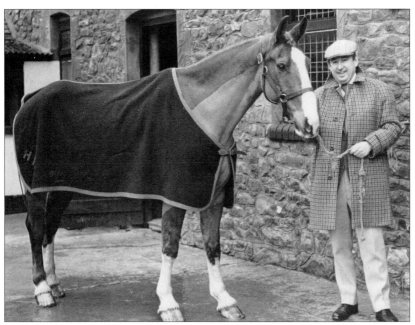

Dad with his Irish cob Rory. This wonderful patient horse seemed to take great care of my alcoholic father.

Left. With Lulu in the garden of the Kilchoan Hotel in Ardnamurchan. Lulu used to accompany me to school and was the first of my many beloved pet sheep.

Below. Ben Hiant, with the ruin of Mingary Castle (since fully restored) overlooking the Sound of Mull and the ancient oak woodland where I have spent so much time.

Kilchoan Hotel around 1969, after my parents had refurbished it.

My mother's mother, Bo, who shared the same birthday as me and who was the kindest person I have ever known.

Mum, who was nicknamed 'Knickerbocker Glory' and Annie Ruadh in 1980, during our time in Ardnamurchan.

Left. From a very early age, Freddy was used to sharing our lives with the various wild animals and birds that were brought to us for rehabilitation. Tawny owlets have always been frequent casualties.

Below. Berry with Rosie, a roe fawn whose mother was killed on the road.

Left to right: George, James and Freddy setting off on an adventure of a lifetime – the Mongol Rally in 2007.

Iomhair in a Perthshire pinewood with our three generations of collie – Pippin, Maisie and Molly, and Freddy's dog Milly.

Kalli, a small collie cross mongrel, with two puma cubs that she successfully reared as her own.

Joe taking the ewes down to the lambing field one miserable March afternoon.

Back home the week after Dad's funeral in 1984, I found Sorrel, a young kestrel in the field in front of our house.

With a young male snowy owl that landed on a BP oil tanker crossing the Atlantic from Canada to Scotland, 1989.

With Freddy and one of our many pet lambs on our farm in Kincardineshire.

Freddy aged four with Border collie Tibby.

With the dogs on the side of Beinn Eighe in Torridon, an area I have loved since schooldays.

With Ruby, a hand-reared red deer hind who came to me as a two-week old calf. She loves to be hosed down on a hot day.

Freddy and me on Ben Lawers in Perthshire with Molly and Pippin. Time in the hills together is always at a premium.

Beside a horizontal oak in Ardnamurchan with a tame tawny owl.

glorious drama of Cairn O' Mount and far into Deeside to deliver the orders.

Live deliveries were more complicated. We inherited an elderly horsebox with a redundant dairy bulk milk tank. To this were fixed oxygen cylinders and an array of rubber hoses, all of which, like the transport, were long past their sell-by date, the rubber perishing and pressure gauges unreliable. Once an estate had put in their order for, say, one hundred approximately ten-ounce trout, we had to grade them. We used a large brush to gently sweep the fish into a net, and one of us then handpicked each trout and put it in a large black dustbin filled with water until we had enough to load up the bulk tank on board the pantechnicon. It was time consuming and was sore on our hands, leading to gaping hacks, particularly in winter, even though we wore rubber gloves.

Hitched to the pick-up, the horsebox was then towed to the various customers. This was a challenge, for our route was over some of the steepest roads in the country, and the stench of clutch and brake fluid dominating our journeys was alarming. It was also alarming to feel the peculiar rocking motion when accelerating, as the water in the tank rolled back and forth. Its pressure on the downhill runs was far scarier than on the ascent. Then it pushed the vehicle harder, and on the north side of Cairn O' Mount, at Bridge of Dye, we had many heart-in-mouth moments as the pick-up gathered momentum until nearly out of control, goaded on by the sheer weight of the trailer behind. We were fortunate that there were no serious incidents. It was blatantly clear that we were taking major risks. Whilst the alterations to the house and buildings were costly, it was not long before we were forced to take out what felt like a second mortgage on a new pick-up and a purpose-built fish transportation tank specially fitted for it.

I loved doing the live fish deliveries as they took us into some of the finest estates in Deeside and Strathdon. Due to the inaccessibility of some of the lochs, often the fish would have to be transported to their final destination lugged by two people, in the big black plastic dustbin – an infallible piece of equipment that was to prove significant later on.

Once the fish were safely delivered, there was usually soup or a delicious tea with keepers or estate owners; this was the main perquisite of the task. The people we met were welcoming and generous, their hospitality was unsurpassed, and we learnt a great deal about the fauna and flora of the area, and in particular heard many stories involving red deer.

I have never forgotten the tale from one stalker, who hand-reared a red deer hind calf. 'Aye, she was a beauty indeed. She often travelled with me in the back of my van. Eventually she would even follow me when I took clients out to shoot other deer, but lay cudding peacefully close by waiting whilst the shot was taken. She would come for miles out on the hill with us, and once the stalk was over, she would then follow us all back home. She was an astonishing beast and surprised me by even seeming unperturbed by having one of her fallen kin in close proximity.' He wiped a tear from his eye. 'I had her for many years and she had calves of her own for several years.'

His love for the deer and for their wellbeing was something I will always remember. He was one of the old school of traditional stalkers – true countrymen who knew the ways of the wild.

Whilst the live fish deliveries were enjoyable, fish gutting was another thing altogether. The converted ex-army ambulance we used as a gutting shed was a health and safety officer's nightmare. Squeaky cleanliness was impossible. Appropriately, given its former life, we soldiered on. Financially we had no alternative.

I had recently met a woman my own age who was looking for part-time work. Stella, a Cumbrian, was typical of many of the people I have come to know from that particular area of the British Isles: earthy, hard-working, generous, resourceful and, moreover, someone who could turn her hand to anything. She eagerly agreed to come one morning a week to help us gut and prepare the trout for the hotels. I do not think I would have stuck working with Joe for as long as I did without Stella. She was never late, and could help us with sheep, fish or any other job around the place. She did not care how hard or dirty the work was, and best of all she had an unsurpassed sense of humour.

Stella was a godsend, and her presence made all the difference. Together we laughed our way through disaster after disaster. We couldn't afford to pay her much. I look back and feel guilty that she worked so hard for so little, but I hope she always knew that she was the star of the show, a joy to work with and someone we could not have done without. Importantly, she became a loyal friend.

Gutting fish was not a pleasant job for one simple reason – we were always cold. Though we had a heater in the shed, our hands went blue even beneath two layers of gloves, our feet went numb and we soon developed chilblains. Joe was always late and there was usually a row on gutting days as he failed to appear at the allotted time. Stella and I would work on, lifting the heavy loads of fish out of the tank, clouting them on the head quickly with the priest – an implement designed for killing fish made of either wood or sometimes antler, as I explained earlier. Then we set to the gutting preparation work, and still there would be no sign of 'himself'. I would have to remove all my stinking, dripping waterproofs in order to go into our cosy newly done-up house to try and extricate him from bed. The routine was ever the same. Nothing worked. Once, I was so angry I threw a bucket of cold water over the bed. However, I was the one who had to clear it up, so that backfired. Whilst I was usually in bed by 10 pm following a day's physical labour, Joe on the other hand would be up every night far into the small hours. I was never sure what he was doing – reading, usually. Whilst I was on Greenwich Mean Time, he appeared to be working in an Australasian time zone.

Some days we also had to deliver trout to the fish shop in Montrose – a half-hour drive from the farm. The fish had to be almost wriggling with freshness and needed to be with them before opening time so as not to miss out on any potential customers. We started early on those mornings and on one occasion had a disaster with a sick ewe that meant we were running late. Meanwhile, Joe was still abed. Stella and I had been racing about like two manic wasps, catching extra-large fish for the shop, and were in the throes of gutting them when Joe appeared looking dishevelled and half asleep, whilst intensely puffing on a fag. He leant on the shed door and looked at his watch.

'You seem to be extremely late,' he said. 'Why aren't these fish ready yet?'

The method the three of us used for gutting was to slit open the fishes' belly with scissors, and then to cut the innards free before scraping along the backbone with a teaspoon, and finally washing each fish under cold water. I had a two-pound trout in my hand and had cut it open and freed the innards, but they were still inside the body cavity of the fish. I had had enough, and I just raised the big fat trout and threw it as hard as I could towards Joe, who was still leaning on the doorpost. I am not much of a shot, but it hit the target perfectly with a satisfying resounding slap. The bloody guts then dribbled slowly down the side of his face. Stella turned away, pretending she was washing her trout under the tap, but I could also see her shoulders shaking violently. Joe, to give him his due, just walked off whilst puffing a little harder on his fag.

'My God!' exclaimed Stella. 'Good shot. I have been wanting to do that for months.' She still reminds me of that moment every time we speak, and it still makes us weak with laughter.

The irony of the matter is that Joe was not lazy and was incredibly talented and practical, and was also far more academically intelligent than I will ever be, but there was his issue with timekeeping and responsibility – it was something he simply could never deal with, while I (and the farm) needed routine. It got worse and eventually made many aspects of our small farming business unworkable. It would drive us onto the rocks in the end.

For now, though, our little business began to thrive. We increased our fish output and rented more ground close by. We had fifty smart mule ewes (a cross of Blackface with Bluefaced Leicester), including Bean as the matriarch of the flock. Bean had several sets of twins and proved herself to be a great mother. Previously she had been at liberty to wander around the farm in the winter and could usually be found in the feed passage of the byre, sharing the turnips with the calves. Once, we lost her and found her wandering about with a bucket stuck on her head, bumping into silage bags in the field. She lived until she was thirteen. She was one of many animals that left an indelible tattoo on my heart.

My three other pet lambs had joined the throng and were very productive too. Myrtle was another extraordinary, sweet, affectionate sheep and during her lifetime had an astonishing seven sets of triplets before retiring and living on until she was fourteen. Joe also bought in diminutive Blackface and Cheviot-type lambs from the Western Isles and Shetland to fatten indoors, and he had secured a contract with a large butchery firm near Aberdeen for producing a certain weight of lamb every month. We had bought a high-powered electronic weighing crush, and the buyers visited us regularly to guide us and check on progress. Then a huge lorry came to fetch the fat lambs, which were taken directly to the abattoir at Portlethen.

On some occasions we took others to the abattoir at Brechin, and it was here that I had a most embarrassing incident. Joe was away fencing, so I agreed to deliver the consignment of lambs instead. But we had a new double-deck Ifor Williams sheep trailer that I had never used. I arrived at the destination and stopped in the large yard, and then went into the office to ask where they wanted me to offload the lambs. A cheery man pointed, 'Just back your trailer down that bay there to the left, lass,' and then he disappeared. It looked fairly straightforward, but I was relieved that there was no one about to see the total mess I made of my reversing efforts. The bloody trailer kept on jinking round to meet me, and I was miles off the bay. Each attempt seemed worse than the last. At one point I even ended up facing the wrong way round. I spent a long time getting hot and bothered, jack-knifing the trailer, until eventually, after dozens of failed tries, I managed it. Just.

The lambs were offloaded, and the cheery man told me to go back into the office to get my delivery line. I could see he was laughing at me, and I felt myself turning red. When I entered the office it was lunchtime. There were five more men with their feet up on a big table, drinking coffee and eating their sandwiches noisily, whilst watching a CCTV screen revealing the activities of the entire yard. They were all laughing.

One of them looked up, wiped his mouth on his sleeve, sniffed, and pointed to the CCTV camera on the wall and said, 'That was great, lass. We haven't had such a good laugh for a long time – you've made our day. We presume you've actually passed your driving test?' And then there were peals of rowdy laughter.

I was mortified and turned scarlet as I took my receipt and rushed out. I returned straight home with the empty trailer and set up a narrow slalom course with bales in one of the fields, and put more all around the yard. For the next couple of days I practised endlessly. I was certainly not going to go through that again.

Gutted

Mum was always rude about Joe. She stirred up a lot of trouble and constantly complained to me about him, and about how lazy and useless she felt he was. She told me almost daily when we spoke on the telephone that she had never wanted me to marry him in the first place, despite the spectacle of a wedding that she and Geordie had insisted upon. Though I knew we had problems, her input made it far worse. 'I am so fed up with you – why on Earth did you marry someone like him? He's so idle.'

Joe certainly could not have been accused of being idle – he simply worked in a different time zone.

Then I would defend him and the response was always, 'You are becoming so impossible, Polly.'

Whenever Mum visited, which was fairly rarely, she always got the knife in and found fault with something he had done or, more often, not done. And no visit to her was without a barrage of criticism of both him and me. Increasingly he was indeed always late for everything, but I didn't require any reminders. Bo, who was living with them, was also constantly criticised, and seeing as Bo was such an easy and grateful person to look after, it seemed unfair. Poor Bo often felt quite miserable about it but like me dared not stand up to her, for the backlash was too awful to contemplate. Mum's temper was getting even quicker.

I had always wanted to have several children, and now, having been married for four years and being in my twenty-seventh year, seemed a good time. Joe felt the same. I had also convinced myself that a baby might really help our shaking marriage. I knew within days that I was pregnant for I immediately felt different. I loved being pregnant and found the experience overwhelmingly exciting.

As soon as I told Mum though, there was doom and gloom: 'It will be a disaster, you are a bloody fool, and anyway being pregnant is ghastly, it makes you feel so ill, and you will get really fat. I was ill for most of my pregnancy with you, and giving birth is hell too.'

This is really what you want to hear from your mother. Mum had always said that she was several stones too heavy. This made her miserable.

Finally, she added accusingly, 'Babies are nothing but trouble, frankly. You were a bloody nuisance from day one and you still are – you worry me so much. Do you know all the weight I piled on was entirely due to pregnancy? Then don't forget there is postnatal depression. Breastfeeding is very difficult too, and you will probably become incontinent – pelvic floor exercises don't work, you know.'

Great!

I suppose some of it was tongue-in-cheek, but it's not the best thing to be told when you are nearly three months pregnant, your hormones are doing an Irish jig and your emotions are to the fore. However, I felt ecstatic about being pregnant. I knew that it was not going to be easy but naively felt that perhaps having a baby would alter everything, make Joe and me a real family, and he would see fit to get up at a reasonable time to help. As with millions before me, and millions after, this theory was swiftly to be proved wrong.

That year, 1987, we had many more sheep to lamb. The lambing was hectic, and we had numerous problems, with our mule ewes having multiple births and large lambs. Then, one glorious warm April day when the countryside was dancing into vibrant life and the daffodils were in bloom, I had a fright.

The fields all around Kincardineshire were smiling festive yellow, with lines and lines of commercially produced flowers. Easter was late that year, and unusually we had an endless stream of visitors to the farm to buy fresh trout straight from the tanks. We had also had an extra-large order from the fish shops, and Stella was away. Joe was out transporting live trout, and I had been delivering lambs all morning, up to my elbows in birth fluid most of the day. By late afternoon I was unusually exhausted and felt giddily weak. Joe was still not home – it turned out he had had a puncture, miles up a remote hill track. Then another car appeared with friends calling in for a cup of tea. I was so worn out I could barely speak, but made tea and chatted feebly to them whilst attending to various needy ewes.

As their car drove away around 6 pm, I felt a warm, sticky sensation and wetness, and rushed into the loo. There was a considerable amount of blood, and my immediate reaction was that I was having a miscarriage. By the time Joe reappeared, I had rung our doctor and she had come out immediately and arranged for me to go to hospital. I was convinced that I was about to lose the baby. I felt devastated.

We had a miserable drive to hospital in Dundee. I felt squeamish but put that down to excessive tiredness and worry. I had a depressing wait in a maternity ward with the shrieks and cries of various women echoing around. Eventually, after further examinations, I was taken for a scan. At twelve weeks, babies are still small enough so that the whole baby can be seen on the scan. On my scan it was clear that ours was very much alive. I could see it in the typical foetal position with tiny hands in fist shapes, almost waving. I could hardly believe it, and now the thought of losing this minute new being was too much to contemplate. Though all appeared to be well, they kept me in overnight under observation.

A young woman with large pink, perky nipples clearly visible below her transparent négligée came and sat next to me, 'Christ I am gasping for a fag,' she said. 'I have had four miscarriages already but I hae three kids onywise – aye, they all hae different faithers, I am just waiting now to be knocked out so they can do the works.'

The works? An abortion, I supposed. I didn't dare ask. 'Oh, you poor thing,' I commiserated.

'Ach dinnae bother, hen, it's nothing new.'

She had regaled me with this information in a casual matter-of-fact tone that unfortunately sent me into a total panic. Then I felt light-headed. Muffled sounds of birthing shrieks filled the night, and my heart was sprinting. Being absolutely ravenous didn't help, and I realised that in the chaos of that long day at home, I had missed several meals. A sympathetic nurse with a lilting, comforting Southern Irish accent appeared at 2 am and brought tea and toast with Marmite. But there was no sleep, as I tossed and turned on the uncomfortable thin mattress and obligatory rubber sheet, sweating and fretting.

Cardboard cornflakes appeared at dawn accompanied by luke-warm milk, but the offer of a rubber egg was politely declined. After another long wait, I was taken for a second scan, and then sent home. I was also instructed to go to bed for a few days. Having conferred with my own doctor, we agreed that whilst I should take it easier, as I was a fit person this was unnecessary unless I felt like it. There was no more bleeding, and the rest of the pregnancy went perfectly.

*

Our business seemed to be working. We were growing organic pars-nips too because they were locally in demand for the hotels and small shops, and faithful Stella came to help us harvest them. They made excellent weapons for hurling at my tardy husband appearing in the field with fag in hand. The quail were productive, and many of the hotels took some of their delicious little eggs every week. Mum and Geordie ate most of them. The fish were thriving, and we were seeing positive returns from our hard graft. I was also boosting our income considerably with writing and photography.

My desire to be a vet had never dwindled, and I took in injured owls and birds of prey, as well as other wildlife including red squirrels and hedgehogs, in the hope of rehabilitating them and returning them to the wild. Joe, too, was very keen on wildlife and was extremely good at fabricating pens and boxes for various creatures. After I had found Sorrel, my kestrel, I had to apply for a licence to keep him in captivity due to regulations of the Wildlife and Countryside Act. Then an inspector from the Department of the Environment came to assess our set-up, and my name was added to their list of Licensed

Rehabilitation Keepers (LRKs) – I could therefore take in other rare birds – raptors in particular.

I had met our local SSPCA inspector, who had an interest in birds of prey and owls too. Soon he was bringing me various casualties, including tawny owlets, buzzards, kestrels, sparrowhawks, and sometimes peregrine falcons. I had bought a little wooden shed to use as an animal and bird hospital, and we had built aviaries in a quiet place behind the farm buildings, including one for Sorrel.

The SSPCA inspector also sometimes brought us seabirds: guillemots and razorbills blown off course, found inland, thin and disorientated. Herons too were brought to us, though these were less welcome. We had to invest heavily in having special covers made for the fish tanks, as herons appeared in large numbers, understandably lured by the prospect of a free fish supper. It was not so much what they ate but what they damaged, as they stabbed at the fish, leaving large gaping wounds and making the afflicted trout unsaleable. The new covers worked brilliantly and that largely solved the issue, but there was one rogue bird that mastered the art of getting his bill in. He'd arrive before dawn and busily stab at the fish until we rose. We tried to scare him off, but eventually I am afraid to say he simply had to be removed. The ground was very hard at the time, so Joe disposed of the bird behind the shed in a large dung heap. It was the only bird we ever had a problem with, and we felt guilty but hoped no one would find out, particularly as we were besotted with all wildlife. With the exception of the rats.

One morning, as I saw the SSPCA van coming down the drive, I wondered what the inspector had for me this time. It turned out to be a young tawny owl. Once we had safely housed it, I was making him a cup of coffee when Parsley, who annoyingly would often go off hunting and digging, suddenly came racing through the yard, struggling to carry the deceased heron in her mouth, whilst tripping over its grey, straggly body in the process. The inspector looked at me with raised eyebrows, and I went bright red and stuttered my explanation. Luckily, he just laughed and said he understood, but it was a tense moment.

There were very few LRKs in the surrounding district, so when something unusual or rare was in need it was likely to be brought to me. In the summer that I was expecting Freddy, an elderly lady from near Dundee who was also an LRK died suddenly, and her birds had to be rehoused. I was asked to collect the licensed raptors. She had a large overgrown garden filled with aviaries. I was upset to see birds such as kestrels permanently disabled and with half a wing missing, or a buzzard with only one leg or a broken bill. This was not the kind of work I wanted to do, as I felt that if something was not going to return to the wild, it was kinder to put it down humanely. With the help of the SSPCA inspector, we took all the birds away and he put down those that were in poor condition, with long-term injuries meaning they could never be released.

I also came away with a tiny tawny owlet – it was barely a week old. It travelled in a Pampers nappy box and was so small that we didn't think it would survive. Hand-rearing it was blissful. Tawny owls have two colour phases – rufous or grey, with many colour variations in between. My bird soon became one of the loveliest grey-phase tawny owls that I have ever had, and I have had dozens and dozens of tawnies since. Sage became imprinted on me, which meant that he couldn't be released. However, some years later I received a pet female owl. Sage and Owly lived happily together for many years and every year raised a single fat owlet. I always released their offspring but continued to put food out for them every night. Sage was another creature that became an integral part of the family. When he died soon after his eighteenth birthday, I missed him dreadfully.

The day the SSPCA inspector and I went to collect the various birds from the old lady's garden, her daughter proudly showed me a bulging folder of features her mother had written over the years for the women's magazine, *The People's Friend*. They were pieces about animals and birds, about her work, and the stories of the successes and failures. It suddenly occurred to me that now there would be a void. I wrote to the editor and told him about my own work, our farm and all the animals, but did not expect to hear back. Then the telephone rang and he asked if I would meet him. I was now seven months pregnant and there was much joking about this when we met as he reckoned I was going to be busy. However, it was agreed that I would send a few sample pieces. I began with the story of Bean, and that led on to moving house with a menagerie, and the stories of acquiring Sorrel and Sage.

Sorrel had now been joined by a wild female with a broken wing that had set crooked. She was permanently disabled, but rather than put her to sleep I kept her to see if she would pair with Sorrel. To my delight they quickly established a strong bond, and then soon afterwards she laid a clutch of eggs. I could hardly believe it. If the eggs hatched, then my intention was to release any young birds. One blustery afternoon as I went into the aviary to put out food, the door blew wide open. Sorrel flew straight out. I watched as he flew high up above the trees behind the farm. And then he vanished. A tiny russet-coloured breast feather drifted down on the breeze. I wanted to cry.

Despite long walks around the area searching and calling, Sorrel remained elusive. I left food out for him on the aviary roof and caught sight of him flying in and snatching it hastily before departing with it in his talons. It wasn't long before the female kestrel deserted her eggs. I opened them, but there were no embryos developing – it looked as though they were infertile anyway – this was small consolation for losing Sorrel. Given that he now had a mate in the aviary, I really expected he would return.

Oddly, Sorrel never came back to me. Having now paired with one of his own kind, perhaps he no longer needed me in the same way. And I think I too was ready to let him go – after all, he was a wild bird. Over the next two years, I saw him almost daily as he flew in to take mice and other fresh food off the top of the aviary. Then one day he did not come. For the next few days I continued to put out food, but there was no sign. I spent a long time going around the woods whistling and calling to him. He was now far older than the years of an average wild kestrel. He had done well to survive as long as he did but that thought did little to ease the pain I felt at his loss. Sorrel was a prop that carried me through a crisis and put me deeper in touch with my overwhelming need to feel wanted. And the relationship and understanding we shared would be repeated with many other wild creatures that came to me over the years.

I have been lucky to write for *The People's Friend* ever since that first meeting with the editor. I also enjoy the extraordinary correspondence and friendships with many of their loyal readers. Writing has always proved another valuable escape for me, and animals such as Bean, Sage and Sorrel were the founder members whose stories gave me inspiration for those early columns.

*

It's midsummer. I wake very early as shafts of gold light filter through the bedroom. There is mist in the valley below the farm. Whilst the kettle is boiling I throw the French windows into the garden wide open. The morning is perfectly still, unusually still. There isn't even the sough of a breeze. Birds are silent, hiding away in heavy moult after the rigours of the breeding season. Ewes bleat softly to their lambs, and a dog barks far below at the neighbouring farm. Then all is silent, so silent. Now quite heavily pregnant, I go into the garden and sit on a chair to take in the peace and drink my tea. It really is so unusually quiet.

Then I realise to my horror that the reason for this is because the burn is no longer flowing through the fish tanks, and the usual soothing sound of water trickling through the pipes has died away. I run to the tanks to find that all six of them are grey with dead fish floating belly up on their surfaces. There's no running water, and therefore no oxygen – something has blocked the inlet. As I take a hurried glance it appears that all our fish are dead. I yell to Joe and run to the bedroom to tell him what has happened.

This news certainly motivates him, and he leaps up and races out across the lawn to look. We stand there in our bare feet in total disbelief. It looks as though we have lost all our fish. We also have a large earth pond further down the field, and it too has a morass of pale motionless bodies, whilst others flounder feebly in a last dying gasp. We stand in horrified disbelief clutching at one another. And then we weep.

All we have worked so hard for has gone. The local council has been clearing out ditches on the little road above us, and their silt and detritus has come into our burn, blocking up the inlet pipes. It is a catastrophe we can't afford.

By 9 a.m. we have made a plan. We have to gut every single trout that is of a saleable size. Stella is already with us, and Geordie has come straight over and is planning to spend the day transporting the gutted fish to Montrose when they are ready. He has rung a large fish company there who by chance have a commercial freezer room empty where we can take hundreds of fish. Our own freezers can't cope with the sheer bulk.

The task is soul-destroying. The day looks set to be very hot, so we need to work flat out against the clock before the rising temperatures ruin our fish. Mum, despite her negativity towards our lives at the fish farm, has always been superb in a crisis, and appears laden with the size of picnic that would boost the morale of a flagging army. Stella and I are already gutting fish faster than we have ever done before. The bush telegraph, though annoying at times, also has its uses. One of the old ladies who previously gutted fish here before we bought the farm, has heard our news, and she has biked over to give us a hand. It moves me deeply to see her donning her gloves and getting stuck in. The local Young Farmers, many of whom I have worked with, also picked up our tale of woe on Kincardineshire's Radio Gossip. By lunchtime several of them appear. A posse of pick-ups comes down the drive bearing a crate of iced beer, and an eagerness to help in any way they can. I could weep again as I see their cheery, willing faces. They set to in the earth pond, some of them in waders up to their chests in sludge, others sifting through the sucking, squelching silt on the bank to find either fish we can still use or survivors to be put into another tank. We have found the blockage and have one tank ready for fish big or small.

We work all day long until it is obvious that any fish that are left are only fit for fertiliser. These are duly loaded into dozens of plastic sacks to be taken away by the group of Young Farmers, which has grown steadily throughout the day. None of us have ever gutted so many fish, and by the end of this miserable day we reckon to have clocked up about 1,500 fish each – a grand total of 4,500 trout. My back hurts, my hands hurt, my legs are throbbing, and my baby seems extremely heavy. I simply never want to see another bloody rainbow trout again, dead or alive. And most certainly never on a plate.

A few days later when I go to thank the kind old lady who came to help, she says, 'I wis'nae too grateful when I got hame because my husband who never, ever does ony cooking said to me, "Aye, lass, I kent you would be tired after all that gutting, so I got you a nice piece of fash aff the van and I've made fash and chips for oor tea."' She smiles at me and adds, 'Aye, I'm nay proud to say that I tellt him where he could stick his fash. Puir mannie!'

Needless to say, the council did not want to know. Despite our best efforts, there was no compensation. We hadn't even been made aware of their ditch-clearing operations. Though it was a catastrophe we could not afford, at the end of that dreadful day I went to bed with a warm glow. The support and help we had received more than made up for the misery, and I knew that I had witnessed the true value of friendship and neighbourliness.

II

Freddy

It was 1987, and my baby was due around the same time as Bo's ninetieth birthday, on 23 October. As Bo and I shared the same birthday we wondered if perhaps the baby might arrive on that auspicious day too. Mum had planned a special birthday tea party. Though now very frail and forced to use a Zimmer, Bo remained mentally alert. She was torn because she was desperate for us to achieve a hat-trick and have the new baby with its birthday on the same day as ours, but she also wanted me to be at the afternoon party.

The morning of our birthdays dawned, and I had a doctor's appointment for another check-up. 'If this baby is not born today I will be amazed,' said the doctor, and I did feel that the baby was descending lower and lower, and was now very heavy indeed.

Bo's party went with a swing – Mum had made an extravagant tea and invited various kindred souls. The food and cake were spectacular, the champagne and cheer effervescent. Having been teetotal throughout my pregnancy, I had half a glass and felt most peculiar. When Joe and I eventually returned home I went straight to bed. At ten minutes to midnight, my waters broke. Not much time to get the hat-trick. It looked as though my baby would put in its debut the next day.

There was no rush to go to hospital in Dundee, and we had time for some last-minute preparations. We arrived in the small hours and as soon as I was admitted, a man dressed from head to foot in green medical gear looking surprisingly like Kermit the Frog appeared and asked me if I would sign up for an epidural, as they were running clinical trials and wanted more women to choose this supposedly pain-free option. I declined in no uncertain terms, determined to have as little interference as possible.

It all took a lot longer than I expected, but I really loved giving birth – despite the pesky reappearance of the determined frog who continually enquired whether I was sure, especially as it became a little more painful. I saw him as a devil trying to lure me into his evil plan. I wished he would stop annoying me. Obviously, it goes without saying that giving birth is not the most comfortable experience, but it was so incredibly exciting and I didn't want anything to mar what I knew would be probably one of the most magical events of my life.

Joe paced up and down like a bad-tempered lion. He was fed up with waiting around (as if I had not spent all our marriage and the lead-up waiting for him) when there seemed to be very little progress. He was dying to get back home and kept going on about it even though we had arranged for Stella to look after everything for however long it took.

At 7 am I rang my mother. My upset with Joe must have been apparent. The call was a mistake; I never heard the end of this either, and she later added it to an already laden armoury against her son-in-law. She even told me, again, that my getting pregnant had been a mistake in the first place – a bit late when you are in the advanced stages of labour. 'You are so stupid. What on Earth made you want a baby? Your life is complicated enough, Polly.'

Once things were really on the move, Joe announced that he was going out for a while, to a local DIY store in Dundee to buy a new black plastic bin for transporting the fish. And off he went, though I begged him not to. It lodged yet another blow to our failing marriage. I was concerned in case he missed the arrival of the baby. But he came back in time and, by 4 pm, the day after my birthday, our wonderful healthy son, Freddy, had arrived, and my life changed forever. Joe and I were both euphoric – me more than I have ever been either before or since. And both of us wept for joy. If anyone ever asks me what is my greatest achievement, then the answer will always be Freddy.

Caroline, who had been so supportive when Dad died, was my first visitor the night of Freddy's birth. She beamed in, looking glamorous, bringing with her a glow of positivity.

Mum and Geordie followed soon after. Mum was briefly emotional, and then spoilt it by adding, 'Such a pity you have not had a daughter; how the hell will you cope with a boy?' Was this her way of covering up her emotion? She always seemed to find it so hard to be positive about anything I was doing. 'And now you will have a lifetime of sleepless nights ahead,' she added.

Geordie, in contrast, was thrilled and brimming with happy comments and support, and moreover chuffed that now there was another male in the family.

When everyone, including Joe, had gone, I sat in my room overlooking the Tay Rail Bridge, its lights sparkling on the buildings far below and reflecting on the dark waters of the Tay. I felt engulfed in peace and contentment, cuddling this perfect little human that only twenty-four hours earlier had been inside me. I really could not believe it. Billions of babies are born every day, but somehow it seemed such a miracle – nature's perfection at work again. The night was swathed in a rapturous happiness I had never experienced before. I could not wait to see Bo to tell her all about it. Tomorrow Mum and Geordie were going to bring her in. And we had so nearly achieved the hat-trick.

Despite my mother's miserable predictions, my euphoric state lasted for weeks. I could have gone straight home the day after the birth, but I knew that as soon as I did I would be embroiled in the farm work, frustrated by my stay-abed husband, and would not have the chance of this uninterrupted time with my new baby. So, when I was offered the option of transferring to a small maternity hospital in Forfar, I took it. It was a blissfully happy few days. The nurses were caring and patient, guiding Freddy and me into an excellent routine. They were always attentive and gave us the kind of start for which I have always been grateful.

I knew that poor Mum had not had this positive experience with me, and I felt sad that it seemed to have been so different for her.

She had had postnatal depression and told me that soon I would have it too. At times there were flashes of enthusiasm for her new grandson, but more often she seemed irritable and full of gloom and yet again suggested that my marriage would probably break down: 'Joe is useless. I cannot imagine what made you marry him.'

I was so lucky that Bo lived long enough to see Freddy. She was now incapacitated physically, so Mum and Geordie wheeled her up to my hospital room the morning after his birth. She was, as I had known she would be, ecstatic. Freddy had two great-grandmothers, as Grandma was also still alive; both of them came to Freddy's christening three months later, and my friend Clare became his godmother.

Bo had by this point moved into a nursing home and I frequently took her out. She enjoyed trips in the car more than anything else, and as ever was incredibly easily pleased. Best of all, she liked to go out for a picnic. We would take a drive around the twisty back roads to see what we could find – either wildlife or farm animals near gateways, or merely lovely views and banks and hedgerows exploding with wildflowers, berries and songsters. She liked to have the window wide open so she could hear them. She also loved me to read poetry to her, especially humorous verse.

One afternoon we found two Clydesdale geldings dozing by a gate. One of them was fast asleep with its bottom lip drooping wide open. Bo had a box of toffees she had been given. She was trying unsuccessfully to palm them off on me due to the perils of toffees and false teeth, and we had been giggling about them. She suggested I put a few in the open mouth of the Clydesdale. For the next ten minutes the pair of us giggled as the horse gently awoke and yawned, and shut his mouth only to discover the toffees. He proceeded to chomp and drool with much licking of lips and extraordinary facial expressions. And then once finished, he nearly pushed the gate over, straining across to the car to see if we had some more. Bo loved it. We giggled like two schoolgirls.

Back at the nursing home, Bo had become close friends with two of the matrons; the three of them had Gin and French every night together when the other inmates were tucked up in bed, and frequently made up a bridge foursome with another member of staff. Bo was a brilliant player. This helped keep her cheerful, and I was relieved that she never had the indignity of losing her sparkling mind.

On another occasion we were drinking tea from the flask and sitting chatting next to a field when a huge, black Anglo Nubian goat with pale satanic eyes appeared from nowhere. We talked to it over the gate. It was a devilish show-off, performing high kicks and jigging about on the spot, bleating. Suddenly it took a flying leap from a standstill and soared over the top of the gate, making us gasp. And then it came up to the car and tried to squeeze its bulk in through Bo's open window, its big ears flopping forward, its rubbery mouth probing for titbits. Freddy was in the back in his baby seat munching a rusk. I can still hear his laughter mingled with that of my ninety-year-old grandmother. This was the last outing we had together, and it was typical of Bo that our final foray should be so infused with hilarity, that it cost nothing but time, and that it was such a simple pleasure.

Bo went rapidly downhill after that, though remained cheerful. But in the July after Freddy's birth she took ill and was in bed for the last few days, alert up until her final twenty-four hours, when she became erratic and then fell unconscious. Mum and I were called early, but arrived five minutes after she had slipped away. We kissed her bloodless cheeks and held her cold hands, and then stood there in silence. She appeared to be so serene. She had ninety wonderful years and was the happiest, most balanced person I have ever known. For me, being without her was going to be almost impossible. July is a bitch of a month.

Bo had always made friends from all walks of life everywhere she went. Even though she had fewer in Scotland than she had in England, dozens wanted to pay their last respects to her – from a friend she'd played cards with regularly, and the lady who used to supply her with free-range eggs, to countless children and their parents, the butcher and local newsagent. Everyone loved her.

For some inexplicable reason, however, Mum chose a short, soulless cremation service for her and said that no one other than the four of us could go, though she made an exception for the two kind matrons from the nursing home. It was all over without even a hymn – and Bo loved hymns, especially 'Jesus Bids Us Shine'. No one was allowed to send flowers either. I felt cheated.

Worst of all, Geordie's daughter Mary was firmly told it was 'family' only. This was a disgraceful thing to say. What was my mother thinking of? Mary *was* family. It was a cruel blow, as Mary had loved visiting Bo, and they had both become devoted to each other. Understandably, Mary felt hurt. It was another act of my mother that I couldn't understand. Bo deserved the finest country-style funeral on Earth. My mother was becoming increasingly hard to fathom.

*

Now I can see perfectly clearly that though Joe and I began our relationship with many shared interests, I had fallen into the trap that I recognise as a major pattern of my life. It had begun when as a child I'd thought I could help Dad to recover from his alcoholism. I always believed that things would get better, and when they didn't I fell to bits and became anxious and unhappy. Like me, Joe had come from a broken marriage, and also had a loquacious alcoholic father. His mother, Sarah, was an extraordinary character, of whom I was incredibly fond but, from his point of view, she was an extremely difficult woman and someone whose mothering capabilities were sadly lacking. An author of repute, she had written many books, but one in particular, part autobiographical, part spiritual journey through India, had described how she had hated her pregnancy with Joe and had felt that she was giving birth to the devil. Even when he was born she continued to feel this way about him. A spiritualist and a lay healer, she was outrageously eccentric.

Her visits were infrequent, dominated by whichever alternative lifestyle route she was following at that moment. A flamboyant cook, her arrivals at the station always caused a stir as, dressed in outlandish attire and, with her long flowing hair, she stepped from the train laden with dozens of carrier bags spilling over with a mass of luscious organic delicacies. Sometimes there was meat, while on other occasions when she took charge of our kitchen she cooked only vegetarian delights. After her curries and fungi stews an inordinate amount of pressure was brought to bear on the farmhouse's archaic plumbing. The organic French wine she also brought had the power to put us on another planet for several days. She and I would take to the hedgerows and gather basketfuls of succulent greenery, usually nettles, and fungi with hallucinogenic powers. She drifted about in bare feet, looking fit and tanned, wearing wafting clothing, meditating. Sometimes she stood on the lawn at dawn on one leg looking for the rising sun.

She was different, and I loved her. I found time spent with her enlightening and fascinating since she was incredibly well read and always brought us eclectic books. Her large, quirky house in Putney had a garden pond full of frogs, and she encouraged the local fox population to move in too, though she was a little unhappy about the number of takeaway packages they left behind. She was often to be seen clearing up, attired in a floating Eastern-style robe after doing her meditations at daybreak. She also kept hens and a cockerel, feeding the latter slices of brie out of her dining-room window and, when it was killed by a fox, she is reputed to have made a delicious stew from it. She also owned a house on Valencia Island, off Ireland's west coast, a retreat to where she would disappear to write.

Sarah and Joe's father had been thoroughly unsuited and divorced after a short and disastrous marriage. She was an activist and had fought powerful battles against all aspects of factory farming. She was a guiding light in the organic food movement and the Soil Association, and by her own admission had been exceptionally promiscuous. I was desperately sad when she tried to treat herself for cancer and lost the battle in 1997.

Sarah's obituary in *The Times* was cause for hilarity as there was a story of her car being overly long at the garage, being serviced. She had been forced to travel back from a party on the last bus home instead, only to wake next morning to find herself in bed with the bus conductor. After this inauspicious event she told a friend, 'Really, my dear, it's easier these days to get oneself serviced than one's car.'

I was abroad and missed Sarah's funeral, but she had a green burial in deepest Herefordshire and travelled from London in a cardboard coffin decorated by all the funeral goers as they drove with her, by bus, to her final destination. It was a send-off that typified her, and it sounded wildly beautiful. That was Sarah.

Joe had a love–hate relationship with her, exacerbated by the obvious fact that she seemed to favour his younger brother. When Mum commented that Joe and I were two broken reeds together, sadly I fear there was truth in her statement. I always thought I could make things better and, as I had with my father, I set Joe up to fail and had expectations of him that he was incapable of fulfilling. He suffered from acutely dark moods, and often for no apparent reason he didn't want to talk or communicate, disappeared if visitors arrived and lost his temper with the livestock. I know, too, that I was struggling to come to terms with the premature death of my father, and was guilt-laden and full of consuming self-doubt. I was desperately searching for something I could never find, which made me unsettled and woefully needy.

Joe's mother was fiercely creative, but like my mother, clearly suffered from erratic moods too. From her writings I noted that she often mentioned how her young children drove her mad, and how she could not deal with them and therefore shut them out totally – especially Joe. For many of us, to grow up in a house dominated by the darkness of a parent's ill humour can only lead to emotional confusion. It seemed that both of us struggled in dealing with our need for peaceful, respectful relationships. And noticing how one's behaviour affects someone else takes a great deal of courage and honesty.

Increasingly, Joe and I seemed to do less and less together. I was getting up almost as he was going to bed. Now with a baby as well, I found it even harder to do all the fish-farm work.

12

Snowy Owl

One morning I had a call from the SSPCA regarding an errant snowy owl. It had appeared on a BP oil tanker in the mid Atlantic as the ship crossed to Scotland from Canada. After landing on a patch of oil on deck, the bird was filthy and weak. It was discovered when the ship docked at Queensferry.

My SSPCA inspector friend asked, 'Can you take it under your wing?'

He knew the answer before he made the call.

The snowy owl is an impressive bird similar in size, though not shape, to a buzzard. The oil had spoilt its glorious plumage. We would have to put it through a full oil-cleaning routine. But it was not eating properly and was in no fit state for further stress. It was important to build up its strength before it was subjected to a rigorous cleaning operation but, as it had probably ingested oil whilst trying to preen itself, it was unlikely to be very enthusiastic about food. I therefore force-fed it by gently pushing food down it several times a day, giving it a very high-protein diet. I almost drowned in the deep pools of its mesmerising yellow eyes as it stared at me, clicking its bill in warning, yet clearly appreciative of the food. After the first day, it readily took the meat from my hand.

Caring for this bird seemed different. Not only was it one of the most beautiful owls I had ever been close to, but it also had a calm presence and didn't seem to panic and try to get away from me. I worried that perhaps this meant it was suddenly going to die, as is so often the case with wildlife casualties. Tameness often indicates serious, invisible problems.

By day three it was eating meat by itself. On the fourth day, we took the decision to risk washing it. A couple of experts from the SSPCA's Middlebank Oiled Bird Cleaning Centre near Dunfermline came to the farm. Cleaning oil off birds is a laboriously delicate process, and basic cheap washing-up liquid has, perhaps surprisingly, been found to be the most efficacious tool. The duo from the centre set to work, and after an hour the bird was deemed free of the horrible oil. We were concerned that after this intense procedure it might not survive. They had never cleaned an owl before. We dried the bird well and left it peacefully to recover with a fan heater on to help speed up the process.

Later, we peered nervously into its box cage, fearing the worst, but our patient was looking bright and alert, and was preening its now pristine feathers, re-oiling them from a preen gland beneath its tail. It was a good sign. A little later, the same bush telegraph that had spread the word of our fish fiasco had been working well, and a Land Rover appeared in the yard. A local keeper had brought the snowy owl a still-warm mountain hare, exactly the type of prey to tempt it. By teatime the owl had devoured the majority of the hare and was dozing with its eyes shut and a bulging crop.

Over the next few weeks, the owl recuperated in one of the aviaries on a diet including fresh mountain hare and pigeon breasts. News of the snowy owl had reached the media, and before long the owl had become a minor TV celebrity. Several journalists came to interview me, bringing camera crews with them. We had been concerned about where we should release it, as it was now ready to go. However, due to some absurd law, the Department of the Environment informed us that as it had come from another country, it should be quarantined for six weeks. This meant the bird had to stay put in our aviary during that time. This was farcical. Do all the millions of migrant birds that annually arrive on these shores do the same thing? It was a ridiculous piece of red tape and one that was actually detrimental to the owl: it needed to be back in the wild, sooner rather than later.

The snowy owl is a bird of the high Arctic, usually only seen as a vagrant in Scotland. There are occasional records of single birds in places such as the Cairngorms or Rannoch Moor, and some of the islands. Birdwatching history was made in 1967 when the then RSPB warden for Shetland, Bobby Tulloch, from the island of Yell, discovered the first breeding snowy owls on Fetlar. Now, over twenty years later, there were still three elderly snowy owls on the island, but no male. Fetlar was proposed as a possible release site, but we were still unsure of the sex of our young owl.

Most of us have our heroes. For me, there are few people who have fuelled and encouraged my own passion in natural history more than Bobby Tulloch, because he epitomised all that I love about the natural world. You have to be passionate about wildlife to take a rotting bird to bed with you, or dress in disguise as a pantomime horse in order to photograph owls. Such was Bobby's love of the natural world that when he was a very small child his mother found him asleep locked in embrace with a putrefying puffin, the fishy aroma of which pervaded the entire room. I had always found this story amusing.

His anecdotes delighted thousands of enthusiastic island visitors, his books were incredibly popular and he made a series of captivating programmes with the BBC, all of which as a child I had watched avidly. He could talk to people about wildlife and its conservation on a level where they felt totally comfortable, thus bridging the gap between science and ignorance. And he understood the importance of some of the old lore and beliefs surrounding many of Scotland's wild creatures.

Bobby Tulloch's discovery of the first breeding snowy owls in the UK caused enormous excitement. Once the press had been informed, the reaction was explosive, and a 24-hour guard had to be put on the nest. He and the owls found themselves in the limelight of a nationwide stage. The Fetlar snowy owls bred on the island for nine years and reared a total of twenty owlets.

But it had now been over ten years since they had successfully raised owlets, and, as I mentioned, there was no longer a male present. Perhaps if our owl was a cock bird, it might change that. The

SSPCA and the RSPB certainly thought so. In order to gain positive publicity, Shell, who had large oil operations in Shetland, agreed to pay for the SSPCA inspector and myself to fly to Sumburgh with our precious cargo.

On our arrival at Aberdeen Airport, there was another flurry of media excitement as we gave further radio and TV interviews. After that, we waited for our plane in the airport's VIP lounge. Newspapers had been printing entertaining cartoons: one in particular showed a dapper young male snowy owl dressed in Canadian national costume, arriving on Fetlar surrounded by elderly female owls with walking sticks and glasses. The caption read simply, 'Howdy ladies!' The *Sun*, true to form, produced something even cornier relating to the young bird's arrival on Shetland being a real hoot and having the wit to woo female owls. Pressure was mounting, and it seemed the nation's bird-watching fraternity were following our every move. Had Twitter been on the go, it would have gone viral.

We expected to fly to Shetland on a small plane alongside itinerant oil workers. However, we were the sole passengers on a 76-seater jet, with an air steward apiece. We were so satiated with the food and drink from the VIP lounge that we had to politely decline the offers of further refreshments. We flew to Shetland through an impenetrable cloudbank, until brief misted views of Fair Isle shining silver-wet far below appeared momentarily, and there were glimpses of Shetland's rocky bastions fringing its dizzyingly sheer headlands with a snow shower of breeding seabirds dazzling white on the cliffs.

Arrival by plane at Sumburgh is dramatic, for the runway is right at the island's southern tip. The approach from the south is not for a faint-hearted trainee pilot as the massive bulkhead of rock, is surrounded by tempestuous sea, and the runway comes as a hard full-stop in the middle. We landed with a thud and a bounce. A posse of bird enthusiasts, including the islands' SSPCA inspector and the RSPB warden, awaited us. Soon after, the bird was officially measured. It was deemed a juvenile male. He was marked with yellow dye on his breast feathers so that from a distance he could be easily identified.

Now that the bird's sex was confirmed, we returned to our hotel full of hope. Surprisingly, his appetite had not been impaired by his travelling and he devoured the food I had brought for him. Next day we still had a long journey involving two further ferry crossings before we reached his destination. He needed to keep up his strength.

In the morning we drove north, crossing to Yell and Unst, and then onwards to Fetlar. This tiny island's unique habitat is rich with a varied and abundant flora and fauna. Peat bogs, moorland, rugged sea cliffs and marshes attract a variety of bird life, including the rare red-necked phalarope that breeds here.

Once on Fetlar, we drove straight to the RSPB's croft to meet the summer wardens. A female snowy owl had been located earlier. A steady grey drizzle did nothing to dampen our excitement as we took photographs with our immaculate male snowy owl. Unperturbed, he clacked his bill and opened his perfect yellow eyes even wider. I had a lump in my throat. Then we took him into the tiny primary school to show the children. They told us about the owls they regularly saw perched on the island's drystone dykes, and were intrigued when allowed to view the new owl so close, all of them silent as if hypnotised by his dandelion-bright eyes, and snowy pied plumage. They had produced numerous paintings and drawings relating to the owls and their island story, and had also used this as the subject for a creative-writing project. One little boy with brilliant red hair, joined-up freckles and trousers that were at least six inches too short shyly handed me an envelope. In it there was a pure white stone massaged smooth by the tides of centuries. 'That's for you,' he said and then turned crimson.

And there was that lump in my throat again.

I had suggested that a temporary release pen for the owl would help accustom it to the new area and the resident owls. However, the RSPB wished to release it immediately. Dense cloud pockets wafted over blue-grey moorland, adding a celestial atmosphere to an already supercharged event. From the distance, a warden signalled to us. He had seen a resident female owl nearby. I looked through rain-smudged binoculars and had my first view of a truly wild snowy owl. She was perched on a stone wall, motionless and rounded, almost a quartzite stone like the one I had been given, and then she moved, turning her head nearly all the way around, looking and watching, sharp eyes missing not even a vole shiver in the salt-crisped grasses. We crouched low in the lee of the wall as slowly the RSPB warden walked forward carrying our bird. And then he gently let him go.

The owl's first flight was slow, unhurried. Then he landed on top of grey-green lichen-embellished rocks and eagerly bobbed his head as he absorbed his surroundings to establish his bearings. The resident owl flew over for a closer inspection. They both took to the air and disappeared into a hollow. A curtain of rain spread towards us. Within seconds the view was obscured. There was but a brief glimpse as two owls flew over the horizon; it was as if we had imagined the entire scene.

Now, for me, Fetlar, like all of Shetland, often stuck into an afterthought box on Scotland's map, had become a most significant dot. The ferry left the tiny island, where hopes hung on one vagrant snowy owl. Might there be young snowy owls raised again on its pristine shores?

Later, when we boarded our plane at Sumburgh, we found ourselves amongst some thirty oil workers. The SSPCA inspector now strapped into his seat beside me, said, 'Don't you just hate crowded aeroplanes?' And with that we were shortly back in Aberdeen.

Nature has mysterious ways and setting up a young snowy owl with elderly females was a gamble. Our bird remained on Fetlar but briefly, and was seen on Fair Isle some weeks later. Sadly, like many males, he had the wanderlust and had no intention of staying put. He was a vagrant, a young male searching for new territory. There have been no breeding snowy owls in Scotland since 1975.

*

It was due to the man who came to clean the snowy owl that I had the courage to leave Joe after eight years together. He was the catalyst, and through his concerns for the bird, and a few return visits, we fell for one another. He could see that I was struggling and that the situation with Joe was not working; he was sympathetic and on the same wavelength as me, passionate about all aspects of wildlife and filled with concerns for its future. Try as I might to walk away from an affair, it was not going to happen. I found myself ringing him all the time, and vice versa. Both of us had fallen. The more Joe was away doing other things such as selling lambs in the market or delivering live trout, the more opportunity there was. We started to meet and our feelings deepened further over roe fawns, tawny owlets, fox cubs and seal pups as I helped him with the mass of creatures brought to the centre where he worked, or he, in turn, helped me with the waifs that were brought to the farm.

I have always been a lousy liar, and it was not long before I broke down and told Joe. I promised to give up the affair. I didn't. All three of us were seriously hurt, I had totally lost my heart to this creative, handsome and talented man. My relationship with him showed me that my marriage was indeed over, but despite us having so much in common, it was sadly all too clear that, in the long term, a future together was not going to be possible.

Having taken the decision to leave Joe, I found myself living alone in one of Mum and Geordie's cottages with Freddy, who was now two. We were forced to put our little place, including the farm and the fish farm, on the market and there followed months of worry and uncertainty. But we could not have continued as we were; both Joe and I knew that. He was able to go back to freelance farming work, whilst I was doing a great deal of writing and photography.

I worried myself sick about Freddy, and my sense of failure was appalling. I had support from Freddy's godmother, Clare, but Mum, having done nothing but criticise Joe for the past eight years and constantly badgering me to leave him, did a 360-degree turn and took every opportunity to tell me that I was making a mistake. Thankfully, Geordie assured me it was a very wise decision. There was no going back. I had made my mind up.

13

Not Good Enough

Perhaps one of the saddest aspects of my failing relationship with Mum was accepting that someone who was so beautiful in so many ways, and who had once been so much fun, could now change so radically. It had not happened overnight, but looking back through my diaries I find more and more entries relating to her fierce jealousy and burgeoning wrath. She was jealous any time anyone directed conversation to me rather than her, in particular when people asked me about wildlife or books I had read. She would sigh loudly and say, 'Oh, God, you will soon grow out of all that wildlife stuff. You are such a bloody know-all, so bloody creative.'

Friends told me that she was jealous of both me and my relationship with Freddy. She seemed angry about life in general, and cross that she had been dealt a bad hand, yet she had more to be thankful for than almost anyone I knew. Everything was everyone else's fault. I felt she was depressed but she would do nothing about it, even though I broached the subject on several occasions. It made her fly into a rage. She was like a brooding volcano, and you had no idea when she would erupt; it was often and without warning. And not only with me. She went away to a health farm on several occasions, with Geordie and sometimes by herself too. She wasn't sleeping, and she was putting on a lot more weight.

Mum had been breeding parrots for several years and had free-flying macaws. They were a spectacular sight zipping around the glorious beech woodland that surrounded their Kincardineshire home. She also had a pair of exceedingly rare Hyacinth macaws, a single Moluccan macaw, a pair of sulphur-crested cockatoos,

Australian galahs and her ubiquitous African greys. These were housed in state-of-the-art aviaries with fabulous facilities. She successfully bred from some of the macaws and expertly hand-reared their young. She had tried leaving the tiny parrots with their parents but often the babies died, or the adults abandoned their eggs only days prior to hatching. Mum used an incubator instead and kept the reptilian-looking chicks in a brooder once they had hatched. She watched for hours as the tiny parrots chipped away at the eggshell and, ever an insomniac, rose in the night to care for them. Mum was never a keen reader, but she studied books on hand-rearing and specialist avian diets with unequalled dedication. She was also very artistic and loved painting. She even had a little studio. Perhaps it was not enough. Something else must have been missing. As Geordie once said, nothing pleased her. I worried about her incessantly.

A few years before Bo died, she was in hospital for a week. Mum had been particularly volatile prior to this and was cross with everyone. The only time I ever heard Bo retaliate was from that hospital bed when Mum was rude to her and told her she was awkward.

Bo simply responded, 'I'm awkward, Geordie's awkward, Pol's awkward, Mary's awkward; frankly, I think it is you that is the awkward one.'

Mum didn't reply.

*

It is a Sunday morning and there is frantic knocking at the cottage door. Freddy is still asleep. I race downstairs to open the door. Mum stands there looking pale and haggard. She is distraught and shaking. Geordie has been rushed to hospital.

'Pol, he's taken a large overdose of paracetamol. Oh, what shall we do? He's a bloody fool, what is going on?' And then she sobs. My mouth goes dry, and my hands start to shake. I feel a cocktail of nausea and terror mixed together. 'I have been to the hospital, he's going to be all right and he's not in any danger, but why, why, why, what on Earth have I done?'

Luckily, Mum had found Geordie soon after he had taken the pills. We are both devastated by this turn of events. For me it is a shock of massive proportions. My mind returns to Dad – I had always had it in my mind that suicide might be a possibility with him, with his continuous addiction battles and other problems. Sometimes Dad had been so unstable. But Geordie, oh why Geordie? My wonderful, cheery stepfather, our rock and constant support. It's baffling. Hideous memories of my own excruciating episode engulf me. It's not something I want to relive. Will Mum mention it yet again? I feel as though she might, at any moment.

Understandably, she is inconsolable, and she is blaming herself: 'It's my fault. Why does everyone I love try to kill themselves? Your bloody father was successful, and you almost were. Oh God if someone hadn't found you! And now this. Why? What have I done?'

The pathos of her emotions sweeps over us both like a pall of choking smoke. Freddy appears at the top of the stairs in his pyjamas, sucking his thumb and carrying a heavy book. I scoop him up in my arms as he sleepily asks for a story. His blonde hair smells of soap and shampoo and he nuzzles into my neck. Mum puts the kettle on while I temporarily blot out this unfolding crisis, reading stories from a safer world altogether.

Geordie returns home next day, pathetically apologetic. God, how I know that feeling. He seems artificially upbeat, but what is going on underneath? That is the real question. I know there has to be a reason. He's not someone who will talk about it, nor will he embrace psychology, but there has to be something that has caused this. I have already witnessed Geordie's aversion to talking therapy while his son Malcolm was in rehab. Panic engulfs me but I try not to show it. Geordie means everything to us, and he is obviously suffering from deep unhappiness. That thought is too much to bear, and I begin to worry, a nagging anxiety bringing an edginess that I cannot get rid of.

And what of Mum? When I try to get close to her, it works for a short time, then the venom rises to the surface again, and the savage claws extend and tear me to tatters. In order to protect myself, I step right back. And that, in turn, exacerbates her anger – it is a vicious circle.

*

It's not long after Geordie's saga and I feel in a state of nervous concern. My telephone rings.

'Is that the owl lady?' a broad Scottish accent enquires. 'We have a hoolet here that has been partially canned.'

The voice trails off into a rambling saga of an owl that has been through a pea-canning factory at Montrose and is clearly in poor shape. I am convinced it's one of my friends trying to catch me out with a practical joke. I have had similar teasing calls in the past: pythons in washing baskets, an escaped wallaby, a puma wandering in someone's garden, but something stops me from laughing out loud. I am about to say, 'Oh come off it', but I think back to my late teens, when during my school holidays I worked in that same canning factory doing nightshifts to earn some cash. With the factory's big wide doors flung open at night, perhaps an owl could have flown in by mistake. It's not an impossibility.

'Aye, the puir wee burd has narrowly missed a canning. It's been through most of the process including washing, grading and blanching. It ended up on the conveyor belt headin' for the canning plant.'

Perhaps it is true after all.

'Will you tak' it, as it's still alive? It was spewed out onto the factory floor. I can bring it o'er to you.'

Even before the owl arrives, I remain dubious about the verity of the caller's tale of woe. I half expect that nothing further will happen. Soon, however, one of the most pathetic tawny owls I have ever seen is foisted into my hands. It is a bedraggled feather duster with bent plumes bespattered with a mass of revolting mushy peas. It has indeed been through the grading, washing and shelling processes, but miraculously has narrowly missed the grand finale of being canned. Thankfully. It is comatose and in shock. It lies motionless. It looks dead already. However, I have learnt that injured tawny owls often appear as if almost dead, yet they may be far from it.

I gently wrap it in a towel and place it on a hot water bottle and leave it in a dark box cage in peace. If it survives the next few hours, I will then try to deal with the various problems. It may have broken legs and wings, but I fear if I examine it too closely straight away stress may bring about its demise.

A couple of hours later and Pea Owl is still breathing. The hot water bottle has doubtless helped, soothing away its misery. I pick it up and stretch out each matted wing. Some of its umber-brown feathers are broken but most miraculously appear to be intact, and only one of its flight feathers, with its fringed edges to aid silent flight, is damaged. Peas fall off onto the floor. Neither wing is broken, and its legs seem good too, the long, sharp talons grasp a pencil that I gently place on the leathery sole of each foot. Perhaps there is internal damage.

Tawny owls have an odd trait. It is something I discovered when I worked in the zoo and numerous road-casualty tawnies were brought in. When you stroke the back of their heads, they often relax, it's almost as if they enjoy it. I carefully smooth the owl's head and it tips it back and opens both eyes while remaining motionless. The once immaculate feathered facial disc is tinted green with pea soup. This is a green owl. Thoughts of horrible mushy school peas come to mind.

I give it rehydration therapy, and a small injection of steroids and anti-inflammatories to help it with severe bruising. It's hard to be sure what lies beneath the dense layers of feathers. By evening, instead of properly formed owl pellets it is regurgitating little hard dry peas, just like the ones Bo used to use for soups and stews – 'Bachelor's Surprise Peas', little gems that have long since been replaced by frozen ones.

Cleaning Pea Owl is the next priority and is a painstaking operation involving warm water to soak off the pea residue and then careful drying with my hairdryer. It is so weak it does not even try to struggle, making my task far easier. Kill or cure, I think to myself. Even after three days surprise peas are still being regurgitated – there have been almost enough to fill a whole packet. An owl would never eat peas, so these must have been forced into it as it became entangled in the machinery. Progress is slow, but that is no surprise after such an ordeal.

I force-feed the owl twice a day. Nothing seems to tempt it to eat by itself though I try mice, pieces of rabbit, a shrew, the breast meat of a warm road casualty pheasant, and a bird that flew into the window. Freddy and I joke about its menu – chocolate mouse, shrew pastry, mouse-aka. Losing the will to eat is a bad sign. I need to find something that owls consider really appetising. I reluctantly resort to trapping voles in the garden.

One of many reasons I love tawny owls so much is that, compared to other owls, and raptors too, they become far less stressed in captivity. If a sparrowhawk had been through such trauma, it would probably have died of shock soon after. Buzzards are like tawnies and are also more robust, making caring for them extremely rewarding too. The morning I trap a vole, Pea Owl takes it enthusiastically. We have now turned the corner – and there is hope. Owls love voles. And Pea Owl has an insatiable appetite.

Releasing a wild creature that has returned from the cusp of death brings a sense of achievement, a pounding heart and an inner glow of satisfaction, but it also brings relief – relief from the strangling web of my personal life and my increasingly tumultuous relationship with Mum.

Releasing Pea Owl remains one of the finest wildlife rehabilitation moments I have ever experienced. This bird has made an astonishing recovery. Only three weeks after its gruelling ordeal, I carry it into the woods beside the little cottage where Freddy and I are living. The moon slides into an opaque vortex, against a sylvan tracery of dark branches in a bruised cobalt backdrop. Pea Owl lifts off gently from my hands in slow motion. And flies perfectly. I stand watching as it takes silently to the air and then lands on a branch close by and perches, a silhouette with bobbing head rounded against a sky of apricot and indigo. These are the moments that bring me ultimate happiness – sadly many wildlife casualties will not be this lucky.

*

It's now some six months after Geordie's dreadful episode, and we are sitting up late, chatting. Mum has gone to bed early. Geordie has consumed a good few drams, as he often does. Usually quite shy about personal matters, the whisky has unleashed his feelings.

I take the opportunity to say, 'I worry about you so much; what made you take that overdose? What went wrong? Please tell me.'

There is a long silence. Geordie gets up, follows the well-worn path to the drinks cupboard and pours himself another dram. The silence continues, and he smokes quietly, rearranging himself in his armchair with glass in hand, letting out a sigh.

'Pol, I just never feel good enough. It's as if nothing I ever do truly pleases your mother. She is constantly getting at me, and I find it all increasingly hard to understand and deal with. I am better now. I love your mother so much, and you too, but somehow I really don't feel good enough, ever.'

'How I know that feeling,' I say, and I get up and go over to hug him tightly. 'I love you with all my heart and I so appreciate all you do for me, all the opportunities you have given me, and I always so love being with you. I know you think I should do more with Mum, but I find it so hard.'

There is another long silence; he draws deeply on his cigarette and exhales. The smoke spirals up and out through the lampshade beside him, sending patterns and whirls into the room. We discuss the pain of his attempted suicide and briefly revisit my own experience. Our feelings run remarkably parallel. Not feeling good enough. I have spent all my adult life, and a good deal of my childhood, trying to please my mother, but her approval always appears to have conditions attached. Conditions I am unable to fulfil. Geordie feels the same.

It is now 2 am. He stands up to open the window to remove the smell of his smoking. Mum will be livid about that. She detests smoking. I can't blame her for that, but there will be harsh words in the morning when, with her nose like a bloodhound, she comes into the smoky room. The garden is silent. Cold air rushes in, chilling the small hours, when the bones of gnawed-over problems grow legs.

I am devastatingly upset and feel mounting pain and debilitating anxiety now about Geordie. What if I lose him? He assures me it will not happen again. He is plagued with sadness about Malcolm too, and blames himself for the fact that his son went so spectacularly off the rails on so many occasions and has now gone. Our feelings over that are similar too, because this is how I feel about Dad: so clever; so much to give, so much of life ahead; yet I could never stop him, never change that fatal pattern. That pressing of the self-destruct button. The perils of his addiction leading to the promises, the lies, the persuasion, the continual denial, and in turn the dozens of letters that I wrote, the phone calls I made begging Dad to stop, and my promises of undying love and support. None of them worked – and then after it was all over, the tide-mark of 'If only I had said and done . . . a thousand different things'. Yes, addiction, it pulls everyone into the mire.

We talk these things over. And then Geordie adds his feelings of guilt about his daughter Mary and the years that had passed when he had not seen her. The situation with Mary upsets me too. I have major concerns that Mum has been putting a barrier up against Geordie's new relationship with his daughter; she is often unkind and critical of her. If Mum carries on like this, Mary won't want to come and stay.

The next day, when Geordie is sober again, it feels impossible to refer to our conversation; it is as if it never happened. It weighs heavily on my mind, though; it is a nagging tension that washes over me.

I ask Mum how Geordie is – what she feels the cause of his unhappiness has been. She looks so sad but says that she has absolutely no idea. I choose not to mention the conversation I had with Geordie. It is a hand grenade. Often in the coming years when either Geordie or I are worried about anything we are doing or planning, we will discuss it together but agree not to tell Mum, because she would work herself into a frenzy and then explode. She doesn't like anyone else to ever make any decisions. She has to be at the helm.

*

Over the ensuing years, Mum was to spawn a great deal of misery for Mary, and did indeed cause inflammation between her and Geordie. I tried to fight Mary's corner when Mum verbally pulled her to pieces after she had been to stay; that never went down well. Mary never gave any cause for criticism, always doing her utmost to fit in with Mum and Geordie's plans. I noted that they seldom put themselves out for her. The fact that Geordie had always been so good to me made their lack of support for Mary more obvious, and must have made it even more hurtful. It certainly made me feel uncomfortable. It appeared to relate to the growing jealousy in my mother. Perhaps Mum did not want Geordie's attention to be taken away from her.

I tried to make it plain to Mary that it was never her father that was the problem – it was my mother. Later I discovered that Mary suffered from acute nerves when a visit was pending, knowing that Mum was going to be difficult. It was like walking over a minefield: however lightly you stepped, it was merely a matter of time before you were blown to bits. From the outside, we appeared to be the family who had everything, yet underneath, as is so often the case, all was not as it seemed. We were flies struggling in the strangleholds of a complex spider's web.

When my divorce came through and the papers were finally in my hand, rather than feeling relieved, I felt sadness and failure. Huge failure. When we separated, Joe and I did not have slanging matches. We agreed we would never say poisonous things about one another ever to Freddy. We stuck rigidly to this. For a while afterwards though, seeing each other was difficult and painful. Joe also seldom saw Freddy and when he was meant to come and take him out, he would be hours late. Nothing had changed.

14

A Fawn, Two Collies and the
Flight of the Condom

One day the SSPCA inspector arrived with a tiny, orphaned roe fawn. Her mother had been killed on the road near Grangemouth. At the time, nine pupils from Kilchoan Primary School in Ardnamurchan, with my dear old teacher Mary Cameron, were staying with Freddy and me. They were camping in the garden, and the fawn arrived at breakfast amid squeals of delight from the children. We were heading for the Royal Highland Show, as Mary had won a sum of money for her school and was using it for this special trip. She had been voted Britain's Teacher of the Year, against stiff competition.

The fawn was shocked and vulnerable, and though still dependent on milk she did not want to know anything about the milk I offered to her. Deer, and in particular roe fawns, are of a highly nervous disposition, and I was careful to keep my exuberant bearded collie, Berry, away. Berry was displeased and sulked, looking doleful as though I had just beaten her with a big stick.

All attempts to bottle-feed the baby were hopeless, ending with a shower of sticky milk. I tried a wide selection of assorted teats – lamb's teats, babies' teats, teats from the Natural Childbirth Trust with peculiar shapes, and even the soft plastic bag that is used to ice cakes. I also tried several different milk formulas. I tried giving her milk from a bowl, but still she remained unimpressed. I picked branches from all the trees and bushes that a roe deer relishes – aspen, hawthorn, rose, hazel, apple and bramble – in the hope that she would start to browse. I offered her a delicious-smelling herbal sheep coarse mix, and chopped carrots and apples. Everything lay untouched for several days.

The perfect little creature with her luxuriant black eyelashes and black button nose deteriorated at an alarming rate. Her once bright eyes, like peaty Highland pools, grew listless. I rang a friend who works with deer, explaining my problem. He listened patiently whilst I listed all the things I had done, the formulas I had tried, and the selection of assorted teats that had been shunned.

There was a hesitation, and then a serious voice at the other end of the line said, 'Have you tried a condom?'

For a moment I was unsure whether he was asking me a personal question.

'Polly, I am not joking – have you tried her with a condom?'

You could perhaps say that there was a 'pregnant' pause at my end.

'Simply wash a new condom out thoroughly, fill it with warm water and pierce the end several times to make a teat. It is definitely worth a go, because the end of a condom when filled with milk is much softer and more like a deer's nipple.' He was obviously speaking from experience.

I put the telephone down with a smile. When a friend called by at lunchtime, I was standing at the kitchen sink trying to prick holes in a condom with a large needle. It is perhaps a relief to discover that this is not nearly as easy as it sounds. The unattractive rubbery-smelling teat substitute was then filled with warm goat's milk and battle ensued once more. The hooves of a roe deer are vicious weapons; in a short space of time, I had added several more bruises to my growing collection, and the flight of the condom and its contents left me in no doubt as to the fawn's disdain.

Every battle led to more stress for the fawn, more chance that she was a step nearer to death. As I sat next to my beautiful, sad little waif, gloopy with milk and feeling frustrated and concerned, the door burst open, and Berry leapt into the pen. I was now so despondent I didn't think it would make much difference. She began licking all the milk off the fawn's messy coat, massaging it up into waves with her tongue. The baby squeaked in delight and nuzzled up to Berry.

I sat in silence, not wishing to disturb the scene. Then, with Berry still in attendance, the fawn stretched herself and began nibbling at the leaves. Half an hour later, she had also taken some milk from my condom teat substitute – without a fight. From that moment on she improved rapidly and, though a dainty eater, picked continuously at her food and began to drink milk from a bowl. We could now give her a name, and as she loved rose leaves, Freddy chose Rosie.

Berry lavished Rosie with great affection, washing her with her tongue after every feed. However, Berry herself began to act neurotically, refusing all her food and opting for the fawn's vegetarian menu, which was based largely on carrots, apples and rose leaves. She was having a false pregnancy, something that occasionally happens to bitches; often they will start to lactate and will mother toys as if they were puppies. At least her comfortable figure would be none the worse for her self-imposed diet.

Motherhood suited Berry well. The pair were always pleased to see one another, playing tig for hours whilst I was gardening. However, Rosie was wary of all other dogs. There is little doubt that, had it not been for Berry's intervention, that particular roe fawn would not have survived. Freddy and I had hours of pleasure watching them racing around together. And it is comforting to know that should you ever have a needy roe fawn, there is a secondary use for a condom. As for Berry, her need for contraceptives was a thing of the past and I had to have her spayed due to continual false pregnancies. However, it improved her character no end and backed up my theory that hormones are nothing but trouble.

*

I first met Kim, a diminutive Border collie, in late January 1997. She blew in on a gale on a night of torrential rain. She had a piece of frayed orange baler twine around her neck. Her coat was matted and muddy and she smelled terrible. She was cowed and terrified and I had to lure her into the stable, where I made her a clean bed of straw, as she was too scared to come into the kitchen. I fell in love with her from the first second that I saw her. She was different from any other dog I had ever had. Her eyes were extraordinarily trusting. When I stroked her, she gave a quiet, soft whine of affection and raised a back leg up towards her head as if she was embarrassed.

I wondered who might have lost such a lovely little dog and half-heartedly rang both the local vets and the police station. There were no stray or lost dogs reported. I was hoping no one would come forward because already the thought of losing her was too much to contemplate. I thought, even hoped, perhaps she might have been dumped – an unwanted Christmas dog. However, two days later a Land Rover pulled into the yard. And out of it stepped a gruff bear of a man with grubby facial hair. He was dressed in filthy oilskins and had a frayed tweed bonnet askew on his large head. And, like the dog, he stank.

He went straight to the point: 'I hear you have my dug, Kim.'

The moment we walked over to the stable and the dog saw him, she buried her head in the straw and pulled her tail down between her legs in fear. When she heard his voice, she whimpered. It was a totally different noise from the one she made when I stroked her.

I asked if I might buy her, but he refused my offer and said, 'She's a disobedient wee bitch and I am going to have one last attempt to train her, otherwise she is going to be chucked in the river with a large stone around her neck. She's useless, but I will try again anyway.'

I really think he meant it too. He grabbed hold of her and dragged her to the back of his filthy vehicle and gave her a heavy boot up the backside as she launched herself in like a stone out of a catapult. I wanted to kick him as he did it, but I thought better of it.

As he drove away in a fug of heavy diesel fumes, I willed that dog to return. It wasn't long before I heard that she was regularly running away from him. Rumour had it that he had been seen beating and kicking her, and his roars had been heard across the fields as she fled in terror. People had seen her on the back roads wandering aimlessly about, dicing with traffic.

In March a friend rang to tell me she had passed Kim on the road looking terrified but heading back in the direction of the farm where she lived. I knew exactly where this was and had already found her owner's phone number. It was teatime – he'd probably be home already.

The familiar gruff voice answered, 'Yes, what is it?' After I had explained he said, 'She is the worst dog I have ever owned, and she needs shot. If you want her she's yours but you better be quick before I change my mind.'

'How much do you want?' I asked.

'Nothing She's a dreadful dog and you will have nothing but trouble It's up to you.'

I grabbed a bottle of whisky from the cupboard, leapt in the car and sped to his cottage. Kim was cowering in the back of the Land Rover. She looked dirtier than ever, and even more terrified, and she was thin too. I swiftly handed over the bottle and in return he dragged her out by the scruff and booted her in my direction, giving her one final kick as she skidded into the back of my car. Never was there a better exchange for a bottle of whisky.

Thus began the start of the finest friendship I will probably ever have. It took me almost six months to stop her from leaping into the back of the car, banging herself badly on the door before it was properly open, but other than that, Kim was perfect. She proved more loyal and affectionate, more gentle, obedient and calm than any other collie I have owned, and after only two days of sleeping in the stable, crept gingerly into the kitchen. She badly needed a bath but that could wait. First, I had to build up her confidence. Within days she settled into life with us as if she had always been there.

Kim became my faithful companion and came with me wherever I went. She rounded up my small flock of sheep with ease and on several occasions helped with gatherings in the Hebrides when I was there on holidays, or for my increasing writing and photography work trips, proving far more steady and useful than many of the other dogs on the gathers. Like me, she adored Ardnamurchan, and I quickly taught her to lie and wait for long periods while I stalked seals and other wildlife. She never moved or caused any disturbance until called. She loved the sea and galloping on the beaches, and seemed to enjoy our regular trips on Caledonian MacBrayne ferries, and in particular a treat of one of their canteen sausages on each voyage. Everyone adored her – her obedience was astonishing and her willingness to please rewarded me for my rescue efforts day after day.

Over the twelve years I had her, Kim was to be seen in countless articles and I included her in my photographs whenever I could. She was on the front cover of the SSPCA's calendar and *The Scots Magazine*, and was much loved and admired by readers of *Tractor Magazine* and *The People's Friend* too. She was with me in happiness, and at my lowest points too. If I was sad, upset or lonely, I would suddenly feel her soft black nose gently pressed into my hand and hear her almost silent whimper. I admit that I was battling with myself more and more, and worrying too that my own unhappiness might have been transferring to Freddy. Walking with Kim and spending time watching wildlife always helped to keep my confused emotions at bay. Being with a canine companion has the power to salve so many things that cause us pain, loneliness or sadness.

My early unhappiness had deepened further but, not long after my divorce from Joe, I got married again, to one of my closest friends. This marriage, too, did not last, although there's no doubting at any stage how much I loved him. Though we were together for eight years, and much of that time was incredibly happy, now that I reflect, I know how emotionally needy I was and how difficult that proved for both of us. I was endeavouring to build a relationship while still living in the past, hammering myself by going over all the mistakes that I felt I had made. They wore away at me like rats chewing on the bottom of a rotten door, and like rats, were brutally destructive. I knew it was a trait my father had suffered from too, and I equally knew that I should stop as it only led to more unhappiness. It needed addressing. Our relationship breakdown was incredibly sad, and it was certainly not his fault.

The failure of that second marriage did nothing for my self-esteem. I felt that I had failed Freddy badly too. What would all this be doing to him? Kim was always at my side, saving me from despair.

A dog's love is sometimes the finest and most uncomplicated love of all. It comes without conditions.

It's easy now, after hitting the bottom on several occasions, to recognise that trying to have a secure marriage when I was so unstable was never going to lead to a successful outcome. I was constantly filled with self-doubt, undermined badly by Mum and suffering far too much from continual anxiety. I really didn't know what I wanted half the time. I am fortunate that when my second husband and I went our separate ways, once the rawness had eased we remained dear friends and there was no animosity. We simply got things wrong. I think he had a great deal to put up with. However, what was clear was that I needed to work on myself and deal with my confused emotions. Kim had come into my life at exactly the right moment, similarly to Sorrel, the kestrel I had found in a poor state soon after Dad's funeral.

Now I see that behind what should have been contentment, I was still constantly seeking approval from my mother. There was guilt too about the loss of my father, and the continuing unanswered paternity issue. I wanted to know the truth. Together, these issues negatively controlled my psyche. I went to the doctor and sought help but rather than accept the proffered pills I asked if I could see a psychologist. For some people talking about things is hard, but I found it very helpful and was fortunate to be referred to an excellent specialist. We discussed the problems associated with addiction – Dad's addiction to alcohol, and the fallout from losing a parent to suicide. What-ifs, if-onlys, and I-wish-I-had-said-and-dones. They were still there.

15

Making an Ass of Myself

Giving people animals as presents is a risky business, and giving my mother an animal she had not chosen herself was one of the most stupid things I ever did. Mum was going to be sixty in March of the coming year, and in my constant efforts to please her I wanted to give her something memorable, something unusual; something she would appreciate. Nothing obvious had sprung to mind.

Then one afternoon when I called in, she was in a state of great excitement. 'Pol, I watched a wonderful programme about donkeys. Did you see it? You know I have always wanted to have a donkey, and I have made my mind up. I'm going to try to find one, perhaps one that needs to be rescued.'

Here was the perfect solution to my present problem. I didn't say anything to her but, as soon as I was back home, I scanned the For Sale columns in the local papers looking for donkeys. Inevitably there was nothing. I rang various contacts, and then our vet told me that there was a badly neglected donkey in a field next to a supermarket on the outskirts of Aberdeen. He would try to find out more. He eventually rang me back with a number and suggested I give the owners a call. A grumpy voice listened to my garbled tale and then informed me that the donkey was not for sale. However, I heard a shrill voice in the background butting in, 'She might be if the money's right, but it would need to be cash.' Three calls later and a deal had been struck.

I took off to have a look at my unseen purchase. The vet had already told me that she was a very pretty little donkey. Her name was Pixie. She was indeed lovely, but as I had also been informed, she was neglected. Her hooves were like Turkish slippers, turned up at the toes, tripping her up and in dire need of trimming. I had made arrangements to hide her away at a nearby farm until Christmas Day; this was going to be a big early birthday surprise for Mum.

Pixie was set to make an ass of me from the outset. Firstly, getting the chocolate-brown fiend into the trailer proved challenging. A friend had come to assist, and though we pushed and shoved, cajoled and dangled carrots and pony mix enticingly, and rattled a bucket of oats, she dug her Turkish toes deep into the mud and refused to budge in any direction.

Suddenly her ex-owner (I had handed over the cash by now), dressed in a most unsuitable white fake-fur coat and garish red stilettos, announced, 'Do you know our dear little donkey will *always* go into a trailer if you give her a honey sandwich.'

This comment was unhelpful. I did not usually go to move donkeys armed with such fare. I laughed rather too cynically, and then realised that she was being serious. She fluttered her long, fake eyelashes and pulled a wounded expression. I guessed that she was not going to do much to help in case she chipped one of her equally long immaculate red fingernails. She obviously spent a great deal of time and care on her own manicures while overlooking her donkey's need of a pedicure.

Battle continued. The more stubborn Pixie was, the more regret flooded through me like too much fuel in an engine. I was beginning to wonder if this was an awful mistake. A carload of boozy, red-faced men steamed past, and waved cheerily at us. Then they stopped and reversed back to us. A fat face not dissimilar to that of a large pig beamed out of the open window, 'Having problems, hen?'

I nodded.

They pulled over onto the verge and came over, laughing and guffawing. They looked like rugby players, with physiques that would move a mountain. Now desperate, we were over-effusive in our acceptance of help. Shortly, with our extended workforce, the little darling was manhandled into the trailer. I made a mental note to take honey sandwiches for all future donkey manoeuvres.

I had to fork out more cash to lure a blacksmith to come in the frantic pre-Christmas rush to trim Pixie's hooves. After deep grooming, and a thorough de-louse, the surprise package looked beautiful, even angelic. Christmas Day loomed. On the morning of the festivities, I pretended I had problems with some of my sheep and disappeared to fetch my Christmas donkey, leaving Freddy with Mum and Geordie. At the farm, my angel had rubbed bald patches round her eyes and shoulders. She looked dejected, as if she was wearing a moth-eaten charity shop fur coat. And then, despite some honey sandwiches, the wretched beast refused to enter the trailer. The farmer and I wasted ages cajoling and enticing until finally his bodybuilding son appeared, and once again Pixie was manoeuvred with brute force. By now I had been away considerably longer than anticipated. When I reached my parents' house, before taking Pixie from the trailer I went into the kitchen where Mum was basting a turkey as large as the Bass Rock. She looked flustered and hassled; she looked cross too.

'Where the hell have you been?' she snapped.

I had primed Geordie, who had now taken Pixie out of the trailer and was holding her on a long rope. He rang the front doorbell and then hid beside the house, leaving the beast standing in wait.

'And who the hell is that disturbing us on Christmas Day? It can't be our visitors already, they are too bloody early,' said Mum wiping her hands on her apron and throwing a cloth across to the sink.

I slipped out of the side door whilst she went to the front to investigate.

Pixie did look adorable. We had put tinsel around her bald neck, and she stood meekly on the doorstep and politely took a carrot from Geordie. Then there was the sound of the door unlocking as Mum flung it open. Clutching an oven glove in one hand and a knife in the other, she exclaimed, 'Jesus Christ!' Given that it was Christmas Day, this was perhaps not so inappropriate. She then hastily slammed the door.

Geordie, now puffing on a cigarette, laughed and said, 'She's a very sweet little donkey, isn't she?' He was quite tickled by the whole episode. Pixie was taken to one of the stables.

Later Mum went off on a tirade about where the hell had I been, leaving her with Freddy when she had the lunch to cook, and asked very little about her joint Christmas and birthday present. She had dismissed it. The bloody donkey had backfired.

Geordie had a Clydesdale stud run by a man who had worked with heavy horses all his life. They had been excelling, showing all over Scotland. One of the mares had won the coveted Cawdor Cup at the Royal Highland Show. Prior to Pixie's arrival I had made sure that there would be plenty of field space available for her. On Boxing Day, Pixie was put out into the field with the show-hopeful for the forthcoming season. It was a day of iron-hard ground; wet areas had become treacherous glissades. The mare took one look at the donkey standing innocently by the fence, snorted disdainfully and took off with her tail high in the air. Finding a sudden burst of speed, she performed an impressive gavotte around the field, her tail bristling in bottlebrush fashion. The donkey took no notice and continued quietly munching hay by the gate. Then she looked up and brayed loudly. The sound split the crisp air like the howl of a banshee, it echoed on long after, with added squeaks, moans and squeals from Pixie. Then, to finally clinch all my mother's doubts about her special present, the mare, frightened by this sound, slipped on the ice and badly cut her leg. Now Mum was livid.

The donkey stayed until after New Year, when I realised my fickle mother really didn't want her, and I had to quickly find another home. But the story had a happy ending, as Pixie was bought as a companion for a friend's donkey, was much loved and lived on to a ripe old age. And I had learnt a hard lesson. It was not a good idea to surprise my mother with the gift of an animal – in particular a donkey. Indeed anything!

*

Throughout his childhood, I involved Freddy in as many of my wildlife encounters as possible, always trying to take him with me for any releases. The triumphs matter because of the endless failures. I wanted to share the natural world with him and give him the best side of the childhood I had myself relished in nature. But there was always an underlying nag that perhaps history was repeating itself with my own failed marriages, and that might be bringing him instability rather in the same way as my parents' divorce had probably affected me. This made me increasingly anxious.

Freddy grew up in a household dominated by animals. From an early age, orphan hedgehogs, a peregrine falcon with a broken wing, tawny owlets and young blackbirds or buzzards surrounded him, and there were always pet lambs. One morning on our way to school, we saw what we thought were paper bags blowing in the breeze on the distant verge. It was a family of young stoats. We sat and watched entranced as the lithe, sinuous bodies of these rapturous mustelids cavorted and danced, leaping high in the air, rolling over and over in the feathery grasses, chasing one another through a maze of undergrowth, before re-emerging to perform aerial acrobatics, high kicks and balletic dancing. It seemed they were doing it for the sheer thrill, honing their elasticated bodies for a future of stealth and murder. Stoats are reputed to mesmerise their victims, particularly rabbits. Freddy and I were certainly mesmerised. It made Freddy an hour late for school. But he has never forgotten it either.

One morning there was an early call about a badger in a snare. Freddy had never seen a badger. I rang his school and told them that he would be late. I learnt early on that there was no point in making excuses. I told his teachers exactly why, and I think they gave up trying to convince me that being late, or even occasionally missing school altogether, was a bad idea.

I once rang to say, 'I am afraid Freddy is going to be ill a week next Tuesday.'

Silence at the other end of the telephone, and then came a chuckle and the response, 'That's fine.'

Knowledge and love of the natural world is the best grounding for a stable education that there is, and I have always been aware that nature holds the key to everything. For my own mental stability it has been vital. Sadly, nature education in schools is now almost non-existent, and in order to take a class out for trips there is a protracted rigmarole of risk assessments and miles of red tape that have to be tackled, causing a total loss of spontaneity. Teachers clearly begin to lose the will once they are forced into climbing an insurmountable mountain of paperwork. Few children play outside any more, and more and more adults spend little or no time in nature. The rise in mental ill-health as a result is a worrying trend.

At Freddy's first school, they did understand that wildlife matters were of extreme importance, and I frequently took animals and birds into the classrooms, much to the delight of the pupils. Freddy's first school report read: 'Freddy brings a carnival atmosphere to the classroom.' And he often brought animals in too.

Freddy's first teacher was a gem and regaled the class with extraordinary things. She was intensely creative and some of the projects and artworks Freddy came home with are still with me now. On one of the rare occasions when Mum collected him from school and he was sitting in the back of the car thumb-sucking, he removed it as he did when about to pass comment, and said, 'Granny, did you know that slugs are hermaphrodites?' I don't think any of us did. He was five at the time.

When his teacher hatched out ducklings in an incubator in her classroom, Freddy volunteered his mother to have one of the end products, and eventually it joined our flock. 'This is Apricot Buff-Orpington,' he announced grandly as he foisted her upon me. Apricot turned into quite a good layer.

Freddy had a love–hate relationship with our hefty Brahma cockerel, Onslow. When home from school and still wearing his uniform shorts, he frequently pottered up to the henhouse to look for eggs. One day I was cooking tea when there were blood-curdling shrieks. I shot out of the door and saw poor Freddy at the top of the bank being attacked from below by the feisty cockerel. He was scratching Freddy's bare legs with sharp claws.

'Run away quick!' I yelled.

Instantly Freddy replied, 'I can't, Mummy, I'm far too busy screaming!'

We had frequent trips to Ardnamurchan and stayed at Ockle on the north coast. On one visit a dead minke whale had been towed across from Skye to Ockle, as it was supposedly more remote and would be less of a problem for Skye's burgeoning tourist industry. Brimming with excitement on our arrival, we rushed straight to the headland to have a look. But the whale had been deliberately blown up. It was a repulsive mess: grey-pink flesh spewed everywhere, stinking and putrid amid shattered pieces of bone. A repugnant aroma pervaded the whole area, and bits of pink sludge and slime coated the rocks.

Freddy, then aged six, had clearly, like me, been expecting to see a complete whale, and commented, 'Mummy, this is not a minke whale, it's a manky whale.'

We did find an enormous piece of bone and lugged it back up from the headland, and he took it to the school nature table where it inspired awe in the other children and made the legs of the table buckle.

*

I had everything, but not the one thing I constantly sought, and that was a happy relationship with my mother. At times there were still glimmers of her fun and humour, and she could be generous and kind, particularly with Freddy, but her constant criticism wore me down. The more I wrote and took photographs, and the more my work was published, the more she commented, 'Oh God, you are turning into one of those impossible creative types. How will you keep this up? What happens if your writing is not good enough?'

Most writers worry about that and don't need reminded.

16

More Misunderstandings

My Uncle Archie had moved to Scotland with his family to become a prep-school headmaster some years earlier, but even though he was now nearer, I seldom saw him and his family. Running a school allows little or no spare time, and I knew how occupied they all were. Occasionally I called in, but our lives had leached in different directions. Then in 1996 my great-aunt, Grandfather Munro's sister, Freda, died at the age of ninety-five. Childless, she and her husband Cecil had always taken a great interest in my life and followed my written work avidly. Though we rarely saw one another, we kept in close contact with long letters. Cecil was a fine ornithologist and when I was a child he taught me that, to really know and understand birds, you must first learn to recognise their individual songs. It proved to be excellent advice. Archie and I drove south together for Freda's funeral in Wales.

Long car journeys provide an extraordinary chance for uninterrupted private conversations. The time we spent together proved to be very important to us both. We talked about my parents, about the years of sadness with Dad's drinking, and my own battles now with my mother. Archie suggested that much of my self-doubt and insecurity might be due to the fact that I had not dealt with the guilt and sadness I felt regarding Dad's suicide. I had written to Dad the day he drove south the last time I was with him, but that letter never reached him. I had known how desperate he was about his future, and I'd feared for him and told him how very much both Archie and I loved and cared about him. His girlfriend, Kate, returned the letter to me, although not without opening it first. The date on the postmark was 9 July. The day of his death. It had arrived the day after. This wore away at me, as I continued to ask myself if, had he seen it, it would have made any difference. Would he still be here? Kate sent me all Dad's papers, together with some of his remaining belongings. It was in a bulging file of letters I'd written to him from boarding school. He had religiously kept every one of them.

I couldn't bear it when after the eight-hour drive north again I dropped Archie off at his school. I had the same feeling I used to have when Dad came to take me out from school – when might we meet again? I didn't want Archie to go, ever. He was the only person who remained who really understood the reasons for my parents' failed marriage – and more. By the time I was back home, once again nothing seemed to piece together, Archie's story was different from my mother's. Yes, it was very, very different.

After the funeral, as I had been driving back up the motorway with Archie beside me, there had been long pauses and then he had said: 'I loved your mother very much indeed; she had a lot to put up with and I witnessed her terrible unhappiness.' I had briefly glanced over to him, but he was staring straight ahead. 'Pol, I think you probably suspect already that I am most likely to be your father. I think you know how much I have always loved you. Your mum and I both loved each other deeply too, but she also still loved your dad. It was a very difficult and complicated situation. It all happened long, long before I met your aunt. Dad understood too and in some ways that made it worse. Dad and I were so close – always.'

I had wanted to stop the car, to pull over and park somewhere quiet. I had wanted to cry. Mum had told me about an affair, but not this part. I had not expected this. Not at all. Instead, I drove on, fearing that if I did stop, I would break down emotionally and be unable to continue. Numbness engulfed me. A steely coldness had taken hold.

Two years later, in 1998, soon after Archie retired from a life dedicated to education, he had a massive heart attack. He and my aunt had been hoping to return to live peacefully in their cottage in a remote part of Herefordshire. He was only sixty-two. Dear, patient, kind Geordie stepped in and drove Mum and me south to the funeral.

My uncle and aunt were renowned for having ancient rusting cars that constantly broke down – usually in Scotland at the start of the school holidays en route to their home in Herefordshire. I used to receive priceless letters from one of my cousins, regaling me with their hair-raising trips south. The AA's Relay services were in big demand, and the family frequently travelled up and down the country on the breakdown truck. In fact, they were well known and knew many of the drivers personally.

My young cousin wrote to tell me about one instalment of their car fiascos, when they'd arrived the day before Christmas Eve, some twenty-four hours later than planned. Unlike today, when Christmas preparations infuriatingly begin in November, or even earlier, they were ill prepared for the festivities. Firstly, the children were adamant that they had to acquire and decorate a Christmas tree, next they had to source a turkey. Passing a farm with a sign advertising free-range turkeys, they had gone on Christmas Eve to find that a few were still running around fit and fully feathered. 'Which one do you want?' asked the farmer. Their chosen bird first had to be killed, and then they were all lost in a sea of feathers, as they had to pluck it themselves. There was no time for the unfortunate victim to be hung for a time to help tenderise its expansive body.

Later, Archie's own description of events was one of the funniest things I had ever heard. The more I laughed, the more he embellished the tale. It was typical of him – he was someone who always retained a wonderful sense of the ridiculous – particularly if the tale was against himself. This was one of the many reasons why I loved him so much. Now, knowing what he had told me in the car on that long journey, I had reason to love him even more. Whatever the truth, Dad would always remain Dad to me. Nothing would change that.

I joined my aunt and cousins in a huge black car that took us to the beautiful little Herefordshire church for Archie's funeral. There was a glass panel between the driver, who was wearing an austere top hat, and the passengers. One of my cousins had to sit in the front. We all piled in feeling miserable and nervous. And then the car wouldn't start. There were half a dozen ominous bronchial splutters from the engine, and silence. Almost under my breath I said, 'Never mind, we can get AA Relay to take us to the funeral.' The black beast filled with uncontrolled hilarity. We could imagine Archie guffawing loudly over it too. The driver, however, was unamused. Finally, the stately vehicle reluctantly coughed into action and transported us the short distance. We were still laughing when we stepped out amid a growing number of friends there to pay their respects to someone who was extremely well loved.

The church where my uncle's funeral took place is of the late Norman period. Its bell tower surveys the glorious, unspoilt rural landscape of Herefordshire – miles of orchards, hedgerows, cattle and sheep, secluded, peaceful – extraordinarily beautiful, with farmland rich in the wildlife that was once such a feature of so much of rural England, and has since been tragically lost due to destructive agribusiness and development. Rooks solemnly accompanied the funeral procession as we filed through the little mossy lychgate and on into the church. Inside, there was a stillness amid the scent of wildflowers, and leather-bound hymn books, as the rooks cawed their condolences from the surrounding trees. I heard a wren singing wistfully. After the service Archie was laid to rest in the graveyard, surrounded by woods and fields. In the distance I saw native pigs happily grubbing on the edge of a copse. In spring it is a place sonorous with birdsong. Bo and my father had been cremated, with neither headstone nor memorial. Archie would have a permanent place and become integral to this outstandingly lovely corner of Herefordshire.

Though I had seen so little of Archie in my adult life, I was going to miss him dreadfully. My head was a liquidiser full of all the wrong ingredients, and they didn't combine well.

Months after the funeral, when I asked Mum a second time about who my father really was, she flew into a temper and told me that Dad was indeed my father. But it just didn't stack up. How could he be, if he was totally impotent? And it wasn't what Archie had said. When I revealed what he had told me that day on the drive back from Wales, it made her even angrier. 'Archie was always a bloody fool. He is stupid. He was always stupid. He has inherited the Munro stupidity. Old Grandfather Munro had it too,' she said. 'He was lying.'

But was he? And now he was gone, so I could never ask again. My confusion was worsened by the fact that I never thought of either my mother or Archie as people prone to telling lies. Perhaps I had misunderstood.

17

Geordie

It's 1999. Freddy is about to start at a new school, and I am house-hunting. Eventually I find a beautiful little farm in Highland Perthshire with ten acres and ramshackle outbuildings. I am daunted by the sheer amount of work that needs to be done and, after an initial visit, write it off as impractical – too much work, too great a challenge. Instead, I set my heart on another place close to Loch Ness: not only has the cottage been newly renovated, but it's also far cheaper. It's remote and up a long track, it has far more land and already this is being returned to nature. I could really do things with this.

I show Geordie the particulars. He lights up a cigarette and makes unenthusiastic noises. 'It's far too remote, Pol,' he says. 'We don't think it's a good idea for you to be that far out on your own with Freddy, and it has so little potential compared to the place in Highland Perthshire. I want to come and see that farm with you. Let's make a plan and go tomorrow.'

It's a bleak wintery morning when we arrive in Perthshire. Geordie instantly feels the place does indeed have endless potential. Vision is what is required, he says, 'and I think you have always had plenty of that.' He puffs on another cigarette and pulls his tweed overcoat collar up round his always-red face.

I point out that vision comes with a cost.

'You are still young, Pol, you can probably do such a lot of it yourself.'

And so an offer is put in. And accepted.

*

It often feels as though I have spent much of my lifetime clearing up other people's crap in both senses of the word, but the positive side to this is the feeling of satisfaction, and the fact that manual labour keeps you from thinking too much. Now, every spare moment was spent making large bonfires and filling skips with years of detritus, accompanied by a tough band of hard-grafting friends who came and gave up hours of their time to help. Geordie was incredible, and though he may not have been able for the physical graft, he often came up to help in other ways. His moral support and his wicked sense of humour proved invaluable, and he had had plenty of experience of dealing with builders. 'Most of them are a shower of messy bastards and you have to keep at them.'

The house had to be gutted, as we continued to uncover more rot. It was almost a year before the work was complete and Freddy and I finally moved in.

There were the familiar problems of strategic military-style planning where the animals were concerned, and each visit to oversee the work involved a trailer stacked high with animal and farm equipment accumulated over years. I had sheep and owls to move, as well as three African pygmy goats and Rosie, my little roe deer. I was concerned about how to move her. After discussions with our vet, we agreed on a suitable mixture with which to dope her. This sedative would last for approximately one hour. The journey to our new home would take about forty minutes; there was precious little margin for error.

During her lifetime, Rosie was ill on several occasions. Though tame with me, catching her was a challenge. Like all deer, she moved with the speed and confusion of a hurricane. Once caught, her struggling and the subsequent stress it caused in turn worried me. I used to wonder whether the treatment was worse than the ailment. But for nine years she shared my life, lived in among our sheep and goats, and sometimes came for walks around the fields with our dogs. I had to learn to deal with the occasional bout of major stress that accompanies caring for a nervy, highly strung, wild patient. When I looked out of the bathroom window first thing in the morning, I could usually see her pretty head peeping from amongst the long grasses, or she would be there wandering around, grazing with the rest of my flock.

The morning we moved her to our new home, I was filled with doubts. It took two of us a long time to catch her, and she was even more wary of my male assistant. When we finally grabbed her, trying to get the injection into her struggling form was hazardous. His ample backside was at severe risk. A misaimed needle might ruin the day. Eventually, after a short struggle amid flaying hooves, the needle was in, the plunger down, and mission accomplished. After this indignity, Rosie fled up the field in terror. The injection was said to work almost instantly. But it didn't. She battled against its effects, nibbled at the grass and still appeared alert. And was as jumpy as a kangaroo. Eventually, after a protracted time lapse, she lay down and slept. We carefully loaded her into the waiting car and drove away through the hills to Highland Perthshire, with me praying that I had no puncture, or breakdown, or met any hazards.

By the time we reached the farm, it was dusk. Rosie was still in a deep slumber as we gently lifted her into her new field. Now I merely had to wait for daylight. Of course, I didn't sleep and went out several times in the night with the torch to see if she had recovered, but couldn't find her anywhere. Next morning, I was up before daybreak, feeling as if I had a hangover. With relief I found her at the top of the steepest field, looking dazed and dopey, but she was chewing the cud. And she was calm. I sat on a large rock and watched as daylight broke to the east and a sleepy sun rose from its bed, splaying rays of gold light to carpet the Tay Valley below.

Rosie didn't venture down to the bottom of the high field for several days. Then one afternoon, she rejoined the rest of the flock and followed me around our new fields like a dog. She settled better than I could have hoped. Oddly, she also became tamer as well as calmer. We had fitted her with a large white goose collar in case she took flight over the fence into the surrounding woodland, and we had informed local gamekeepers about her presence. One of them nicknamed her 'the minister', for it looked as though she was wearing a dog collar.

In 2001, soon after we had arrived on the smallholding in the Perthshire hills, another devastating outbreak of foot-and-mouth disease erupted and spread to many areas of the countryside. Dumfries and Galloway, and Cumbria were particularly badly hit. All livestock movements were grounded, walkers were told not to go out in the countryside, and repercussions of the outbreak caused acute misery across the farming community, as they had done previously.

My intention on the farm was to restore some of the badly degraded and overgrazed habitat, and I had plans to plant a great many trees and hedgerows. I wanted to turn it into an undisturbed wildlife habitat. Due to the foot-and-mouth epidemic, a friend who worked for a forestry organisation was unable to go on to various large estates to plant, and he had several thousand bare-rooted broadleaf trees going to waste. Did I want them? he asked. I eagerly accepted, even though it was June and not the best time for planting, and the forecast was for a heatwave.

Kim and I set to and put over a thousand bare-rooted plants in over a few days. Kim was an expert digger, and, whilst busying herself looking for voles, assisted me more than she realised for her neat scrapings were ideal for me to put trees into. Almost all of them survived despite the drought. Perthshire is extremely fertile, and in our south-facing position with a high rainfall, the young trees grew fast. I have continued to plant trees and hedges on the farm ever since, and it has brought extraordinary results.

The area soon became Rosie's favourite haunt. Some days I did not see her at all, secreted away perfectly as she was in the long feathery grasses and the flag iris I had also planted on the fringes of the little burn that ran through the field. Kim could always find her.

I had seen Rosie the previous day browsing happily, but on one particular morning, despite persistent calling, for some reason I knew that she was not going to come. After a few minutes, Kim and I found her lying dead underneath a large alder tree in a bed of iris. Deer occasionally suffer from pneumonia that is hard to detect, but it was also possible she had simply succumbed to old age as roe deer do not live very long. Kim accompanied me when I returned, weighed down by a heavy heart and a spade, and dug a last resting place. Once Rosie had been buried, I sat on a rock with Kim's black nose pressed into my hand and thought of the pleasure that the small roe doe had given me. For nine years she had been a part of me, and, as ever with all animals, the void she left was hard to fill.

Next morning when I looked out of the window, the field seemed empty, but I knew Rosie had done well to live as long as she did. Animals break my heart, but for me a life without them is unthinkable.

*

Mum was beginning to fail. She was putting on more weight, had a couple of bad falls, was having serious problems with her eyesight, and she also had high blood pressure. She looked frail, but battled on. If anything, her tongue was sharper. One day I heard her telling the gardener, who had politely queried something she told him to do, to fuck off! She was becoming more demanding and erratic. She was understandably terrified that she might have her driving licence taken away due to her rapidly failing sight.

Geordie looked tired. He didn't seem well and appeared to be struggling too, running about doing the shopping whilst endlessly trying to please her. Neither of them would go to the doctor, and he in particular was adamant that they were managing.

After they sold Ardnamurchan, neither of them returned. The place had meant a great deal to Geordie, but not half as much as it did to me and Mum. I continued to return as often as possible, though sometimes years would pass before the opportunity arose.

In Mum's case, she always said, 'I can't go back because I know it won't be as I remember it. It will have changed, everything's changed.'

But Mum always wanted to know all about it whenever I returned from a visit. Though there was a continual tension between us relating to my doubting her story about who was my father, and what she saw as the problem of my free spirit, when it came to Ardnamurchan, we were united.

'I don't ever remember being happier anywhere,' she added wistfully. 'Mingary was the loveliest house I ever lived in, and we could never equal that view, could we?'

If home is where the heart lies, then I have no hesitation in saying that for me Ardnamurchan will always be home, even though we only lived there for a brief period of my life. Most of us have a place that is dear to us, a place that we treasure above all else. Ardnamurchan provided the backdrop and foundation for my greatest love of all. It has always enhanced my thinking and fired me with a burning passion for wildlife, the wilderness and the way of life in a rural crofting community. It has also always been the place to which I run when life becomes too hard to deal with. It has been, and will always be, the place where I am able to replenish my equilibrium: between a beautiful, wild, windswept rock jutting far out into the Atlantic, and the hard places I have found myself emotionally. It is here that I find harmony within myself, something I have battled with most of my life. And it is here that I find the true wildness that feeds my soul. It is also a place where I have often escaped to write. With no mobile phone reception in the cottage at Ockle, and no internet, there is peace that lends itself to creativity as storms rip in off the sea, and the slates dance on the roof.

*

It is March 2004 and I have escaped again with my collies, driven down that long and winding road heading ever west. For me, whatever wildness the elements hurl in my direction, this is my road to the sun. I feel worn down with the mess I seem to have made in every direction. Now not one but two failed marriages, a complex relationship with Mum and this bloody lingering paternity issue. Why does it gnaw at me so much?

This morning I am sitting high above the shore beneath the ancient oak wood that sprawls its way up the side of Ben Hiant, the highest hill on the peninsula overlooking the Sound of Mull. Ravens are calling nearby; they are already sitting on eggs. They have used the same shambling cliff-site nest through generations of birds, alternating it with another close by on a lower rock face. I have found solace here, watching, since I was a child. Both great structures are made up of flotsam and jetsam from the beach, padded with sheep's wool and deer hair. They are garish with the ever-increasing plastic detritus that accumulates on the tideline.

Far below me an otter steams effortlessly out into the bay, flipping and twisting in the swaying bronze weed before emerging with a succulent crab. It's so still today that I can hear the crunching sounds of its sharp teeth, the strong jaws pushing through hard shell. Deer are high above me, an old hind watching my every move. I can hear the soft mewing contact call of a hind to her calf. I don't move, for I am too comfortable, lost in peaceful thought. A grey seal bottles and snorts; through my binoculars I can see the saltwater droplets on its whiskers. My two collies, Kim and Pippin, are beside me, quaking with excitement, but they have learnt to keep still and wait patiently. They will soon fold themselves into neat pied doughnuts and doze, oblivious to the activity around them. A golden eagle appears over the tweed gold of Ben Hiant's flank, and a snipe jinks away, emitting its staccato two-note call.

I am so absorbed in this world that I forget the other. I forget the things that usually prey on my mind like greedy maggots in rotting flesh. I know the mind is a powerful tool and I should have control. Sometimes I don't. It needs work. Adders and other snakes shed their skin – if only I had the ability to shed my old self that easily. It does indeed need work. I don't always like what I see of myself either.

By the time I return to my car and pick up a fleeting phone signal from the Isle of Mull opposite, I see there are more than a dozen missed calls from my mother. There are also several from my close long-term family friend Sue, whose cottage I always stay in at Ockle. I sense all is not well.

I ring Mum immediately. She is calm, distant, matter-of-fact, under control. She is in deep shock. She and Geordie had been going out for the day to a special event, had had early-morning tea together, and then Geordie had gone to shave. He didn't appear for breakfast. She called him to no avail and then went to see what he was doing. She found him fully dressed in his suit, clean-shaven and lying peacefully on the bed, arms folded across his chest. Like Archie, he too had suffered a massive heart attack. He had never had a day's serious ill health in his life, and, compared to what lay ahead for my mother, I think it must have been an easy departure. But not for us.

*

I return to the cottage to pack up. My heart is laden with so much sorrow, I can't think. As I begin the beautiful three-hour drive home, every twist in the first section of road bordering Loch Sunart brings a deluge of memories. Memories of my stepfather, who, like Ardnamurchan, where first he entered our lives, always proved an anchor that never dragged even in the harshest storms.

The last time I saw him I had been concerned that his usually ruddy complexion appeared grey, his lips blue. He had come to the farm, and I told him that I thought he looked tired. 'I am, Pol,' he said. 'I find your mother increasingly hard to handle. She's not very strong physically, and I think soon we will have to try to find some extra help, but I will continue on as long as I can.'

I had agreed to visit more often, but when I said I was also struggling with Mum and that she wouldn't let me help, he hadn't replied. She was so determined that she could still cope and was always defensive over having more assistance. Yet she would also beg for it, and when it came, rebel against it.

Geordie had looked worn down with dealing with her. I had again suggested he went to the doctor, but he had always had an aversion to the medical profession and tended to steer clear; he wouldn't have done what they told him anyway. He drank too much caffeine, consumed far too much alcohol, smoked too much, and took no exercise. He was not one of the many to be found knocking on the surgery door on a Monday morning. Geordie was a bon viveur, a person who usually loved life. He was the mainstay of a party – always cheerful and full of fun – generous and loving, and he had always treated me as if I were his own. And he adored Freddy.

I feel a griping panic grab at my heart. I had not had the chance to say goodbye. Had I told him often enough how much I loved him? Had he died feeling unhappy, as he had felt when he took the overdose? Had he been in pain? Rather than going home, I drive on, straight to Freddy's school, forty minutes from our house. When I arrive, it is evening, Freddy is in his study working peacefully, and is thrilled to see me, but within minutes his happy expression has crumpled as my awful news alters his world. He and Grandpa had had a very deep bond.

In the weeks that follow, Mum is extraordinary. She remains calm and organised and rallies in the most incredible way. This is shock. I go over almost daily, but there are few tears, and outwardly she is strong and very much in control. I know, though, that this is not what lies beneath the surface, that she is terrified now that she might not be able to live by herself and might be forced to move elsewhere – something she would refuse to accept right to the very end of her life. She knows that if she goes to pieces then it will make things harder. Her independence is fiercer than ever, and she clings to it like a clump of marram grass on a gale-battered Atlantic sand dune. Though it did make things difficult, I will always admire her for the determined resolve that she manages to muster.

18

Mongol Rally

Towards the end of his time at school, Freddy seemed to be under constant pressure to go on to university, together with many of his peers. He certainly never had any pressure from me. I firmly believe university doesn't suit everyone. When he came home and told me he had made the decision to go to Liverpool to study politics, I was surprised. From when he was very small, he was always mechanically minded. He used to infuriate my mother by immediately taking all the gadgets and electronic or clockwork toys he was given to pieces, and then putting them back together again. 'Fiddle, fiddle, fiddle,' she'd say. 'He can't leave anything alone, can he?' But as he got older Freddy was always the first person she asked to help when something needed to be fixed, and he saved her a lot of money 'fiddling' and sorting out endless things that had ceased to work.

I felt Freddy should be doing something practical, but for some reason he couldn't get on an engineering course that he favoured and told me that this was why he'd chosen politics instead. He also felt that, having lived all his life in Scotland, it would be good to venture south. I had my doubts about that too but decided it was far better to support his decision and go with it.

'You're not very keen on this idea, are you?' he asked me soon after the various forms had been filled in.

We are very close and have never had secrets between us so my doubts must have been obvious. I still felt it was better to let him do what he wanted.

However, towards the end of his last school term, Freddy announced that before university he was planning to go to Mongolia. Naively,

I thought it was simply a question of ringing up a travel agent and booking a flight. I knew he had always been keen on travel, with a particular interest in Russia and Eastern Europe. But there were no flights involved. Instead, he and two school friends planned to take part in the Mongol Rally driving from London's Hyde Park, to Ulaanbaatar in Outer Mongolia.

Freddy had been one of the first of his year to pass his driving test. He had taken an astonishing amount of driving lessons at vast cost. As it transpired, the reason for this was the fact that a) they were a legitimate reason to skive from his increasing boredom with school, and b) he fancied his blonde driving instructress, as did most of the rest of his male school friends. But the thought of having him drive some 10,000 miles on the opposite side of the road, having only recently passed his test, and travelling through numerous war-torn countries, secretly filled me with horror.

But then, Freddy had never been one to do things by half measures. I remembered when we went to a circus when he was only four, how someone asked for a child to volunteer to go and sit on the poor, sad elephant and he went immediately when no one else would. I remember seeing the images from his trip to the Skye Ridge when he was in his early teens too and feeling glad I had not known how treacherous it was until after the event. Though I have always been a very keen hill walker and love climbing Munros, I had only managed a small part of the infamous ridge myself and found it far too exposed and akin to walking on ball bearings, with sheer drops on either side. I kept my thoughts to myself again and tried to be enthusiastic.

If I thought moving house with dozens of animals and the detritus of years of accumulated stuff involved military-style planning, I was about to see military planning on a grand scale. The Mongol Rally, run by an organisation called The Adventurists, requires participants to travel in a small car, with a tiny engine – basically a car that they refer to as a banger. The teams, usually of between two and four, are unsupported; there is no time limit, and no specified route. Racing is not part of the equation. The goal is to get there, and every year dozens and dozens don't. This is mostly due to cars irretrievably breaking down, or major hazards on the way. And those hazards are numerous. One team apparently managed to pass through no fewer than forty countries – that was a record, but perhaps it has since changed. It has been described as 'the greatest adventure in the world'.

Soon the house and a dry mouse-proof shed began to fill with a curious selection of items. Daily, more and more arrived, as we had been chosen as the HQ for Freddy's team of three. I felt it was better to throw myself into this whole terrifying business rather than waste hours worrying. I agreed that part of my financial contribution to it would be to provide a superior first-aid kit for them – this was one of the few things they had been advised to take. And I do not mean a small tin with a red cross on it containing a few non-sticking sticking plasters, a bandage or two, and some paracetamol. Suggestions from previous participants listed an astonishing array of items, including syringes and needles so that if the worst came to the worst they would have their own for emergencies, particularly if they had to go to hospitals lacking properly sterilised equipment. I also had to acquire broad-spectrum antibiotics that could be used if someone had a bad wound, or perhaps picked up a chest infection. That proved more challenging, as our doctor was flummoxed by the whole idea.

Much of my list could be acquired from Boots. Having spent a long time whizzing up the aisles with a trolley, now full, I met a friend who is a hypochondriac par excellence. She looked mightily impressed when she saw my haul: boxes and boxes of pills and tablets for every bug and reaction imaginable, water-purifying tablets, glucose energy tablets, creams, potions and lotions for sunburn, bandages, slings, rolls of plasters and tape, electrolyte replacement, sharp scissors and tweezers, eye baths, eye ointment, and boxes and boxes of Imodium. As it turned out, the latter should have sponsored the entire trip as the afflictions of dodgy water and dubious food meant this was the participants' main problem. At one point they almost ran out and apparently the other teams they bumped into during the marathon would have paid a hefty premium for spare sachets. There were none. It turned out to be a gut-ripping adventure.

Poor Mum. We managed to keep revelations concerning the Mongol Rally from her till there was literally no going back, and then we told her our guilty secret. She quietly nodded, and then I made tea. Her silence was worrying. A storm percolated. Three days later the phone rang. Odd how it seemed to be dancing on its base like a toddler having a tantrum. As soon as I picked it up, I knew I was in for a blast of fury. Mum had worked herself up into a good head of steam, a combustion engine set to burn me savagely. And burn me she did.

I accepted that she was worried but when she said, 'You have to stop him or we will lose him'.

I am afraid I replied, 'If I do stop him, Mum, then we will definitely lose him.'

She asked me, 'What the fuck does that mean, Polly? You are so impossible!'

I tried to explain that it was important for Freddy, who was now nearly nineteen, to be allowed to do his own thing, but this fell flat too.

'Well not in fucking Mongolia for God's sake, Polly.'

For the next few weeks, I was *persona non grata*. She was livid with me and rang endlessly with huge lists of all the things she thought might happen. It was hard not to sink into a decline myself.

The sponsorship plans were going well, and money had been steadily coming in. People were very generous in their support. A minimum of £1,000 at that time had to be raised for charity, but obviously Freddy and his friends were aiming far higher, and it looked as though they would achieve far, far more. A car had finally been acquired – a red Ford Fiesta with a 1,000 cc engine.

Meanwhile, at HQ, the shed was filling rapidly. An army friend had provided clothing and reconstituted rations: enough meals to see them through a long period when they were totally out of contact with any form of civilisation. They had two tents and numerous cooking utensils, sleeping bags and even a few books. They needed a couple of spare wheels, and not just tyres due to the anticipated roughness of the terrain. A roof rack had to be modified and a special reinforced sump cover made. Tool kits were becoming more extensive by the day, and we had numerous trips to buy yet more gadgets.

Route planning was now part of daily life, and my geography was improving as a huge map was regularly sprawled out on the kitchen table and decisions made. Freddy has always been an excellent planner and was clearly revelling in this part. Once this was done, timings had to be precise as visas had to be applied for in each country they were to pass through. Freddy had taken on this time-consuming role too. The three of them also needed to have several vaccinations against many heinous diseases, and needed to stagger these, as some were liable to make them feel ill for a few days. The vaccinations were far from cheap, and the same went for the visas. Mum suggested travel insurance too. However, there was not an insurance company on the planet that would have covered this lot.

There was little time to worry about Mum's hysteria, and in the end she calmed down. I understood exactly why she was in such a state, and I felt so sad and wished I could have helped her more and got her to accept that for a great deal of the time she was in a very unstable mental state. Like Dad and his drink issue, it was simply a case of 'everyone else is wrong'. Denial.

On the evening before the expedition set forth, I cooked a huge piece of beef with Yorkshire puddings, Freddy's favourite meal. From now on it might be army rations, and further into the journey, goat boiled in 100-day-old mare's milk. We had stuck a map on the kitchen wall and the aim was for me to follow the route and mark where they were whenever I had any news. The other two mothers also agreed that we would keep in close contact with one another and relay messages back and forth.

By the time the small red car was packed up and they were all on board, I am sure they couldn't have even squeezed in a pin. It looked bloody awful, weighed down and pressing hard on its axles, covered with stickers of those who had sponsored them, the roof almost caving in under the weight of the spare wheels, tent, fuel cans and tools, tow ropes, tackle and teabags. It was a laden Tardis, and I had a lump in my throat that was now threatening to choke me. I waved the wee red car off thinking it might not even reach Perth and went back inside with my two collies, Kim and Pippin.

The kitchen seemed empty, the map forlorn: eighteen war-torn countries, bandits, crooks and swindlers, an adventure of a lifetime. Time to put the kettle on.

News came in with surprising regularity. The boys were brilliant at keeping us posted. For almost six long weeks, messages were relayed as the map gathered more and more red crosses in places I had never even heard of. My patchy geography and knowledge of countries ending in 'stan' was now improving at a furious rate. One morning at 4.30 am I received a text that read: 'How many Russian rubles to the US dollar?' I had to leap out of bed to check the internet and text back the answer. They were running out of money so as day broke, I was knocking on the bank door (back in the day when we still had a local bank), moving more cash into Freddy's account. Once he was home and had a weekend job, he insisted on paying it all back.

It was not surprising that the boys grew up in that short space of time. On their return they regaled us with extraordinary tales both harrowing and hilarious that emerged by degrees. Their photographs were outstanding; it had been an epic journey. The end of their trip, in Mongolia, involved riding tiny, wiry horses across the plains and a return journey on the Trans-Siberian Express. The rules of the rally at that time were to leave the car, or the wreck of the car, in Mongolia for the use of locals, and to find another way back. I will always be astounded that that unassuming wee red Ford Fiesta made it. It said a great deal for Ford's manufacturing skills during that era. Freddy's diary revealed life-changing events, and I was glad I was unaware at the time of what they were experiencing, for it would have made my hair stand on end.

I knew that after such a trip university would not have much pull. Freddy really didn't want to go but decided to give it a try. The most my son has ever shocked me was in his choice of politics as a subject. To begin with, city life and the wine, women and song must have had an attraction. It was not to last. By Christmas Freddy was thoroughly disillusioned. I had a call in February just as I was about to go away for a week to ask if I could leave him a house key. He told me that he had exam results due, and when he failed as he said he was sure to do having left two exams forty-five minutes early, he would pack it all in and come home. After all, he told me persuasively, he had a job awaiting him with an older school friend who had started a ground works business. We had already done a lot of soul-searching during the holidays and agreed this was a possibility.

A week later, whilst I was walking on a remote beach on Islay, my mobile phone picked up a signal and rang – it was Freddy sounding devastated. I thought something dreadful had happened. He was livid because he had his exam results. He had passed with flying colours. 'Just goes to show that politics is a load of bollocks,' he exclaimed. Now leaving would be harder. My son is the first person I know who has been disappointed to pass an exam.

The lure of working with a plant-hire business, and the JCBs, was strong. I was reminded of carting Freddy and his pushchair up and down the steep hills at Edinburgh Zoo when he was very little, and how, when we got back to the car park, it was a JCB there that made him almost fall out with excitement. So, he left university with my blessing, and for some time I would return home to find very interesting vehicles parked outside the house. Once, when I had some friends for supper, he showed up looking like the coal man bringing the biggest tractor and trailer I had ever seen up the drive whilst rearranging the gravel in the process. I could always tell if he had called in when I was out by either the vast ruts on the gravel, or the oily hand marks around the light switches.

Then an extraordinary opportunity arose: to go to Kiev in Ukraine to spend three months there doing project works management with his best friend's older brother, who lives and works there. He agonised over the decision, worrying that he would return to no job, but we both agreed it was an opportunity not to be missed. Mum was apoplectic but even she agreed he should go.

The three months turned into five years, by which time Freddy had become a director of a new Ukrainian company and had a beautiful girlfriend, Daria. He threw himself in from the outset, and quickly learnt to speak Russian. During a visit there I also learnt that his grasp of Russian building-site lingo was apparently colourful – highly unusual for an English speaker. When he met me off the plane and drove me back to Kiev through kamikaze traffic, slaloming in and out, under- and overtaking, it proved the start of a few days of white-knuckle rides, psychedelic nightlife, vibrant restaurants and the intrigue of watching the behaviour and interaction between large packs of itinerant street dogs. How he coped I did not dare to think, and I made a mental note not to give my mother any details about Ukrainian driving. Lines of crosses by the roadside and bunches of flowers did little to help my own nervous state. Yet, his time in Kiev was vital grounding, and it would be five years before he returned home with Daria to make a new life back in Scotland.

19

Chasing Light

A few years after Geordie's death in 2010, I was in Islay. I had gone to work on various magazine features and was staying in a cottage on a farm near Port Askaig. The first morning, a tall, smiling, blonde man who looked like a Viking appeared from out of a building on the other side of the yard and shouted a cheery good morning. He was struggling on with a pottery business on the family farm, run by his older brother. They had been making a wide range of items, including unique whisky jugs for the island's numerous distilleries. Competition from cheap foreign imports was pushing the business to the brink; he was disillusioned and desperate to escape. He needed to do something new.

The weather was glorious, and I struggled to extricate myself from a long conversation, aware that I needed to capture the island's land- and seascapes whilst the light was right. Chasing light in every sense appears to be a dominant feature of my life. When I arrived back at dusk, there was a note asking me out for dinner. I discovered that Iomhair (a Gaelic name pronounced 'Eva') was not only a skilled potter but also a talented cook. During the rest of the week, in between various creative commitments, Iomhair and I walked and talked, with our dogs running beside us on Islay's eternal beaches.

I had discovered a dead Cuvier's beaked whale on a beach earlier and had told Iomhair about it. As it was highly unusual, he was keen to see it too. We set forth to investigate further. On a storm-bound beach in a remote part of the island, a bulbous, bloated whale lay in a pool of rancid red seawater infused with leached body fluids. A more unpleasant saline broth would have been hard to find. The smell was dire, but we were intrigued, so intrigued and absorbed that we only narrowly prevented our dogs from taking a plunge in the pool with the deceased. They thought the stench was heavenly. It reminded me of my childhood, when I had a morbid fascination for dead creatures. I would turn them over with my foot to revel in the minutiae of beaks, claws, paws and glazed eyes, sodden fur and feathers. I found it extraordinary that some of the long dead seemed to wriggle again. Maggots!

We laughed ridiculously as the pungent pong of putrid whale made us gag, and the fact that despite this affliction we were both enthralled. Iomhair had also spent his life surrounded by wildlife, and birth and death, on their mixed farm. His childhood had many parallels to my own.

Though the whale episode could perhaps be seen as less than romantic, a wildlife encounter a few days later at Machir Bay is as vivid to me now as it was then. We were standing near the ruin of Kilchoman Church. Close by, the ancient Kilchoman Celtic cross was a silhouette looming through pearly diffused shrouds, mist curling in off the sea, low gold November sun breaking cover. We were supping coffee from a flask and enjoying the stillness when the sound of bugle calls drew nearer. From out of the mist a flock of whooper swans emerged, pinions white against a patina of grey, light illuminating the whirring of great wings, the sound like a dozen harmoniously fast-beating hearts. We were dazzled for a moment by their sheer brilliance and the crispness of the sound cutting silence. And then it faded as the birds travelled on out over the sea. The mist lifted, clearing the view, as the eerie, ethereal sound faded. Had the swans been there at all? Choughs wheeled above us laughing and mocking. The silence between us said reams.

Soon after I was home again, Iomhair and I met up in Glasgow. He came to stay and adored the farm and the animals, and clearly felt at home. And after the third visit, he never really left. I had given up all hope of ever finding a stable relationship and put it down to my own intense creativity, demanding nature and previous dysfunctional family life. I was content to be by myself and was certainly not looking for anyone to share my life, but I missed him dreadfully when he was not with me. His stays became longer and longer, and he luckily found a job nearby, and now runs his own gardening business.

It was almost a year before I told my mother about Iomhair because she had entered a new phase of heightened hysteria. If I had added a new male companion into the brew, there would have been further trouble. Cowardly, I lay low, regressing to naughty-child status. My visits were increasingly intolerable and Mum's unhappiness dreadful to witness. I lay awake tossing and turning and wishing I could help her.

As feared, Mum had her driving licence revoked due to her encroaching blindness, and she had eventually agreed, after a protracted battle, that she did indeed need a carer living in. This was not going well. She was already on the third – she'd hated the first two; they had clashed spectacularly. I was devastated for her about the blindness – another understandable addition to her misery. It was a terrifying prospect. Then in 2014, while Freddy was still working in Ukraine, civil conflict broke out and this gave Mum, who was always glued to the news, even more to worry about. I was being nagged because she felt Freddy should come back home to find a job here instead: 'We are such a small family now, we need him back in Scotland to look after us, you must insist he returns.'

Before long the number of failed carers was approaching double figures. None of them could tolerate Mum's cutting tongue and temper, none ever seemed good enough, and on each of my visits she had a long list of complaints: their voices were wrong, they came from the wrong background, they were too fat, too neurotic, too thin, too greedy, too lazy, too busy texting, too in need of time off, couldn't cook, cooked too much, talked too much, didn't talk bloody enough, and one did not know about bloody cucumber plants. Really?

Though Mum had no idea how long I had been seeing Iomhair, she had now met him. He had come with me on several visits and hated the way she treated me. Though he was sympathetic, he told me to stand up to my mother. But my mother was not his mother.

It was too late. It was a pattern that I should have broken thirty years earlier. The force of my mother's control still ran at full throttle. In among the low spots where Mum's state caused so much stress, there were tiny glimmers of her humour. And whenever I was back home with Iomhair there were many moments of great happiness that helped me find my strength again.

*

It is a brutal, squally March afternoon when I collect three tiny, orphaned red squirrels whose drey has blown down in the gale. They have been taken to the local vet. Their eyes are tightly closed and they each weigh less than two ounces. They are huddled together in their moss and lichen-lined drey, and, as is the norm, are crawling with fleas. However, using something as harsh as flea powder on tiny babies is not an option. Hopefully the unwanted guests will swiftly move on.

I have hand-reared litters of squirrel kits before, but the excitement never wanes. I swap their collapsing nursery for a fleece beanie hat and I feed them three-hourly on minute amounts of puppy milk substitute. They suck vigorously, front feet pummelling against my hand as if they are stimulating the flow of milk from their mother's mammary glands. Their tails are not yet bushy, short hair beginning to sprout; their notably large hind feet seem several sizes too big. We are enchanted. They emit soft sounds that instil a feeling of protectiveness in me. As soon as a feed is over, they wriggle and squirm their way quickly back inside, then this squirrel-filled hat is gently placed on a hot-water bottle.

For the first week, I rise in the small hours several times to feed them. Sitting in the silent kitchen listening only to the soft sounds of the little squirrels suckling and tawny owls hooting from the garden is soothing. The clock ticks. A moonbeam sends a patch of light into the corner of the room. I return to bed as silently as I can to avoid waking Iomhair. His regular breathing indicates that he sleeps on oblivious. I edge carefully back between the sheets. Now wide awake, I lie on my back not daring to move. Something is tickling my arm. I gently pat it. A few seconds later, the feeling continues. It appears to be travelling up my arm. My light slaps become urgent until they would awaken the dead. After a few minutes of this torture, a voice beside me says, 'We are not alone, are we?' And we leap out of bed, pull back the bedclothes and put the light on for further investigations. Animal fleas have a particular host, and in this case, these are squirrel fleas. And they make unwelcome bedfellows.

Hand-rearing mammals is fraught – often milk substitute can lead to diarrhoea, which can in turn swiftly lead to death. Happily, this particular brand of milk is suiting the kits well. However, there is another problem, not uncommon in orphaned mammals. The females are using the male's penis as a sucking dummy. Wild babies do this when they are stressed without their mother. I have encountered the problem whilst rearing otter and fox cubs too. However, stopping it is easier in larger animals. I acquire bitter spray and separate the male. However, he pines and goes off his milk. He is missing his siblings, so I have to put him back with them. Sadly, the bitter spray does not work. They don't stop, and the pathetic male finally cannot pass urine. I am devastated to lose him.

Once we are over this setback, things improve. The squirrels' eyes open, and they quickly become more active and in need of space. We move them into a large wooden box. Their antics absorb us, and whenever they wake, they fly around their box like two mammalian gymnasts, even though to begin with there are a few misjudged manoeuvres. I wean them onto a mixture of pulverised nuts, seeds, apple, digestive biscuit and milk. These really are babies reared off a silver spoon. Unlike stainless steel, silver is malleable and may be easily shaped so that the spoon is more pointed and better for tiny mouths to feed from. Nothing is too good for these precious little squirrels.

They paddle in the mixture, making a sloppy mess, pushing and shoving one another in a bid to get into the centre of the dish, sticky babies that need to be carefully washed after every feed to keep those now gleaming gold-red coats in top condition.

Now, the weather is unsettled, and we have late snow, delaying the squirrels' upgrade to an outside aviary as the sheer weight of this heavy wet fall has pushed in the aviary roofs. Hours of maintenance follow as we hammer and patch, replacing the wire around the bases too, cementing it in deep to avoid digging out or digging in by rats, weasels, stoats, badgers or pine martens.

Finally, we line the aviary with fresh Scots pine branches snapped off during the snowfall. It is a squirrel's adventure playground, where we hide a selection of nuts and fruit to keep them busy. This is a temporary squirrel heaven. They race around frenetically chasing one another until they crash and burn, collapsing into their nest box and sleeping until their mad chasing begins all over again. Human contact is kept to a minimum for they need to revert to wildness; it is surprising how quickly they become wary and won't come near.

Once they have mastered the art of opening nut feeder boxes, it is time for them to move on. Some squirrels are released in our garden, but this is always dependent on the situation with the local felines. And sometimes there may be more persistent and dangerous cats around – real squirrel killers so that we are not happy to release them at home. Further down the Tay Valley lies Cluny House Gardens owned by John and Wendy Mattingley. This large sprawling woodland garden overflowing with the unusual, including botanical treasures from the Himalayas, and also famous for its magnificent towering trees, is well away from roads. And the perils of domestic moggies. The Mattingleys nurture their healthy population of resident reds, and put food out for them every day. This is the ideal safe release site.

The night prior to freedom I creep in and shut the kits in their sleeping box so that come dawn we won't need to catch them and cause stress. The last day of May breaks spectacularly, wraiths of mist filling the valley floor with alluring tendrils, amid drifts of bluebells, a smoking haze in the tender new greens of the awakening woodland. The birds are in full voice; a blackbird close to the open bedroom window fills the room with his intoxicating liquid song. The garden is stippled with a thousand backlit dewdrops.

Cluny is magical in all seasons, but spring is its high point, its moment of triumphal glory. Blackbirds and thrushes are garnering worms on the lawn. Shrubberies and borders are busy with birds under pressure from voracious fledglings.

For two months, these little squirrels have dominated our lives, and shortly they will be free. This is the goal that we always aim for. Sometimes we do not get this far. We carry the box to the base of the record-breaking giant sequoia we have chosen for their first taste of freedom. My heart is heavy but light at the same time – emotions running to overload. So many hazards await. Silently we nod. Then without a word we carefully open the door to set free our precious cargo. Two squirrels flash forth like a fizz of champagne froth. And away! They seem tiny – elf-like, oh so small. They fly up the corky pitted bark ever onwards with barely a backwards glance as we stand motionless beneath. How appropriate that they should have chosen something so stable for their first proper tree climbing effort. Then they do turn around and look at us as they climb higher and higher. They are back where they belong. They have the chance to become part of the lifeblood of this arboretum, valuable links in the complex web of life. Our work is done.

We return on several occasions and see our squirrels, though as soon as they moult and transform, they simply blend in with the other squirrels in the garden, and become part of the ecosystem.

*

It was always these interludes, close relationships with animals and birds, that helped me to come to terms with the things that made me so anxious. Their needs seemed to ease my own. I could not venture far without another crisis with Mum, or a protracted tale of distress relating to those who were helping her. Old age doesn't always come easily. No one was ever good enough – the pattern continued as it had for the past thirty years. I had to lie about where I was working and not tell her if I was to be away for a few days or else she would erupt into another rage and blame me for the misery that engulfed her. I felt torn. But my work – my writing and photography – was vital to my stability as well as my financial situation.

'You are so bloody selfish, Polly. All you ever seem to do is work when I really need you here. You are never, ever here when I need you.'

There seemed no point in trying to explain. When I gently suggested to Mum again that perhaps she was depressed, it backfired, and I was accused of trying to have her locked away.

'You just want to get rid of me, don't you? You are always trying to tell me what I should do. I wish you would stop bloody well interfering; you drive me mad, the way you come here and criticise all the time.'

There was no response possible to this tirade because I knew in my heart that I never told her to do anything, ever. Butterflies took flight. I was the child being reprimanded for its naughtiness again.

Mum was now falling frequently and could not be left alone; she was also suffering acute panic attacks. I was desperate to help but came away from each visit feeling vulnerable and ill. If I could have bought myself a rhino hide on eBay, I would have happily done so. Why did I take it all to heart so much?

My drives home through the glory of the Sma' Glen and over the Perthshire hills were often blurred by tears as I was filled with desperate frustration and sadness, and then I would stop because there was always something that caught my attention and pulled me back. After one particularly bleak visit on my way home a red kite soared on the thermals above the road. As it rose, its distinctive forked tail acting as a rudder, its rich red and grey plumage glinting in the late afternoon sun, I thought of how close this glorious raptor had come to total extinction. There would often be deer silhouetted on the crags above, or perhaps a dipper on the burn below the road bobbing and curtsying, disappearing under the swirling black eddies and reappearing with a tiny larva in its bill. In early spring, I watched a ring ouzel – the mountain blackbird, a bird that is becoming increasingly rare. Wearing its ministerial white collar, it perched on a crag and sang a sweet pibroch to its imaginary congregation.

I did not know how to cope with my poor mother, but I knew that to stop and absorb myself in this otherness, even for but a moment, was a salve.

20

Hospital

It's 2015, at 6 am a week before Christmas, and the telephone is ringing. It's Mum's carer. She thinks that Mum has had a stroke, and she's been taken by ambulance to hospital. She fears it is a bad one, but the doctor has suggested I don't go to the hospital in Perth for a few hours until she has been settled into a ward.

My heart is racing. It's something we have feared. I don't know much about strokes, but I am about to learn – the hard way, chucked off a cliff into a boiling sea of medical information.

When I reach the hospital, Mum is in a 'transit' ward, in a bed by the door. She looks grey and her face is lopsided, her eyes shut. She cannot move, but there is a flicker like fading candlelight when she hears me coming in. Despite her growing blindness, she definitely knows I am here. I try not to cry. Her right side is paralysed, and she is not speaking, though tries to mumble. I take hold of her hand, but it's limp, there is no grip, it feels cold. I try the other and squeeze it hard, and she squeezes it back. Now that Mum and I are both in this never-never land, all the upset and disappointment that has consumed me about the decline in our relationship has vanished. Love is all I feel for her. I will be by her whatever lies ahead.

Her breathing is laboured and noisy, like an old horse that has been galloping too hard. It's a grim ward and people in varying states of decline surround us – not all are elderly. The nurses are grey too, frazzled, racing about with clipboards, under serious pressure – it's a motorway junction with traffic merging in all directions. There is no peace. Mum's name is above her bed, hastily scrawled in biro, and they have missed off the 'e' from her name – Anne – and put an extra 's' in Ferguson too.

I sit for some time as nurses come and go, wheeling patients on their beds up and down. And then back again. A woman appears, pushing a tea trolley with a squeaky wheel. Her brow is as furrowed as a ploughed field. Manoeuvring the trolley through this medical mayhem without disaster is a feat. There's the rustle of rubber sheets, and a large backside close by is making up an adjacent bed. She has ankles like tree trunks and is wearing off-white slip-on shoes. Her tired, swollen feet spill over them – pale dough rising in a baking tin. In the next war I want to be on her side. No one has any time, and I can see that my mother may not have much either.

After a while spent floating in this never-never land, a nurse asks me if I am Anne's daughter; it's all first-name terms, and she calls me Pauline – never in my life have I been Pauline; it's a common and aggravating mistake that people assume Polly is a shortening of Pauline when I was christened Polly. I correct her and then she calls me Paula instead. She tells me that the doctor would like to see me.

I am escorted down the passage to a small room full of dog-eared magazines and half-empty boxes of pastel-coloured tissues. There is a water dispenser with plastic cups, and a heap of battered children's toys in a pink box in the corner next to an old-style television. A bear's leg protrudes from behind a cushion on a sofa, and everything is sticky. I am told to take a seat.

Shortly, a doctor appears and smiles kindly, closing the door softly behind him. 'Are you Anne's next of kin?' he asks.

I reply in the affirmative.

He is wearing a white coat and a weary expression and has a stethoscope around his neck. He sits beside me and clears his throat. 'Your mother is a very sick woman. She has had a major stroke, but we do not yet know to what extent, and she will be having a scan later. What do you feel about resuscitation should she have a heart attack or another bad stroke?'

I have discussed this with Mum in the past, and I know that is not something she would want, but somehow it seems so final, as if I am playing God, and the question makes my heart race. My mouth goes dry. I am also shaking.

The doctor explains the options, and it is agreed that she will not be revived if the worst happens. He shakes my hand and says, 'I am so very sorry'.

It's a ghastly scenario looming over me. She may not have long indeed. I return to the ward to say goodbye to Mum before she is wheeled off for scans. I am told that it is better if visitors are strictly kept to close family only until her condition stabilises.

I leave the hospital's depressing car park and drive the thirty-five miles home in lashing rain. Looks like it's not going to be a white Christmas. Then as I cut across country and over the high hill road towards the farm, fresh, wet snow decorates the heather, and I meet a gritter coming in the opposite direction. The salt hits the windscreen with a surge, and I flinch low over the wheel in natural reaction. A beautiful mountain hare lollops across the road in its white winter pelage, and I slow to watch it as it breaks through the fence out onto the heather.

I return home with a heavy heart, wondering what lies ahead. Iomhair has lit the fire, fed the animals and made tea. The room glows warmly, and our collies whine and lick my hands in sympathy. They seem upset too – they always pick up on my mood. I want to bypass Christmas and hibernate until it's all over. The lovely pine tree with its decorations seems to rub salt into another open wound.

I have yet to tell Freddy about Mum's stroke; he is now permanently back from Ukraine and working in Scotland again. He is on the Isle of Lewis and is not due home till tomorrow; there is no point in worrying him when he can do nothing.

When Freddy arrives, he is, as predicted, devastated by the news, and early next day we head to the hospital. Mum has been moved to the stroke unit. We go straight there and find her in a smaller ward with three other patients. This is a different place altogether, away from the cacophony of the main building, almost peaceful. Mum is asleep, having been sedated, but her breathing clatters along irregularly as she has a chest infection. A nurse takes us aside and tells us that Mum can neither move nor swallow, and once the dietician has assessed her, they will fit her with nasal feed tubes if we are in agreement. Freddy and I sit there in total disbelief, surrounded by poor souls so facially contorted they are as gargoyles on a decaying, pallid Gothic building. The ward is pungent with the aroma of disinfectant, urine and death. We are going to find ourselves here almost daily as we endeavour to accompany my mother on her final journey. A different doctor appears clutching a clipboard and informs us that it has been 'a big bleed'. To the uninitiated, that means it's a serious stroke. Nothing has prepared me for seeing my mother like this. Nothing has prepared Freddy for seeing his grandmother like this.

We enter another world. Sometimes she is awake and makes gurgling noises and acknowledges our presence, whilst at other times she is somewhere far, far away. A bag of dark urine fills steadily below the bed; there are tubes and wires everywhere, and a machine strapped to her leg to minimise the threat of thrombosis. The beepings make us jump, our adrenaline surging and minds over-fertile. Some days we find her calm and alert. She reacts almost ecstatically to Freddy and tries to talk. We ask her if she is comfortable, and she always nods that she is. Other days she is in a deep sleep, and once we find her lying half out of her nightie revealing her nakedness, having extricated herself after much thrashing about. She seems too hot, or too cold, and her distress is horrible to watch. We feel powerless. She has to be regularly turned, and she has to be fed and watered through a nasal tube, referred to as 'bridling'. Often when it's time to turn her, we are asked to leave the ward.

After our visits, Freddy and I find ourselves in a café close to the hospital. On the second visit, we simultaneously notice the words 'GOD IS LOVE' on the wall amid various biblical slogans. Neither of us is religious, but this place, filled with genteel ladies, young mothers with pushchairs, and latte and cappuccino drinkers, is comforting. It is a peaceful womb engulfing us in amniotic fluid, temporarily protecting us in our sorrow. There are succulent bacon rolls, and the caffeine fix is powerful. We fall in there regularly to sit and talk, trying to come back to the real world before we drive north again. We talk in depth about things we have never previously covered, becoming ever more closely bonded in our shared misery and the harrowing experience of seeing someone we love in this state of pathos.

The drives to Perth in fog, snow, ice and lashing rain make it harder. We have been called to see the consultant. He is very understanding, though loses us in jargon, and we have to ask him to translate. He does not expect my mother to live long. It could be days. Then he says it is less likely to be weeks. Then he adds he cannot be sure, maybe it will be longer. And then he says that she is very sick indeed, and he doubts actually it will be long. In other words, he hasn't got a clue for such is the uncertainty that surrounds the stroke victim and not even a specialist can be sure of how things will develop. He feels powerless to comfort me. The stroke has been a devastating one, and she is at grave risk of others in the coming weeks. She will be moved to a single room.

On Christmas Day, we set sail for the stroke unit to find it bustling with activity: streamers, tinsel, fairy lights and a brass band are playing carols in the adjacent ward. Smartly dressed visitors are here to see loved ones, bearing gifts that will never be looked at, but in their helplessness they bring them anyway. There are children here too, visiting grandparents, eating their chocolates and grapes. A couple of people are weeping silently in the corridor, the poignancy of a day they should have been spending at home with a parent, or close relative, unbearable. Mum is too poorly to be wheeled in to hear the band, but a line of elderly people in wheelchairs sit listening, some with animated faces, others dozing or with lopsided smiles, their feet encased in oversized slippers, woollen rugs wrapped around their legs, hair standing up like wayward feathers on a fledgling. Freddy has his arm around me, and we are holding hands, moved to tears. There's an extraordinary atmosphere, a strange mixture of contentment and celebration. Mum loves music, and we hope she can hear from her semi-comatose state in the ward close by. The nurses are doing their best, away from their families because they drew the Christmas short straw and landed this shift. All are wearing festive hats, big-hearted and cheery, without a hint of resentment.

Soon after Christmas we ask Mum if she knows where she is and Freddy and I are both sure we hear her replying, 'The Holiday Inn.' We cling to this because that is not a place she would ever have stayed, and we like to think it is her wonderful sense of humour still at work.

The nurses laugh too. 'Well, we've heard it called a lot of things but never that!' one laughs. A place less like the Holiday Inn would be hard to find.

On Hogmanay, we plan an evening in Mum's house, where Freddy and his partner Daria have been living to look after the place and Mum's little dog since Mum went into hospital. They have been busy cooking, and all four of us are determined to make it a happy night. Then I am called to the hospital; it looks like Mum is slipping away.

Freddy and I rush in again and sit with her, holding her hands. Her breathing sounds like someone sawing logs laboriously with a blunt handsaw. But she gets over this new hurdle and rallies again.

It goes on and on, and we are called many more times over the coming weeks. Now they have decided to continue giving her water but to stop feeding her. They have done this before, and then she showed signs of hunger and they started again, but she keeps pulling out the feeding tubes. I have ridden many emotional roller coasters, but this one is proving the roughest yet.

Our days are fractured by hospital visits. Up and down the road Freddy and I travel, mostly together but sometimes alone, scraping ice or snow off the car, driving on a skating rink, through slush and sleet and flooding. It's a seventy-mile round trip. The days I go on my own are hard, but for me they are important too. I sit and prattle by Mum's bed. Once I have taken in clean nighties and put them in the cupboard by her bed, I busy myself by rubbing cream into the dry skin on her arms, brushing her hair and filing her nails. Freddy does the same when he goes alone. And sometimes together we soothe her hot brow with a cool flannel.

After over six weeks in hospital, she badly needs a haircut. I ask her if she would like me to cut it for her, and she nods. I struggle, catching the fallen hair on a towel, and manage to cut around her face, but only on one side. Then she falls asleep. The nurses promise to come and turn her for me, but they are too busy, so she stays with a one-sided hair cut for some days. She was always so proud of her appearance. Of greater concern is that she now seems to have another infection and is sweating too. Freddy is so kind and caring. I am proud of the way he handles everything, proud of his loyalty to both of us. I hope in my heart that I have always been his rock, as he, in turn, is mine.

We have taken in her radio so that, as she always did at home, she can have the constant comfort of Radio 2. It drowns out the racket in the rest of the ward. Some days it's almost as if she is singing along, and the nurses confirm she has indeed been singing. The oddest part of this stroke is that all the discontentment of her previous life has departed, and when aware she seems extraordinarily mellow – maybe it's the drugs she's on. I wonder what has happened to her brain, what thoughts are going through it, what she is really feeling, and how much she knows of what has happened. However, for most of the time all we hear is the distressing sound of her 'chain stoking' – the rasping uneven breathing that frightens both of us. It sounds so terminal.

One morning I find Mum's room empty, the bed stripped. I almost pass out in the corridor and stand frantically checking my phone to see if there has been a missed call. I cannot find my glasses, and the numbers are blurred. My mouth is dry. Then a familiar cheery nurse, whom I like immensely, appears and throws her arms around me, knowing instantly what I am thinking. She apologises profusely. They had to move her in a hurry because someone needed what I now see as the departure lounge. Perhaps the new occupant's plane will take to the skies faster than Mum's. Mum is back in the ward and remains there for some time.

A junior nurse greets us one day, saying isn't it great that Anne is making progress and there is some improvement? I become surprisingly upset by this throwaway comment. As far as I am concerned, she is not progressing in the slightest. I am desperate for her to slip away, slip away from this misery. She cannot move, she cannot eat, she cannot talk, and she cannot ever do anything for herself. The same nurse briefly mentions that she may soon be ready to move on to a nursing home. Our hearts sink, for we fear that she is far too bad for that. It merely adds to our confusion, and we start to worry about where. Which nursing home? Due to her considerable weight, she has to be hoisted from the bed, and it takes several people to move her. How can the nurse say there is improvement? There can never be betterment – return from this is impossible. My guilt trips are refuelled by this new situation, for I feel guilty that I would rather she was dead. There is no purpose to this cruelty. I would not put my animals through this horror, but that thought makes me feel horrible, as if I am heartless.

It is days before I track down the busy consultant. It turns out that, on the contrary, there has never been any question of her leaving the hospital. She is dying, but he is confused because she is also defying all the odds, leaving him baffled. 'Recovery' merely means that in her case she will linger longer, and then he adds 'perhaps', for he really cannot give me an answer. Perhaps the inexperienced nurse was trying to give us hope. Freddy and I remain torn by our turmoil.

Then Mum is moved back to a single room. Perhaps they think the plane will depart this time. At dusk one miserable February day, I sit beside her bed watching the opportunists outside in the car park below: rooks, herring gulls and carrion crows congregate around black bin bags awaiting collection. They peck idly, strutting their stuff and keeping a vigil. They, in turn, are watched by visitors who are standing in the sleet, manically drawing on their cigarettes, close to the shelter of the main door. I have never been a smoker, but I can see the attraction to help soothe frayed nerves. Being in this half-life, half-death situation is the ultimate test. And I feel I am beginning to fail spectacularly, revealing great crevasses in my character that I really do not like. Perhaps I may fall into them.

It is now over two months and I have been called more than half a dozen times with the message that my mother is about to die. But something makes her hang on; it is as if she is still not ready. It is hell on the nervous system. Selfishly, I do not know if I am coming or going, and clearly neither does she. At least she is in a single room again. For all of us, this is better. For someone like Mum, a private death is important. I sit beside her bed and tell her what a great mother she has been, I apologise to her for all the things that did not work out, and I go over stories from the past that I know would make her laugh. I remind her of the fabulous picnics we used to have, for which she was famous, the animals we kept, all the hilarity, and the wonderful things that we did with Bo. I thank her for all the good things, and ask her to forget the bad ones. I tell her repeatedly that she must now let go, that it's all right to die, and not to be frightened.

Sometimes her groans are appalling, and sometimes she thrashes about so that I beg them to give her something to keep her comfortable. I am never sure if she hears me or not, but often there is a good reaction, and she gurgles a laugh. Some days Freddy and I have been in and found that she is talking a little, but rather than being pleased we have found it depressing. We don't want her to be aware of this final hurdle, especially when she has hated her last ten years and found them a major struggle, firstly with her failing health, the cruel loss of sight, and then with the loss of Geordie in 2004. It would be so much better if she remained oblivious.

Then, whilst always trying to keep calm, I have panic attacks, knowing that it's now too late to ask her anything, to do anything with her again, and to show her things. I wish I had done more but am reminded when I am back home with Iomhair that she made it totally impossible. 'Stop beating yourself up,' he says. 'You know how tricky she was.'

I do, but much healing has taken place in my heart over these past miserable months. I know that, though latterly I dreaded her increasingly irate and usually rude telephone calls, now she will never ring me again. Never.

It's the beginning of another end. And then there is calmness as

I sit there alone by her bed with the rain battering on the window and the dim lights from the car park throwing eerie shadows onto the pavement outside. The raindrops on the windowpanes are like tears, and sometimes the light catches them as they roll on and on over the glass. The chief nursing sister often comes in when she sees me sitting alone. A cheerful Irish woman, she brims with empathy and tea. She knows how hard this is, for she has seen it hundreds of times, and there is the sweet effervescent young nurse who often gives me a hug and chats to us.

There is so much time to think: a melancholy peace dappled with memories of a life, as I chat beside my mother's bedside or fall silent, my mind flitting back and forth over well-cropped pasture.

*

Mum was a country child, a tomboy, wandering off for hours with a trike and a terrier called Paddy. She spent time with a family of gypsies and claimed they were the finest people she ever met. She never forgot that it was the gypsies who taught her to ride or gave her a taste of baked hedgehog. Later in life she became passionate about hedgehogs, but rather than eating them she bought a microwave oven purely to thaw out Marks and Spencer's chicken drumsticks for the young ones she had rescued. Any other brand was considered inferior for her charges.

Before this beastly, cruel stroke, my mother was such a feisty character and in her younger years so brimming with vibrance and spark. What is it that makes someone become so embittered? For this is how it was for at least the last thirty years of her life. Was it any one thing? It was more likely to be a combination of factors, all of which I never fully understood. I wish I had. I am convinced mental illness was at the root of it. I wish we could have helped her; why couldn't we? There was a deep unhappiness within, and even though she appeared to have had such a wonderful life with Geordie, she was not at one with herself. It was as if she was troubled and unhappy. Perhaps she was a creative soul trapped within her own lack of self-esteem; I don't think she ever found the way to express herself properly. As she began to fail through issues of age, and perhaps in her own mind losing her good looks and fitness, she was simply unable to handle it.

I loved my mother very much but never pleasing her took its toll, and sometimes there were occasions where I also felt that I disliked her too. Her *pièce de résistance* even began to infuriate Freddy after a few renditions: when she had visitors and was behaving in a ridiculous, grandiose manner, she would say to them, 'Do come and have a glass of champagne.' And when they did and were just supping the vintage nectar, she would add with emphasis, 'Yes, this is rather good, isn't it? It's from Polly's *first* wedding.' It made me embarrassed and ashamed. The last time she said it, Freddy gave her hell; I was relieved to know it hacked him off as much as it did me.

She was so different in character from Bo, and I wanted to tell her to enjoy what time she had left, and to be kind instead of always pulling everyone and everything to pieces and seeing the dark side. But this was clearly something she was unable to do, and for us the wedge deepened. There was, however, a matter that she raised many times, particularly at the end of her life. Bo had a sister called Bid, who was married with two children, Peter and Margaret. They were a little older than Mum, but as a child she saw a great deal of them and always said they were the brother and sister she never had. Margaret was a fine horsewoman, training as a riding instructress and planning to take this to a high level. She was riding along a road when a lorry frightened her horse. She was thrown under the lorry and killed instantly – she was just eighteen years old. Further tragedy followed, as Peter, who was training to be a vet, was called up and went away to the war as a bomb aimer. The Lancaster plane he was on went missing without further trace over the North Sea on 30 January 1944. Peter, who was part of 514 Squadron based at Waterbeach, was never found. Bo, too, spoke often of Peter and Margaret, and her sister Bid, whose husband had died from gassing in the First World War. She said they were a wonderful family – but that after so much tragedy Bid died of a broken heart. I know my mother never got over their loss. But was this the reason she was so angry against life in general? I fear she suffered from depression but was frightened to address it.

*

Now as she lies benign and at death's door in a hospital room, the ceaseless rain driving down on the floodlit car park below seems to wash away a great deal of the pain of years. And despite the continuous bustle of the ward, the protracted wait for death, healing begins to take place.

It's almost the end of February, just a week to go until Mum's eighty-fourth birthday. Deep inside I wonder if this is the day she will choose to go; Freddy says he is wondering too. On her birthday, I go to the funeral of one of my parents' closest friends, Lord Mackie of Benshie. He was over ninety, so it is a wonderful celebration of a long and successful life, followed by a wake in the Kirriemuir Town Hall, the very venue supposedly where the 'four and twenty virgins came down from Inverness, and when the ball was over there were four and twenty less'. I know how amused Mum would be about this, as it has been a standing joke since I was a teenager. Then I frequently came to dances here; the hall is filled with memories and faces from the past, many of whom I have not seen for years, older and more battered by life's bruises, but still here, smiling, thrilled to see one another.

It is an event that will stay in the memory, a farewell celebration to a great man – a coming together of dozens of kindred souls old and young. Tea, food and whisky flow without cease, and tousled great-grandchildren belt up and down playing games under the trestle tables. The atmosphere is buoyant and lachrymose at the same time. Everyone asks after Mum, and I try to be cheerful yet also tell them that she is very fragile, that I don't think she is long for this world. So many have been through similar experiences; all are deeply sympathetic. They are filled with anecdotes of the times they spent with her and Geordie. I feel my own mortality.

Afterwards, I stop at the hospital in the vague hope that Mum may be alert enough for me to tell her about all her old chums and pass on their messages. I know she would love this. I walk into the ward and sing 'Happy Birthday' to her. She tries to join in, and the effort it takes brings a huge lump to my throat and a ghastly feeling of finality. I am choked with tears. Then she falls instantly into a deep and noisy slumber. I sit beside her and tell her about the funeral and the party anyway. Then she opens one eye and clearly says, 'Poor Jacqui.' Jacqui is George Mackie's widow. I am astonished. Then Mum falls asleep again. The dark world of the stroke victim – it's so hard to understand what lies beneath these murky waters.

The weather is deteriorating, typical of March – heavy wet snow and surly gales. It's roaring like a lion, and the early lambs on the hill road look miserable. Everything plays into my negative mental state, and I am finding it impossible to stay upbeat. I am worn out by my trips to Perth, and I feel as if that's selfish, but I am struggling to work and write anything that makes sense. I have not taken to the high hills for weeks. Freddy is back working on the Isle of Lewis, storm-bound in Stornoway, and I miss his companionship badly.

Having not seen my mother since all this happened, Iomhair offers to go to Perth to give me a day off. He has continually offered ever since the beginning, but Freddy and I decided it would be better for Iomhair and Daria not to see Mum in this state. Iomhair returns home pale. He had gone into Mum's room but had to go out again to check the name on the door. The Anne he knew had vanished; the person lying there did not resemble her in any way. He cannot believe she is still living. He is deeply shocked and tells me he really thinks this cannot go on much longer. I know of many poor families who struggle through this hell for years. We have only had three months, and I am desperate for Mum to be relieved of such misery, for us all to be relieved of such misery.

It's now over seven weeks since Mum had food, and that feels burdensome too. Up and down I go for the next few days, and then the weather is so brutal that I miss a day. I have said my goodbyes so many times, told her endlessly how much I love her. Please God, she knows what I feel. I have had a bath and am heading for bed. Suddenly I notice that there is a light flashing on the answerphone.

I must have missed the call whilst in the bath. It's the hospital asking me to ring them. I stand looking at the telephone, about to dial the all-too-familiar number but not daring to. Then it rings again just as I go to pick it up. This is it. At 10 pm, having tucked Mum up for the night, the nurse went back into her room to collect something she had left and found that she had finally let go. No one was with her. After all the hours we raced to be with her so she would not die alone, she has chosen to do just that and slipped away silently. The kind nurse says she is very sorry, but we agree it is a massive blessing, and we both hope she is finally at peace.

Numbness sweeps over me, just as it did in 1984 when I heard news of Dad's departure. Iomhair appears and I put my head onto his chest as he holds me. Now suddenly Mum has gone, and I am the oldest member of our family. I have no parents any more. There is deep sorrow, yet indescribable relief that her battle is over. Tiredness engulfs me, yet I am too awake to sleep. We have tea, and then I stay up into the small hours emailing and writing to my close friends and relatives to tell them. I write dozens of emails, for it saves having to speak, giving me the chance to write things about my mother and to scan old photographs and send them too. For me, it's part of the process. The wind tugs at the roof tiles, and the rain batters on the Velux windows as one of my precious owls hoots from the garden. There is stillness. I find myself coming to terms with not only the past three horrible months but also years of worry with my mother. Now it's reached an end. Nothing is forever. In the dark of the small hours, a mouse scampers between the roof rafters. A vixen calls eerily, far off down the valley.

I think of my father, and of Archie, who were always close, and wonder which one of them is responsible for my being. And I also think that it no longer matters, for I will never know for sure – I loved them both equally. And after all, they were brothers. Was it Mum's story that was the truth, or was it Archie's? Tight genes either way. The night stretches out – soft as black velvet – until the grey areas of my paternity drift into oblivion and our cockerel announces the arrival of dawn.

21

Frogs

By morning, I have had just a few hours' sleep, but my system is fired by adrenaline. The choke is full out; the engine will flood sooner or later. We have rung the undertakers and have an appointment. First, I have to return to the hospital to collect my mother's death certificate. Going back into the stroke unit for the last time is another milestone. The familiar nurses are so kind, offering words of sympathy and hugs, whilst handing me a bag of things belonging to Mum, including the solace-giving radio. Then they give me the envelope containing the piece of paper that makes it official. Mum has gone. Already some other poor soul occupies her bed, and I secretly hope that their departure is less turbulent.

As Iomhair and I are early, we find ourselves heading for the haven of the familiar café before we meet the undertaker. The weather closes in. The world seems monotone, the roads are treacherous, and even with the car heater on high we shiver. The dark dankness of death seeps into our bones.

Sleet and hail pummel the car, savage blasts of wind buffeting us. We are both fragile, and I have permanent butterflies. As we try to park in a small space adjacent to the funeral home, a long, white van turns into the one-way street. A scruffy driver slews it roughly across the road and endeavours to squeeze into the space close by. He thumps the parked car in front, breaking the light and making the bumpers of both vehicles droop, and then mounts the pavement and reverses out again at speed. I pull back. His jaw has the set of a pit bull terrier, and his teeth are bared in similar fashion. He is a force to be reckoned with, and I think we need to steer clear. He swerves in for a second attempt. Once stationary, he leaps out and kicks his own bumper back into position before sliding open a door to extricate a large box. We see him visibly mouthing an exasperated, 'Fuck it!' as he rushes through a side door into the undertaker's premises. The gale pushes us violently, as we struggle to open the car doors preparing for what lies ahead, yet tittering over this White Van Man interlude.

The funeral parlour is comfortingly warm. Quiet music plays amid an aroma of waxiness. A sombre, dated carpet with whorls covers the area, and there is an immaculate three-piece suite as well as a table and several chairs. Each highly polished side table has a new box of tissues on it. The ambience is reminiscent of an airport lounge from the 1980s. A smiling woman appears and shakes our hands, and we sit while she fetches the main man. He enters, red-faced and shiny, and shakes our hands too. His black shoes are shiny, his black suit is shiny, and he has just come in from polishing an already shiny black hearse. I note that though smart and pristine, every stitch of his shiny suit is doing its duty. It's comforting, and we feel we are in safe hands. Clearly there is money in death.

Over the next hour, we are taken through a procedure by his colleague – she can take this whole deadly business out of our hands, and do so with the utmost efficiency. This part at least is a surprisingly pain-free experience, accompanied by a great many questions, none of which I am prepared for. Do we want gold inlay or brass handles on the coffin? Do we wish to come and see the deceased once she has been prepared? Are we bringing clothes in for her to wear? Do we wish burial or cremation? Do we want to have a large black car to take the family to the service? Do we want flowers? On it goes, so many questions, so few answers. The woman is superb. She is exactly the right person in the right job. We encounter some stumbling blocks, but she calmly says she will find out about them and returns smiling – she sorts it without any fuss. She should be running the country. She is an angel in undertaker's black clothing, and we are impressed and grateful.

We ask her to put Mum's death intimation in two national papers as well as the local one. Luckily, this is a thoughtful woman, and she returns a few minutes later and asks politely if we are sure, as she hands us a piece of paper with the cost for these insertions – £500 each plus VAT. We wince and ask 'really?' before agreeing that £1,000 plus VAT for two announcements is crookery. We will only put the few humble lines in the local paper. There is indeed money in death. My nocturnal emails have paid off, as I have already told most of Mum's few remaining friends in the south.

The day of my mother's funeral dawns bright and sunny. The weather has changed again, and now it is spring-like. Fickle March! We congregate at the crematorium in a haze dominated by shiny shoes and blackness. Freddy's best friend Kyle, now a fully fledged Church of England priest, and someone who knew my mother well, is conducting the service. Kyle is superb and I am so proud of him; I know how pleased Mum would be, for she loved him too. He and Freddy have been friends since they were five years old. We have the committal first, and then afterwards proceed to a large function room adjacent to the football ground which is conveniently next to the crematorium. Mum would have laughed about this. But we have hired a perfect room for the service; the time slots at the crematorium – a meagre twenty minutes – are too brief to do my colourful mother justice. We want to give her a good send-off; it's important to us. It is something she would have really enjoyed – all her old friends sitting in comfort with a dram, and later tea and sandwiches as Kyle takes us through a beautiful service filled with humour.

'Not too much of your fire and brimstone, please,' jokes Freddy before it all starts. Kyle looks worried and bites his lower lip. I know he is tense because it's hard for him to do this for us.

We sing some hymns and tell some stories. Freddy reads a poem I have written for Mum, and I tell tales from her childhood. It's harder than I ever thought possible, but I am surrounded by kindred souls, many of whom I saw little more than a week ago at Lord Mackie's funeral.

After it is all over, Sue and Dochie, my close friends from Ardnamurchan – almost family – come home with us, and so does my best friend Clare. The day after my mother's funeral, it is Iomhair's fiftieth birthday, and there is a total eclipse of the sun. In the middle of the morning, we stand in the garden watching the extraordinary solar powers at work; eerily the day darkens, it is shrouded in mystery, and the sky fills with weird, ethereal light, the sun like a half moon, a crescent, a child's painting. The moment is surreal as we peer at the haloed phenomenon through special glasses, and also use a welding mask that reveals the luminosity to perfection – nature is indeed perfection. I feel too numb to take it in. The sky is still dark, the sun dressed in a shroud. Everyone is looking out for me.

*

Afterwards, Clare and I take off to the pond close by. For this is frog season. The water is a veritable Scotch broth of amorous amphibians. Bog plants imitate vegetables in this vast vat – shades of orange are carrots, rich yellows are turnips, and verdant greens are chopped cabbage. And there are a dozen shades of brown for meat. It is a boiling cauldron of action that suddenly grows silent as our shadows stretch out over the water's surface. As if on command, hundreds of lovelorn frogs and toads disappear under a tangle of waterweeds, leaving bubbles and silence whilst the pan goes temporarily off the boil. We withdraw from the edge and step back to crouch motionlessly; if we keep our shadows at bay, they will think the threat has gone. Then the heat is turned up and again the soup waltzes, accompanied by a rhythmic concerto of croaking, whilst heads and rubbery legs jostle for position.

They come annually to this place, exhausted and cumbrous with eggs and intent, often collapsing on the way before becoming a temporary part of the frothing concoction. They use the routes they have always used, which are becoming more and more hazardous; many die under the wheels of increasing traffic. But driven by the force of the breeding urge, they continue regardless.

I too have been coming here each year, usually between heavy showers, some winging their way from the west, whilst those from the east are bitter and sleet-laden, leaving face and hands smarting as I dodge in and out, returning to the pond for the lulls when the sun paints everything with her tangerine glow. Shiny spawn trails grace the grasses where a casualty has fallen in the fray. Foxes and badgers have been here for easy pickings. It is not only the French who like frogs' legs on their menu. We bend to scoop up exhausted frogs, taking them the few last yards to the water – singly they seem weightless, fluid, aquiline and elegant. Long splayed legs and flipper feet effortlessly glide through the nutrient-rich murk. In heaps they appear swollen, the bulk of the larger females topped with several struggling males clinging on with all they have, melding patterned skins to one another in a glutinous mass. In the toads' case, an egg-bound female may have so many rampant males piling on top of her that she will be strangled in the mêlée. Nature has gangbangs too.

There are also perfect little newts. They attach their tiny eggs to underwater plant life, while the frantic frogs leave clouds of spawn: enormous cauliflower heads in meaty stock. The bulbous female toads leave theirs in neat chains. A heron appears. This will be a buy one, get one free meal bonanza. The pond surface blistered with tiny heads is suddenly smooth as the seeing eyes dive underwater for cover. The heron jinks gracefully in a low pass, turns sharply and with gangly legs outstretched flies away. Clare and I sit on the bank. I tell her that once I saw a weasel dashing back and forth with pairs of frogs in its mouth. It was clearly stockpiling them in the ancient, crumbling dyke. The toads, though, are a less favoured repast, for they exude toxins from their warty skin to help protect them.

I tell Clare that one dawn, perched on a crooked hawthorn, there was a turquoise kingfisher encased in a sunbeam. The rising sun illuminated plumage of shot silk as the tiny bird was revealed like a feathered topaz. And the water on the pond had not even a wrinkle. The frogs were lying low. Clare smiles, loving every second, her eyes sparkling with tears.

Red deer stags in velvet come here in the evenings to graze. At this time of year, the high hill behind remains barren, grass slow to grow. There are signs of movement, ferns begin to unfurl, and reeds grow daily. Soon celandine, yellow rush, marsh marigold, the spears of flag iris and the prehensile-looking early forms of mare's tail will change the scene again, as the brief fornicating frenzy ends for another year. The first swallows will appear any day, swooping low over the water, drinking and feeding after long, arduous flights back to Britain.

As the seasons unfold, butterflies flit silently, orange tips, peacocks, fritillaries, red admirals and later speckled wood. Pond skimmers, water boatmen, and iridescent dragonflies and damselflies will grace the water. Underneath the surface, fat tadpoles metamorphose into hundreds of perfect, minute frogs and toads. And so begins this extraordinary cycle all over again.

We watch whilst inhaling one of nature's finest spectacles. For me it soothes away the grief, the numbness, returning me to reality, to new life, new beginnings. Clare is as enwrapped as I am, since she too is a child of nature. The beauty of being with her is that therefore I have nothing to explain.

22

The Horizontal Oak

My need to return to Ardnamurchan became great as I came to terms with the death of my mother. It was as if being back there would bring the whole episode full circle and give me the time to think, to put the gnawing anxiousness of the past into the place where it belonged. So much good, so much forgotten and forgiven, a salving of bruised shadows that had so dominated much of my life with both my parents. Once more I thought that they did the best they could under the circumstances they, in turn, had to deal with. Now I needed time to be by myself in the place I loved most. I needed to set things back on track. I needed the force of the gales, the lashing rain and the salt air, the views to the islands, the savagery and peace of that sea-girt rock – my rock.

*

In late March, Ardnamurchan is usually still lying under the auspices of winter. The deer are moth-eaten, raggedy and thin, desperate for a fresh green bite. If spring is wet, then there will be many casualties. Weakened by winter this is the time they will succumb. Moors and hills are threadbare and faded, but despite this nature is indeed stirring. I have always regarded March as one of the hardest months of the year. Wild things are at their lowest ebb, but the birds are beginning to sing and soon they will be attired in their best breeding plumage. For me it really is time to move on. Nothing is forever. It's a new beginning.

Rain is battering in from the north; it carries a sting. I fall into the cottage with bouncing collies, weighed down with our supplies.

Daffodils on the bank tinge the dreary afternoon, like sunbeams piercing dense cloud. At night I lie in bed listening to the comforting roar of the Ockle burn. The wind is teasing the slates and they rattle rhythmically on the roof like piano keys. I often see otters from the windows of this windblown little house, and have watched them cleaning salt-coated pelts in the racing fresh water. I wake in the small hours. A storm. It is angry, wild and erratic with gusts coming and going. The almost silent lulls are eerie in between great growls of fury. I have always enjoyed storms here, yet often they cause mayhem; structural damage is all part of life on this remote, exposed peninsula.

By morning the wind has died to a whisper. I take the three collies up the sheep track past the house, to a ruin where rowans, ash and bramble thickets have colonised the lichen-covered walls, and where wrens and chaffinches find safe nesting sites. Pine martens come here to feast on the rowans in the autumn, but for now the trees are still undressed. However, spring is close. The dogs snuffle along burnsides stippled with primroses and celandines, excited by the pungency of creatures that have passed this way. A sparrowhawk circles above the ruins. The sun is not far away and sends apologetic rainbows across a sea of Prussian blue with beams of light to melt cloud from distant snow-speckled hills.

I think of my mother, for she loved this place too. I wonder, had she stayed, would her life have been any happier? I think so. She hated leaving. I believe that she was at her most content here with her house and her life in Ardnamurchan. Once she and Geordie left, she found it impossible to return. Though Geordie is such a part of this story, it is really Mum and Dad who I have to thank for bringing me here in the beginning, to the place that means more to me than any other, to this wild peninsula engulfed in its abundant wildlife. I have Mum and Dad to thank too for letting me run free as a child. That freedom in nature has given me the most powerful tool of all. It has given me the ability to survive.

In the afternoon, I head to the familiar outline of Ben Hiant and wander down to the bay of Camas nan Geall. I follow the rocky coves through a corridor of massive rocks, some the shape of great dinosaurs. Rocks I have known most of my life. Otter spraint and gull pellets cling to rocks beside the path. Wind simmers to the boil, swirling and whisking the Sound of Mull into frothy paint-splash waves. My favourite aged oak tree appears ever more horizontal; last night's gale has nagged at its roots. I sit with my back against its trunk, fissured veins in an old man's guiding hand. A raven calls. There is another lull, merely the soothing breath of sea, and the feel of the salty damp coats of my three generations of dozing collies lying close beside me. Then I see my mother and Geordie, and remember the time they spent here west of the sun, where it all truly began.

I can see Mum now, crossing over the Choire Mhuilinn burn on the Mingary side of Ben Hiant. We are at the cricket pitch, so nicknamed because it is flat and grassy, a smooth, almost level, sheep and cattle-cropped sward dappled with wildflowers at Ben Hiant's feet; it is blue and yellow in spring, yellow, white and pink in summer, bronze in autumn, tawny in winter. We are having a picnic and have brought the Land Rover along the rutted cart track that follows the shoreline to the far side of the burn. We have ferried the food between us across the water. My school friend and I are standing in the middle, passing bottles and baskets to Bo, Geordie and Malcolm on the far side. The dogs are rummaging gleefully, cooling their tummies in the water and rootling on the bank, lured by the smell of vole and otter. A seal bottles close to the mouth of the burn where it hurries over glistening jade weed to the sea. Fascinated by our activity, it snorts and rises higher from the waves for a better view. Lulu, my pet sheep, is there too, grazing greedily, snatching at the better grass between continual interruptions, being a nuisance whilst sticking her head into one of my mother's huge picnic baskets in search of biscuits. Mum's picnics were legendary, a riot of wonderful food and colour. She always thought of everything – hard-boiled eggs and celery salt, homemade pâté with lemon wedges – and she never forgot the wooden pepper mill. We plan to spend the day here. Geordie has his priorities right; already the white wine is cooling in the burn above us, wedged between the stones. Everyone is sunny.

Once all is in situ, Mum remembers she has left a pie in the back of the Land Rover and wades back across the burn in her bare feet. Her jeans are rolled up and she has her sunglasses on, her red hair glinting in the sunlight. The dogs follow, splashing her as they chase excitedly in hot pursuit. I see her returning across, clutching her beautiful oven-browned pie in its tinfoil dish. She reaches the middle of the burn, and then she slips on the weed as viridescent as crème de menthe, tries to save both herself and the pie, and lands with a dramatic splash, sitting on a rock with water lapping around her. Then she laughs, and we all laugh, and the dogs bark their excitement. I rush over to rescue the pie from her hands amid eager dogs also keen to assist, spraying water, lip-smacking in anticipation of the pie, and wagging. Mum looks fit and happy. She is still laughing uncontrollably but is now on her feet again. Her jeans are sodden, but she doesn't care. This is the beautiful Mum I knew and loved; this is the Mum I will always remember.

The wind is fretting, worrying itself into another frenzy. It's time for me to return to the cottage. Rain drives in off the Sound of Mull; a great, grey curtain closes over the scene, ending my musings. Mull vanishes. I rise from my perch against my horizontal oak tree and stretch, zipping up my coat and pulling up its collar whilst mustering the dogs. We walk with our backs to the pelagic storm as it quickly blows through. Memories, like the rain, seep into every crevice. Ardnamurchan, west of the sun, where rainbows and reflections are born. Ahead lies a new road to the future.

Epilogue

Children begin by loving their parents; as they grow older
they judge them; sometimes they forgive them.

Oscar Wilde

I have been as honest as I possibly can, but the truth is complicated.
The past is hard to dislodge, but when we revisit it perhaps there is
a chance to reassess and view it from a better angle. And we have to
learn, too, that we cannot always save those we love; there's a great
deal you cannot change when you are a child.

Is it only when you reach an ending that you start to think about
the beginning, the middle and the bits in between? Reflecting now
that my parents and my stepfather Geordie have gone, I know that
I used to believe I could change things; that I could fix Dad's problems, and later I thought I could help Mum. I don't blame them for
the things that went wrong. They, in turn, had issues to deal with
that were not of their making – it is the same for all of us. And life
is far too short for bitterness.

I will always be grateful to all of them for the role they played
instilling in me a passion for the exceptional things that have made
my life happy: nature, animals, hill walking and livestock farming,
and also for their sense of humour and the extraordinarily beautiful places where we lived. Mum, and my stepfather Geordie,
in particular, also gave me incredible opportunities. My time at
Gordonstoun proved invaluable and enhanced the activities I loved
already. It was a school where they encouraged a wealth of life skills,

and importantly, *Plus est en vous* – 'There is more in you'. It's been one of the most useful mottos for life.

Best of all, my parents gave me freedom, something that few children today will experience in the unique way that I did. This allowed me to be unfettered, a true child of nature. Ironically perhaps, under the circumstances, it was the most potent tool that they could have given me. It is this more than anything that has carried me through. It is one of the dozens of reasons why disconnection from nature is detrimental to us all.

Acknowledgements

My grateful thanks are due to many people for so many things.

For listening and advice – my publisher, Hugh Andrew, Fergus Crystal, Lou Radford, Linda Cracknell, Jim Crumley, Anna Price, Sir John Lister-Kaye and the late Sam Morshead.

For moral support and loyal friendship (as well as advice) – Caroline Jauncey, Clare Mackie, Peter Harris, Alasdair Gordon-Gibson, Les and Chris Humphreys, Mark Stephen, Breege Smyth, Angela Gilchrist, Anne Hamilton, David and Enid Holiday, Ian Craig, Robert Harris, Miranda Mitchell, Stella Dey, Tom Bowser and Evelyn Veitch.

To my dear friends, almost family, Sue and Dochie Cameron. It is at their wild and windswept cottage on the north coast of Ardnamurchan that I have done so much writing and thinking over the past 25 years.

To my treasured godmother, Heather Ewbank, and her husband, Will, and my sorely missed ex-neighbours, Tim Wynne Williams and Pippa Catling, now residing in Canada.

To my inspirational teachers at Gordonstoun – Mike Nolan and David Spooner taught me English, and John Pownall helped promote my passion for hill walking; the late Jocky Welsh and Barney Robinson both stoked my love of the outdoors.

For their editing skills and general help and patient advice, thanks are due to Ailsa Bathgate, Helen Bleck and Anita Joseph, and, of course, to Andrew Simmons of Birlinn, who is always a joy to work with.

To my lovely, positive agent Jenny Brown, who believed in this book when I sent her the first tentative draft, and to Rose Cooper, who captured the essence of the book in her beautiful cover design.

To three incredibly special women: Drs Fiona Lyell, Anne Jarvie and Debbie Shann. I will always be grateful to have benefited from your incredible wisdom and understanding at various stages in my life

To my long-suffering, kind, witty partner, Iomhair Fletcher, who loves the wild and our eclectic flock as much as I do. Thank you with all my heart for all you do to make my life wonderful, and for all the support you give the animals we share our lives with. I love you.

And, finally, to my son Freddy, of whom I am immeasurably proud. You are my rock and road to the sun. I love you more than words can say. Thank you.